HEARTS & HANDS

Gathering up the Years

HEARTS & HANDS

Gathering up the Years

An
Illustrated History
of
Woman's Missionary Union
of
Virginia
1874–1988

by
Frederick Jarrard Anderson

Woman's Missionary Union of Virginia
Auxiliary to the Baptist General Association of Virginia
1990

Written by:
Fred J. Anderson

Managing Editor:
Don J. Beville

Editor:
Moira J. Saucer

Designed by:
Dennis Michael Stredney

Production Coordinator:
Donna Hughs

Library of Congress Catalog Number
89-051569

Printed in the United States
of America

Fine Books Division
William Byrd Press/Expert Graphics
2901 Byrdhill Road
Richmond, Virginia 23261

Acknowledgments

or the past three years the compiler has been gathering up the years of Woman's Missionary Union of Virginia, sifting and sorting through the vast number of papers which chronicle the organization's progress. He has perused the minutes of Virginia WMU, the "Women's Page" in the *Religious Herald*, and the voluminous papers in the collection of the Virginia Baptist Historical Society. The sketches, stories, and photographs which appear in this volume reflect WMU's development.

For a male who only observed WMU from a respectable distance, the project of compiling a history has been an education. Gathering up the years, one by one, necessitated learning the intricacies of the woman's missionary movement.

Actually, the compiler declares that he was a member of WMU since early childhood. As an unashamed Mama's boy, he frequented the "missionary meetings" with his mother and aunt and became appreciative of the loyalty exhibited by "the girls" of Circle No. 10, the Irwin Parker Circle of the WMU at First Baptist Church, Albany, Georgia.

I grew up listening to my mother and aunt rehearsing their parts in the missionary program, cutting out pictures from *Royal Service* for geography class scrapbooks, and hearing my mother speak of letters she received as a young woman from a faraway missionary named Margie Shumate. But it was not until my mother died and my aunt needed help that I learned that the strongest ties within the WMU are the loving friendships for each other within the "circle." Although the groups are no longer correctly called "circles," I can never forget my appreciation for "the girls in the circle." They taught me the importance of a missionary society.

In 1979, I began a different appreciation for WMU. When I began work as executive director of the Virginia Baptist Historical Society, I discovered its other dimensions. I worked in a building constructed through the generosity of Virginia WMU, and all around me I saw evidence of their support of the Society's work and of the very cause of preserving and proclaiming Baptist heritage. I had an internship, so to speak, with two ladies who once worked for Virginia WMU and then served the Historical Society. Ellen Douglas Oliver and Bessie McGahey made certain that I learned more about WMU. And through the years I met a number of WMU leaders. As an adult male I was acquiring a new attachment to an old love, "the girls in the circle."

Despite these attachments, it is an oddity for a male to compile the history of a female organization. My resources have been those produced and preserved by the women themselves. In gathering up the years I have merely given form to the substantial works the women have left behind.

A chief person who deserves appreciation but who cannot receive it is Bessie Spraggins McGahey; she died in 1988 but not before she had heard several of us express appreciation for her heroically saving so much Virginia WMU memorabilia. She was accused of keeping every scrap of paper her boss, Blanche Sydnor White, ever touched and it's true! Those scraps form the heart of the vast WMU collection at the Virginia Baptist Historical Society, a horde Catherine Allen calls the largest file of WMU periodicals and papers outside of the WMU, SBC, headquarters in Birmingham.

Another person who must be appreciated posthumously is Blanche Sydnor White who led Virginia WMU for 25 years and whose influence was keenly felt for at least another 25. She wrote some 50 histories chiefly related to missions and WMU and left a large body of papers which form a gold mine of WMU material. I could not help sensing—as I compiled this history—that Blanche Sydnor White was nearby, peering over my shoulder. It was not without fear that the author chose to break with the formerly accepted style and use "Virginia WMU" (no periods) instead of the correct but lengthy, "Woman's Missionary Union of Virginia." After all, a note written in 1971 had surfaced from Miss White to her "Elect Ladies" in which she wrote: "Virginia W. M. U. (note that I do not write it WMU and take warning). . . . "

Invaluable assistance was given by Rees Watkins, the gracious former editorial and research secretary of Virginia WMU, who is a walking encyclopedia of missions lore. She can tell the who, what, when, and where, and quite often, the why as well. For years, she wrote the WMU page for the *Religious Herald* and remains a guardian of WMU heritage.

Others who performed yeoman service included Helen Doherty, Sharon Tucker, and Becky Dale, all of whom typed the original draft from the compiler's poor handwriting. As well, the compiler's sons deserve appreciation. Chris Anderson reproduced 1,110 photographs culled from old publications and the Historical Society's files for use in the book. Matt Anderson and the compiler's "other son," a friend named Donald Collins, photocopied hundreds of pages of source material. Cathy Banton of Virginia WMU retyped the manuscript onto the computer in record time. Emma Hutchins handled much of the background planning, especially for distribution.

The compiler is indebted to Kathryn Bullard, executive director, for her guidance and confidence. A committee including Alma Hunt, Christine Gregory, Jean Woodward, Jane Clarke, Kitty Martin, Rebecca Cridlin, and Margaret Wayland offered vital direction. Among those at William Byrd Press who carried the book to completion were Don Beville, publishing consultant, Moira Saucer, editor, and Dennis Michael Stredney, designer.

Sources for items in *Hearts and Hands*: *Gathering Up the Years* include the official minutes and the photograph files of Virginia WMU; the back issues, page by page, of the *Religious Herald*, Virginia's state Baptist newspaper, from 1874 to 1988, especially the women's page, which was published under one title or another practically every week from 1898 to 1984; the official magazine of WMU, SBC, *Royal Service*; and the biographical and photograph files of the Virginia Baptist Historical Society as well as its large collection of personal papers including the papers of Blanche Sydnor White, Carrie S. Vaughan, Eva Sanders, Fletcher Mae Howell, Louise Fletcher, and others. While in the midst of the project a double bonanza came to the Society's archives in the form of the photograph file from the *Religious Herald* and the photograph collection compiled by the late Josephine Carroll Norwood, former Virginia WMU staff member and executive secretary of Maryland WMU from 1954 to 1978, who produced some 5,000 slides, many of which were of Virginia WMU personalities and activities.

Published sources of inestimable value included *The Baptists of Virginia* (1955) by Garnett Ryland; *History of Woman's Missionary Union* (1964) by Alma Hunt and *A Century to Celebrate* (1987), Catherine Allen's definitive and superb history of WMU, SBC, and Mrs. Allen's companion volume of collective biography entitled *Laborers Together* (1987); the earlier history of Virginia WMU, *From Strength to Strength* (1949) by Mrs. E. D. Poe and Juliette Mather's splendid *Light Three Candles* (1973).

Gathering up the years from 1874 to 1988 and placing them between covers may produce something like a scrapbook of thoughts, concerns, lives, and events, large and small, which shaped Woman's Missionary Union of Virginia. It is often through examining the "scraps"—gathered and affectionately saved in books—that one really sees the larger picture. In her biography of the missionary leader Fannie E.S. Heck, Minnie James stated: "Show me your scrapbook and I will tell your biography. Not indeed where you were born and when, nor the schools and other places of learning you frequented, nor the many activities in which you engaged, but the real you." Perhaps in this scrapbook, through these fragments, we can each form our own idea of the real Virginia WMU, the organization which welcomed women to respond joyfully to the divine call. If the scrapbook presents one story, it is the high drama of hearts and hands, individually and collectively attuned to missions through the Woman's Missionary Union of Virginia.

Fred Anderson
August, 1989

Preface

*F*or over 100 years, Woman's Missionary Union (WMU) of Virginia, auxiliary to the Baptist General Association of Virginia, has been effectively guiding women dedicated to missions involvement, missions education, and missions support. It was in 1874 that Virginia Baptist women organized the state missionary society for the purpose of focusing on missions. Woman's Missionary Union continues to be a dynamic instrument through which women and girls of every age in a local Baptist church can be involved in prayer, study, giving, and ministering for the cause of missions.

Today, as a member of WMU, it is a privilege to stand on the shoulders of such a noble heritage and view the fruits of the labors of our early members. It has not been an easy pilgrimage; the road to each victory has been strewn with rough places, roadblocks, sorrows, and joys. The backward glance leads us to view the present and provides us a perspective from which to regard the future.

Frederick J. Anderson, executive director of the Virginia Baptist Historical Society, was the choice of WMU of Virginia to author her history. With his love and abiding interest in preserving history, the astute author has done a masterful job. He has spent months researching biographies, letters, speeches, articles, minutes, histories, and other memorabilia of WMU of Virginia.

Hearts and Hands: Gathering Up the Years, a pictorial history of WMU of Virginia, introduces us to the beginning of the work. The founders, those zealous women who manifested determination and courage as they attempted the task of undergirding missions for the denomination, are featured in "The Founding Years, 1874–1899."

The early years of the organization—the tensions, struggles, anxieties, and the perseverance of the women to provide missions education for all ages—are depicted in "The Hopeful Years, 1900–1924."

In the division, "The Expanding Years, 1925–1949," we sense the excitement of WMU's growth under the dynamic leadership of Dr. Blanche Sydnor White.

We enjoy seeing the harvest of those early laborers as we view the numerous happenings and accomplishments of "The Fulfilling Years, 1950–1974," with Ellen Douglas Oliver and Carrie S. Vaughan providing distinguished leadership.

"The Years of Expectation, 1975 to the Present," under the capable direction of Dr. Kathryn Bullard, have been characterized by effective changes: the innovation of new methods, materials, terminology; the introduction of church-wide missions offerings; the enlargement of the state WMU staff; and the building of a centrally located missions camp.

Hearts and Hands: Gathering Up the Years is not a book to be read only once. It is a book to be enjoyed often, as we turn to it again and again to find within this single volume the highlights of WMU's heritage and history in Virginia. Space limitations have prevented inclusion of many photographs, personal experiences and interesting stories. Yet the pages that follow offer a distillation of the great moments, the influential leaders, and the choice experiences from the lives of many people. Emerging from this historical search has been the realization that WMU of Virginia represents the culmination of the efforts of many women who through the years have been faithful to missions.

Woman's Missionary Union of Virginia is proud of her legacy. We are grateful for the heritage given to us. We trust that we have built upon that strong foundation, adding our worthwhile contributions. We transmit that heritage, augmented by our commitment to the future, confident that those who come after us will continue to create an environment through which women can hear and respond to God's call into missions.

Margaret B. Wayland

Margaret B. Wayland
President
Woman's Missionary Union of Virginia

"*Gather*
up the fragments
that remain that
nothing be lost."

—John 6:12

Table of Contents

Prologue

William Carey, the English cobbler-turned-missionary, became the father of the modern missions movement.

he tiniest, tenderest, earliest roots of the women's missionary movement are found at the very source of Christian life. Robert J. Willingham, who was a leader of the Foreign Mission Board (FMB), once encapsulated the idea when he wrote: "When Christ was here, some of those who served Him best were women, and so it has been for all ages and will be until He comes again."

From the beginning to the close of Christ's earthly ministry, women were there. They were part of the crowd along the mountainside who were told in Christ's sermon to let their lights shine. For two millennia the good works of women have illuminated Christendom. Judged innately inferior by society, women were regarded worthy by Christ and He called different ones—the woman of Samaria, Mary Magdalene, Mary and Martha—to unique opportunities for service. In modern ages women have responded to the Great Commission with a fervor and a devotion which has equalled or even excelled the missionary spirit of their brothers.

Womankind, last at the cross and first at the tomb, believed the Great Commission was also for them. John Bunyan extolled Christian women in his *Pilgrim's Progress:* "I will say again that when the Saviour was come, women rejoiced in Him before either man or angel. Women followed Him and ministered to Him of their substance. 'Twas a woman that washed His feet with tears and a woman that anointed His body to the burial. . . . They were women . . . that brought tidings to His disciples that He was risen. Women, therefore, are highly favored and shew, by these things, that they are sharers with us in the grace of life."

> The glow of morn about us,
> Life's gladness all before,
> In sisterhood of service
> We count our mercies o'er,
> O Master, give Thy blessing
> And guide us as we try
> In sisterhood of service
> To lift Thy banners high.
> Let not thy Kingdom tarry,
> Nor let it suffer loss,
> Speed on the day of glory,
> The conquest of the cross!
>
> Margaret E. Sangston
> **Royal Service**
> September, 1917

In 1800, Boston women organized the first missionary society in America fully "two months before William Carey baptized his first convert in India." They gave themselves an illustrious and ambitious name, the Boston Female Society for Missionary Purposes. Their missionary interests encompassed much of the world, from the United States frontier to India and the work of English Baptist missionaries.

A history of this pioneer society concludes that "the richest treasure" it bequeathed to the women's missionary movement was not in "contributions nor example" but the "inspiration" of its secretary and treasurer, Mary Webb. Crippled and bound to a wheelchair, she pushed herself around the city, "wherever there were human needs to be relieved or human hearts to be redeemed." Even from her "hand-carriage," as it was described, she could write. Her appeals went far and wide, resulting in the formation of over 100 other missions groups. She regularly corresponded with some 60 organizations and launched "a monthly concert of prayer" among these scattered bands. Writing to Christian women in 1812 and calling for a day of prayer for missions, she asserted: "It would have a tendency to cement us together in the bonds of Christian fellowship and establish a union never to be dissolved."

In 1912, Mrs. Julian P. Thomas, an early leader of Virginia WMU, placed on the woman's page of the *Religious Herald* the following tribute: "The 'Mary Webb spirit' covered the whole ground at home and abroad. She well stressed the unity of all Christian endeavor [as a] 'oneness' of worldwide missions and [concluded] that charity begins at home and never fails till it reaches earth's remotest bounds."

In the same year of Mary Webb's prayer meetings, a young couple wed in Massachusetts and in February, 1812, departed America for the new mission fields in India. Ann Hasseltine Judson and her husband, Adoniram, would become the leading figures of America's Baptist foreign missions work, but in 1812 they were Congregationalists. During the long ocean voyage they read their Bible, anticipating questions from the English Baptist missionaries about baptism. Much to their surprise, they became convinced that the Baptist concept of believer's baptism was aligned to New Testament teachings. Ann Judson confided in her journal an entry dated September 1, 1812: "I have been examining the subject of baptism and, contrary to my prejudices and my wishes, am compelled to believe that believers' baptism alone is found in Scripture. If ever I sought to know the truth . . . I have done so during this investigation. We expect soon to be baptized. O may our hearts be prepared for that holy ordinance."

On arrival in Calcutta, they were baptized and became members of the Baptist church organized by William Carey. A compatriot of the Judsons was Luther Rice who had a similar revelation and also was baptized upon arrival in India.

Sent and supported by New England Congregationalists, the missionaries turned Baptist could no longer be identified with their sponsors. Luther Rice returned to America to seek financial support from the Baptists, although they lacked an organized missions board at that time. The Judsons also decided to settle in Burma. Judson persevered despite all manner of opposition, persecution, and imprisonment. He devoted his primary attention to translating the Scriptures into Burmese. Ann Judson shared the perils faced by her husband and became a singular figure of devotion and piety. The story of the Judsons remains a poignant chapter in Christianity echoing through the ages to inspire the mission-minded.

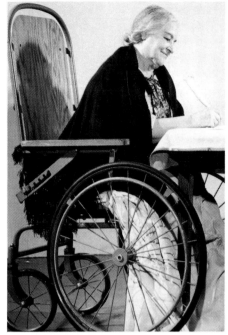

Mary Webb, the Boston woman most instrumental in organizing American women for missions, was portrayed by Mrs. G. Paul LaRoque in Virginia WMU's 75th anniversary pageant, 1949.

Ordination of Adoniram Judson and Luther Rice and three others for missions work.

Adoniram Judson, truly a hero of the faith.

Ann Hasseltine Judson.

Luther Rice's only known likeness is this silhouette, cut by a Virginia girl from Caroline County prior to 1830. Although reproduced many times, the photo shown here is from the original cut.

CONSTITUTION
of the
Fredericksburg Female Baptist Society,
for
FOREIGN MISSIONS.

Constitution of the Fredericksburg Female Baptist Society for Foreign Missions, 1814.

Boston led the way in forming a missions society to support the Judsons and others who followed but Rice believed a larger national body to support missions was needed. In the fall of 1813, he began a series of missionary journeys up and down the eastern seaboard, eliciting help, organizing local societies, and collecting funds. While in Richmond on October 28, 1813, he organized the first general missions society for Virginia labeled at first "The Baptist Mission Society of Virginia," and later the longer "The Richmond Baptist Mission Society for propagating the Gospel in India and other Heathen Countries," and finally, in 1826, "The Baptist Mission Society of Virginia." The organization of the Virginia society followed Rice's plan, as he wrote to Judson, of "forming one principal society in each state and others auxiliary to that and by these state societies delegates be appointed to form one general society."

But even in October, 1813, the Virginia General Missions Society was not the first such organization in Virginia. Two seasons earlier, in the spring of 1813, the Female Missionary Society of the Richmond Baptist Church (*now known as First Baptist Church*) was organized; it was, according to Blanche Sydnor White, "the first Baptist society organized in the South specifically for the support of foreign missions." (*The women's society at First Church, Savannah, Georgia, was organized in the same year and two years earlier, 1811, the first report is made of the Wadmalaw and Edisto Female Mite Society in South Carolina.*)

Fannie E.S. Heck, one of the most effective developers of WMU, SBC, and one of its early presidents, reflecting upon the Richmond Society's centennial in 1913, declared: "In the heart of its origination was the germ thought of a State Central Committee, similar to those out of which WMU grew 75 years later. Better proof of the program to unite the women of Virginia for Foreign Mission work . . . is the fact that their words and example brought forth speedy results in another part of the state." These "speedy results" referred to were the formation of the Fredericksburg Female Baptist Society for Foreign Missions, with the "explicit intention" to "aid the sister Society for Foreign Missions in Richmond."

According to its printed Constitution, the membership in the Fredericksburg Society was open to "any females who wish to promote the glory of God." Giving to missions was considered a part of membership and "subscriptions" were to be "at least one dollar annually." Contributions were to be forwarded to the Richmond society.

After 175 years, the names on the Fredericksburg document—the oldest known printed constitution of a female missions society—still bear testimony to those missions support pioneers. The sparse rules give evidence of early organizational patterns. The first meeting was held at "the home of brother Alexander Walker" and Susan Walker was elected as the chief officer called "Directress." Eliza Smith was the "Recorder" of the minutes. Fifteen women were chosen to serve as Managers.

Rice had continued to pursue his intention of a "general society" and on May 18, 1814, 33 delegates from 11 states and the District of Columbia met in Philadelphia to form "the General Missionary Convention of the Baptist Denomination in the United States of America for Foreign Missions," or quickly nicknamed "The Triennial Convention" because it met once every three years. At the organizational meeting Robert Baylor Semple of Bruington Church, King and Queen County, and Jacob Grigg, who operated a school in Richmond, represented the Richmond-based Virginia society.

The Triennial Convention agreed to support Judson and appointed Rice "to continue his itinerant services with a view to excite the public mind to engage in missionary exertions, and to assist in originating societies for carrying the missionary design into execution." Rice was their agent, and he repeatedly visited Virginia to promote and collect funds for missions as well as to distribute missions literature and promote the new Baptist school, Columbian College, to be located at Georgetown in the nation's capital. He visited and preached in Baptist homes. Often when the women-folk would take pity on the poor traveling missionary and wash his clothes, they would discover the fabric was threadbare. Many made new clothes for their valued guest. The women also gave liberally of their means. In his journal of 1819 to 1820 there are numerous entries of Virginia women's gifts: One dollar "fr. a Lady, for Indian reform"; in Salem the collection included "a gold ring & a silver ring"; at "Sister Mrs. Alin Temple's" house in Eastern Virginia he noted a collection of seven dollars after preaching; and at Moore's Ordinary outside Richmond he received "a pair of woollen socks by Mrs. Smith." In Lynchburg in November, 1819, after he preached one evening on the Scripture, "Verily, I say unto you, wheresoever this gospel shall be preached in the whole world, then shall also this, that this woman, hath done be told for a memorial of her," the appreciative Lynchburg Female Missionary Society gave $20.67 for the cause.

The women of First Baptist Church, Richmond, "outdid all others" in love gifts. They equipped him with a coat and hat; and once in Richmond, he discovered in his lodging room "two excellent cravats" and a pair of socks.

From 1813 to 1834, Richmond Baptist women, along with those in other Virginia communities, forwarded their gifts through the Richmond Female Missionary Society. The women's money also would go through the Virginia Baptist Missionary Society or in the hands of a delegate to the Triennial Convention or directly to the agent, Luther Rice.

In 1822, women of First and Second Baptist Churches, Richmond, organized the Female Judson Society to undergird the work of Ann Judson in Burma. In April, 1823, she acknowledged a gift from her Virginia "sisters in Christ" for "female schools in Burma." She wrote: "On my own account and in behalf of ignorant females in the East, allow me to express my thanks. . . . I am convinced that, when American females are induced to contribute of their worldly substance to enlighten their own sex on the other side of the world, their prayers and their influence also are joined. May your society prosper and increase. May your hearts 'ere long be gladdened by the intelligence that your bounty was not bestowed in vain."

Virginia women felt a special kinship to the missions saga of Henrietta and Lewis Shuck. As a young woman, Henrietta Hall of Kilmarnock began her search for Christ after a teacher presented the piercing question: "Where will you be a hundred years hence?" As a Sunday school teacher in First Church, Richmond, she met her future husband, a student at the Virginia Baptist Seminary, Jehu Lewis Shuck, who had been reared in Alexandria. It was Shuck who at a missionary rally quickly searched his heart and wrote on a slip of paper for the offering plate: "I'll give myself." Two days after their marriage, Shuck and his bride were set apart for foreign missions in a service conducted at First Church, Richmond.

The story of their labors in Macao and Hong Kong fill the annals of missions history. Henrietta, long concerned about helping humankind

From the oil portrait of Yong Seen Sarng, the early convert made by the Shucks in China. He visited America from 1846 to 1847 and became a favorite friend of the missionary society at First Church, Richmond.

through a lasting contribution, opened a school and pioneered in the instruction of Chinese females. Lewis Shuck was the forerunner of a long line of American missionaries to labor in China and his work established a firm foundation for future efforts. Later he again pioneered missions work among the Chinese in the United States when he worked in California. Henrietta's missions career ended abruptly with her death at age 27 in 1844, following the birth of her fifth child. She was buried in Happy Valley Cemetery in Hong Kong.

Virginia women never forgot their sister or her contributions and her brief yet inspiring life. In death, they gave her heroine status. She was cited as the role model for young Virginians, and the Shuck Centennial of 1935 became the ultimate focus upon the pristine lives of Henrietta, whom Virginia WMU literature called "our Fairest Flower," and her husband. Henrietta became to Virginia WMU what Ann Judson was to Baptists of America in general.

A fascinating supporting player in the Shuck drama was Yong Seen Sarng, an early convert who served as a language teacher for the Shucks. Although once "a bigoted adherent to Confucianism, Taoism, and Buddhism," he became a Christian minister himself to the Chinese people. Following Henrietta's death, Lewis Shuck felt compelled to visit America for several reasons, including the search for a wife. He also wanted to raise funds for a chapel in Canton and so he carried with him the best advertisement, a living curiosity from the mysterious Orient, Yong Seen Sarng. From 1846 to 1847, the pair toured the eastern United States speaking to various Baptist groups including the newly-formed Southern Baptist Convention (SBC).

Yong caused quite a sensation. In his native attire, including a long gown, skull cap and "fantastical" shoes that curled at the toe and with his long plaited hair, he was a sight to behold! Along the way he made lasting friendships with mission-minded women. Since he was likely their first contact with the foreigners whom they had labeled as "heathen," they would not soon forget the Chinese convert. The woman's missionary society of First Church, Richmond, remained devoted to Yong. They paid his return traveling expenses, provided him with warm clothing, and collected funds for a year's salary. While he was in Richmond they even commissioned his portrait. For years, Yong and the Richmond Baptist women corresponded. In his old age he once wrote them: "Through your kind love, I have been enabled to exercise this ministry and to preach for many years. Every year the number of believers has increased."

Another early figure in modern missions with Virginia connections was a black man who had purchased his freedom so he could tell his own race in Africa about the true freedom found in Jesus Christ. Born about 1780, Lott Cary was a native of Charles City County and came to Richmond in 1804 at about the age of 24. He was converted under the preaching of "Father" John Courtney of First Church, Richmond; almost immediately after his conversion, Cary began to preach.

Another influence upon Cary was William Crane, an ordained Baptist deacon, who in 1812 began teaching young Negro men the rudiments of reading, writing, and arithmetic as well as unfolding the Scriptures to them. In 1815, he was instrumental in the establishment of the Richmond African Baptist Missionary Society.

Cary, who was working as a tobacco warehouseman, and another black, Collin Teague, had been taught by Crane, and they joined the African Missionary Society. In 1819, Crane introduced the two men in a letter to the

William Crane, at right, *looks on while Lott Cary signs the church constitution for the Liberian Church in Crane's home in Richmond in 1821. (Sidney E. King, artist, VBHS)*

American Colonization Society: "Ever since the missionary cause began to be agitated, these two men have wished they could do something to aid their unhappy kindred in Africa. They have determined to go themselves."

In 1821, Cary and Teague and five others, including their wives and Teague's 14-year old son, met in Crane's home and constituted the Providence Baptist Church of Monrovia, a church which Blanche Sydnor White calls "the first Baptist church of missionary origin on the continent of Africa." She also described the Liberian missionaries as "converted, educated, equipped, supported through Virginia Baptist initiative [with] white and colored Baptists cooperating in their support."

Lott Cary was supported in his work by the prayers and gifts of Virginia women. Even to the present, organized missions work among black women has been known as the Lott Cary Missionary Society.

Another great missionary force began in the 1820s and continued without interruption. It was the Baptist General Association of Virginia, a successful attempt after earlier failures to unite the scattered congregations of Baptists. In time its State Mission Board, later simply called the Virginia Baptist General Board, supported the work of many missionaries across Virginia, including religious book distributors called colporteurs, evangelists, and the forerunners to today's "church planters." In the 1800s, the General Association was controlled by men. Only once in its early years was a woman listed as a "life member," and she possibly purchased the membership for her pastor. In the 1920s, women began appearing as delegates, later called messengers, from the churches. In 1930, they began serving on the State Mission Board but not until 1972 was a woman elected an officer. In 1982 and again in 1988, women were elected as presidents of the General Association and, automatically, as chairmen of the General Board.

But in 1823, the General Association was new and its missions service was for the future. The state Baptists needed to know the religious climate across Virginia so they appointed two young men to serve as the first state missionaries. In 1823 and 1824, the two traveled throughout Virginia preaching wherever they could gather an audience. Jeremiah Bell Jeter and Daniel Witt were boyhood friends from rural Bedford County and called themselves appropriately "the Bedford Plowboys." They journeyed into every corner of Virginia including places where a Baptist witness had never been felt. Along the way those who did hear and respond included the women of Virginia.

The first account of organized missions work by Baptist women in Virginia appeared in the *Religious Herald* on February 10, 1828. It was a report of the Fifth Annual Meeting of the Richmond Female Judson Society, which had met in the home of Mrs. George Roper. There were numerous others. One early Virginia Baptist historian stated: "Long before the organization of the General Association, the ladies had certain missionary societies and at the first service of the General Association in 1823, the Female Baptist Missionary Society of Goochland reported a contribution of $80, the Female Baptist Missionary Society of Fluvanna, $32.50, and the Louisa Missionary and Bible Society, $20. There has been no period that the influence of the organized women's work has not been felt in our church development. There has been no missionary effort, no great or challenging denominational undertaking, that has not received the unstinted support of our noble women."

In tracing the development of education among the Baptists of Virginia, Frederic W. Boatwright, who for 52 years served as president of the Uni-

First state missionaries, "the Bedford Plowboys," Jeremiah Bell Jeter, at left, and Daniel Witt were equipped with "reliable horses" by the new General Association and commissioned to tour Virginia from 1823 through 1824 to determine the religious climate of the state. (Sidney E. King, artist, VBHS)

versity of Richmond (UR), reminded his readers that "early in the life of the Virginia Baptist Seminary [in the 1830s] it was suggested that auxiliary Female Education Societies be formed to assist the Virginia Baptist Education Society in raising money for [its] support." He added that "the remarkable financial success of the Seminary and the early college [Richmond College, now UR] was due to the devoted and sacrificial gifts of Virginia Baptist women." He suggested that free-will gifts to the Virginia Baptist Seminary offered the women "lessons of liberality" which were precursors to their later missions gifts.

The devout Baptist women of King and Queen County, about 50 miles northeast of Richmond, early caught the missionary fervor and became examples of effective organizational support. Fannie E.S. Heck brought the obscure Priscilla Pollard to national attention when she extolled Pollard's virtues in her book *In Royal Service*. "Priscilla Pollard inspired the women of a wide section with missionary zeal," wrote Miss Heck, "reorganizing in 1832–37 the Bruington Society and acting as first president of the St. Stephens and Mattaponi Societies and reorganizing the Society of Beulah Church." Baptized by Robert Baylor Semple and a member of Mattaponi Church as early as 1833, and possibly one of its constituting members in 1828, Pollard was an early dynamo among Virginia Baptist missions leaders. As Mrs. H.M. Wharton wrote in 1938, "The Mattaponi Society early took the whole world into its view, putting Home Missions on the same footing as Foreign. In 1842, it decided to retain the right to bestow funds as may be deemed most expedient, whether for foreign missions [or] state or any part of the American continent. For years Mattaponi Church proudly displayed a little chair which had been used during the missionary meetings by Priscilla Pollard. The chair bore the initials of "P.P.," and Mattaponi's Baptist women insisted that the initials really stood for "Perfect President."

The missionary societies offered Virginia Baptist women opportunities for service. While they could and did send their contributions to the General Association beginning with its founding in 1823, they were denied representation in the body for nearly a century. The limitation of male delegates only was not lifted until 1919.

Despite the blatant discrimination of the times, Virginia Baptist women found ways to serve. Blanche Sydnor White once summarized: "They taught in the earliest of Sunday schools; brought their mites and organized fairs and feasts to pay current expenses and building debts of the church. Where there was no Baptist church in the community, women frequently led in establishing a Sunday school, nourished it until it was ready for organization, prayed into the pulpit the man of God's own choosing, then proceeded to provide money for a building." Within many of the churches, benevolent organizations usually called Ladies' Aid Societies were organized. They frequently raised funds by holding church suppers for such causes as building improvements.

Blanche Sydnor White noted that "no one objected" because the Ladies' Aid Societies were not perceived as threats "to the solidarity or sovereignty of the church." Yet she exclaimed that "animosity reared its head when the conscience of Virginia Baptist womanhood was stirred in behalf of Christian missions beyond the local church"; and missionary societies, composed usually of the same women who were active in the Ladies' Aid Societies, came to be seen as "dangerous and divisive."

Yet Blanche Sydnor White concluded that vocal opposition to "woman's work for woman" was actually "found in the heart and on the lips of a minority." She cited a long list of leading figures in Virginia Baptist life who were supportive—"a great host of ministers, deacons and other laymen who encouraged 'Woman's Work'; editors of the *Religious Herald* without exception have been champions [of women] in every good work; Robert Ryland, the first president of the University of Richmond [who] stimulated the organization of female education societies; secretaries of the mission boards and missionaries . . . to these friends Woman's Missionary Union (WMU), under God, owes her very existence and her continued growth."

Indeed opposition was quiet during the six decades of localized work, from 1813 to 1874, but with the development of a state organization a perceived threat stirred the flames of discontent.

An important early leader in the woman's missionary movement was an unlikely person, the modest Ann J. Graves of Baltimore, Maryland, mother of an early Southern Baptist missionary to China, Rosewell Graves. Her son wrote impassioned letters home explaining the need for "Bible women" to visit Chinese homes. She took her son's pleas to heart and organized "A Female Missionary Prayer Meeting for the Support of Native Bible Women Belonging to the Canton Mission."

Ann Graves

In 1868 when the SBC convened in Baltimore, Ann Graves suggested that the women who had accompanied their husbands meet to discuss missions. Mrs. C.D. Creasman, the woman who popularized WMU history through pageants, called the gathering "the first general meeting of Southern Baptist women in history." Among the women at the meeting was Mary Catherine Jeter of Richmond, who was the wife of the editor of the *Religious Herald*.

Soon afterwards there was organized in Baltimore a group called "Woman's Mission to Women," and other meetings were subsequently held in connection with the SBC.

The quiet Ann Graves found a way to be heard loudly. In a circular to be distributed across the SBC, she described the organization of the Baltimore branch and boldly declared: "We now appeal to the women of our Baptist churches to sustain this union by their prayers and contributions. We support the organization of branches in each state, to attend to the business, and missionary circles in each church or neighboring churches united, to meet regularly for prayer and dissemination of missionary intelligence."

In the 1870s, several Virginia women went abroad as missionaries, and their support became a rallying point for organizing women's missions work. In 1871, Kate Evans of Amelia County went to Burma under appointment of the Woman's American Baptist Foreign Mission Society. The following year an Albemarle woman, Edmonia Moon, was sent by the FMB of the SBC to China. Her appointment broke the 20-year ban against sending unmarried females. Mary Catherine Jeter invited the women of the seven churches in Richmond to meet and discuss the support of Miss Moon. On April 4, 1872, women from five Richmond churches met and organized the Woman's Missionary Society of Richmond. Their initial raison d'etre was to aid Edmonia Moon. Any Richmond Baptist woman could join if she agreed to contribute at least two cents a week.

The constitution of the new organization stated: "Grateful for the social and intellectual education of women . . . impressed with the importance of carrying to the homes and hearts of our oppressed and degraded sisters in other lands that Gospel which has done so much for us, we . . . desirous to promote by our gifts and prayers . . . here associated ourselves togeth-

When this photograph of Lottie D. Moon was given to the Virginia Baptist Historical Society in 1979, it was said to be one of six known original likenesses of the beloved Virginia missionary to China.

er." Juliette Mather's study of missions history declared it to be "the first cooperative organization of Baptist women from more than one church, south of the Potomac."

In 1873, Edmonia's sister joined her at Tung Chow, China. Charlotte Digges Moon, affectionately and popularly known as "Lottie," would become, despite her humility, the most celebrated missionary associated with Southern Baptists. At the time of her departure the native Virginian, along with a friend, had been operating a school in Cartersville, Georgia; she easily had the potential support of mission-minded women in two states. The Cartersville women organized a missionary society to aid Miss Moon. Henry Allen Tupper, corresponding secretary of the FMB, requested Mary Catherine Jeter to stir Virginia's support through the Richmond Society. Specifically, a building was needed to serve as a residence for the missionaries and for a school. "The Moon House" became the common goal that rallied the women.

Mrs. E.D. Poe's history of Virginia WMU gives at a rapid clip the succession of events which culminated in the traditionally accepted founding of the state organization. She begins with Dr. Tupper's appeal printed in the *Religious Herald* of March 19, 1874, in which he outlined the financial crisis limiting the FMB's support of the Moon sisters and seeking help for improved living and working quarters. Tupper spoke at the General Association meeting held in Fredericksburg in June, 1874, and J.C. Long, president of the FMB, added a plea in his report on missions: "The wants of our China missions are great and very pressing. The Misses Moon need a school-house. Cannot our Virginia women undertake the task of building the house for them? The cost will be $2,000."

Before an SBC meeting, Tupper suggested the formation of coordinating bodies among local missionary societies in each state. The name "Central Committees for Woman's Work" had been employed. Virginia, through its Richmond Society, would become a testing ground.

Mary Catherine Jeter accepted Tupper's appeal and called upon Virginia women to respond. One account credits the *Religious Herald* as providing the date of August 14, 1874, as the founding date of Virginia's Central Committee. Mrs. Poe stated with much certainty that "we do not know where or when," yet surmises that the first meeting was "in late August or early in September" and likely at Mrs. Jeter's residence at First and Grace Streets in Richmond. On September 7, 1874, Mrs. Jeter published in her husband's paper, the *Religious Herald*, an open letter addressed "to the Baptist Ladies of Virginia." She expressed the Moons' needs and explained that "a circular has been sent to each of the Baptist churches in the State by the 'Woman's Missionary Society' of [Richmond], requesting your aid."

The Virginia Central Committee was, in reality, the Richmond Society and in the early years the Richmond Baptist women were the mirror image of the state organization although Tupper was quick and correct to point out that "no organic connection [existed] between them." It is further evident that the Virginia organization existed earlier in the 1870s because it was "reorganized" in 1878, when it became an auxiliary of the FMB. Mary Catherine Jeter was again president and other officers in 1878 included Mary Thomas Curry, Mrs. Edwin Wortham, Mrs. Richard Adam, Mrs. J.B. Turpin, Mrs. H. Theodore Ellyson, Mrs. W.E. Hatcher, Mrs. A.B. Clarke, and Mrs. J.B. Hutson.

Juliette Mather stated that the purposes of the Central Committee were "to organize missionary societies and by the circulation of periodicals to cultivate the missionary spirit." An early appeal in the *Religious Herald* urged: "Experience has shown that women, when they work independently of men, yet in harmony with their plans, accomplish more than when they labor with them. We wish to secure the largest amount of means for the prosecution of our missionary work. . . . Will our sisters in every church make immediate arrangements for organizing a Society?" The appeal was signed by Mrs. Jeter, president, and Mrs. Wortham, corresponding secretary.

As for the Moon House, Virginia women raised at least half of the over $2500 collected with contributions of $700 coming from Richmond women. But the Moon House was never built. Edmonia's health was broken and she returned home. In time the funds were used to provide a house "at the Cross Roads" for Lottie Moon and a chapel at Tung Chow.

Soon the clamor would be heard for the support of other missionaries appointed in the 1870s. Among these were Virginians Susan and George Boardman Taylor, who founded Baptist work in Rome, Italy, and the Davids, who served in Africa. Nannie Bland David of Chesterfield County became another early heroine among the Virginia missionaries. Inspired at age twelve to serve as a missionary, in 1879 she accompanied her husband, W.J. David, to Nigeria where she pioneered the work of child care among native women. She died in 1885 with the parting and poignant words, "Never give up Africa."

The tempest of organized woman's work was swirling. In 1885, the SBC recommended that the state Baptist bodies assume the connection to the women's Central Committees rather than the FMB. In 1886, the General Association considered the matter and referred it to the Committee on Co-operation. The committee sharply debated the relationship of woman's work to the state body. The committee was still divided internally when it reported to the General Association meeting held in November, 1887, in Lynchburg's First Baptist Church. J.T. Ellyson, chairman, reported for the committee, reminding the delegates that the committee's charge had been "to take such measures as in our wisdom we might think effective in organizing the sisters of the churches for more direct and personal work." Ellyson hit the raw nerve of the issue: "We are aware of the objection made by many good brethren and sisters to the tendency to disintegration in our churches by the formation of societies working apart from regular church methods. But we have no idea that the women who are thus en-

Nannie Bland David speaks of her missions commitment at the Ladies' Missionary Sewing Circle of Bethlehem Church in Chesterfield County. (Sidney E. King, artist, VBHS)

Scene from the Diamond Jubilee pageant shows the Virginia brethren reacting to the perceived threats of a woman's organization. In hot and furious rhetoric some likened it unto a second civil war and predicted the ruin of the race.

gaged in society work would, for a moment, intentionally foster any plan which would compromise the teaching of our one Master—Christ. They are devoted to their churches, and we believe, also, that all Virginia Baptists, whether men or women, are desirous of promoting that beautiful and helpful unity of sentiment and effort which has always made us strong. We should remember that these societies are composed of members of our churches; that they are legitimately a part of the resources of this body, and the point for us to consider is whether they shall be brought into organic connection with the General Association, or left to pursue their work in an irregular way."

Ellyson urged the appointment of a standing committee, "The Women's Missionary Committee of Virginia." The new committee would promote "the missionary spirit among the Baptist women of the State" and receive funds from donors. Local societies would be encouraged to cooperate with the committee. The recommendation contained a disputed provision to allow representation by local societies in the Baptist General Association of Virginia "upon the same terms and conditions of the churches."

The divided committee had Ellyson's majority report and a minority report signed by four members. To save his report and its recommendations, Ellyson struck the provision of representation. Despite his move, the minority report won with its call for "a select committee of five" to further investigate the matter of women's organizations. It also cautioned the Baptist women of Virginia against forming any separate organization. Three men, John Hart, C.L. Cocke, and A. B. Evans, were appointed to draft and distribute the appeal to the women, "urging upon them the duty of co-operating with their respective churches in missionary work."

At the SBC meeting held in Richmond in May, 1888, before the Virginia committee could report, Southern women were determined to organize. Virginia WMU hosted a gathering contrary to the will of many of their brethren. The women were cordially welcomed to Virginia, where the Southern women met in a borrowed hall, the basement assembly room of the Broad Street Methodist Church. Virginia "Jennie" Snead Hatcher had talked with her husband, the influential Richmond pastor William E. Hatcher, and he had urged her to defer Virginia's entry in the national woman's organization until the brethren in the General Association could be persuaded as to the wisdom of such an organization. And so Mrs. Hatcher extended greetings and stepped aside. On May 14, 1888, the WMU, SBC, was formed without Virginia's membership.

By November the controversy was raging in Virginia. The five-man select committee may have been "stacked" as it included a chief opponent of organized women's work, Tiberius Gracchus Jones, pastor of First Church, Norfolk. Others were A.B. Dunaway, Edward Harrison, L.B. Johnson, and David Johnston. In November, 1888, the General Association met in far Southwest Virginia at Bristol. The committee's report, finally heard during the Saturday evening session, proved an exercise in anti-women sentiment. The committee endorsed the concept of one missionary society composed of men and women, disguising their resentment by declaring that societies exclusively for women smacked of the "organization-mad, society-mad times." The report claimed: "It directs and distracts attention, prevents a proper concentration of energy and effort, divides and unwisely diffuses resources, and so wastes and weakens strength."

The distraught brethren likened the very idea of a women's organization to a second Civil War: "[We are] threatened with a second subjugation, 'an invasion of ideas,' worse, perhaps, and more formidable than an invasion

In this detail from the Virginia Baptist history mural, the founding meeting of WMU, SBC, is underway with Annie Armstrong speaking before the group. Notice the twin girls in the foreground, the daughters of Abby Manly Gwathmey. (Sidney E. King, artist, VBHS)

of armies; a mental and moral subjugation more to be dreaded than territorial and political." Calling it a "monster evil," they predicted the downfall of families and all good relationships between the sexes. They sternly warned against "departure from 'the old paths, the good way.' " After exhaustive rhetoric, the committee declared that "it would be altogether unwise and inexpedient" for the General Association to be connected with "a Central Committee of women."

George Cooper, pastor of First Church, Richmond, saved the day for the women of Virginia. After the committee's lengthy diatribe he offered a calm and single substitute which carried: "That the General Association hereby recognize this Central Committee." The Cooper motion called for the women to continue collecting funds and to promote their work, submitting an annual report to the General Association. The storm subsided at least publicly, and the Central Committee was duly recognized.

The man who moved the mountain at the Bristol meeting and convinced Virginia gentlemen to do the right thing by women was not a Southerner. Born in Scotland and reared in Canada, George Cooper was educated "up North" and all of his pastorates, except the one in Richmond, had been in Northern states. The young man in his forties had only been in Virginia three years when he led his colleagues to accept women into the denomination's framework.

When the General Association met at First Church, Charlottesville, in 1889, the meeting lacked the previous year's rancor and debate over the women's movement. Jennie Snead Hatcher, president of the Central Committee, very likely compiled the mandatory report. The minutes, with no statement of who presented the report, simply stated the report had been "read and adopted."

The first report to the General Association reported remarkable success. Thirty-two societies had been organized and out of approximately 300 societies, a total of 127 were corresponding with the committee. The women had contributed over $4,600 to missions enterprises. Juliet Pollard, the corresponding secretary, had been extremely busy writing letters to practically all the pastors and local societies, as well as sending "leaflets on Foreign and Home Missions, prayer-cards, programmes of exercises," and copies of the two missions publications, *Foreign Mission Journal* and *Home Field*.

The women, however, found little financial help from the denominational offices. No longer identified with the FMB, the Central Committee felt compelled to seek aid for its work from the General Association through its Committee on Co-operation. They received "courteous and sympathetic aid" but few dollars. Mrs. Hatcher reported: "Realizing that success in arousing a missionary spirit and organizing societies could not be secured without fully and widely disseminating information, the committee resolved to be responsible for its own expenses and set to work to raise a fund for this object." The women collected nickels and soon $34 provided "amply enough for the remainder of the year."

The women were earnest. "It soon became evident," Mrs. Hatcher wrote, "that the correspondence of the committee . . . would be too great a tax on any two or three persons. Volunteer helpers could be had if we could furnish a place suitable for the work." Suitable mission rooms at Fourth and Franklin Streets, over Ladies' Exchange were rented, and Jennie Hatcher and Juliet Pollard, "aided by a half-dozen ladies," spent Tuesday and Thursday mornings "doing clerical work." The "mission rooms" would provide the headquarters for a state-wide missionary organization and Jennie Hatcher encouraged "ladies from the country who chance to be in the city" to visit the rooms and secure missions tracts.

As the work progressed, improvements needed in the organizational framework became evident. By the close of the century, societies, including Sunbeam Bands, numbered 542. The active personnel was expanded to include a Sunbeam Band superintendent, the forerunner of the young people's secretary. Gifts had increased to over $12,000. The General Association's Committee on Co-operation studied the need for reorganization, and by 1899, the following significant changes were effected: the Central Committee would assume the title of Woman's Missionary Union and elect its own board; and the women's annual meeting would be held at a separate time and place from the General Association's. All funds collected would be deposited with the Treasurer of the General Association. In October, 1899, the first annual meeting of WMU of Virginia was held at Salem.

Was the organization an agency or a board? Another word surfaced. As William L. Lumpkin interpreted the history in an address before the General Association in 1963, "A move to make the Central Committee into a Board of the General Association was stoutly resisted. Finally it was accorded the unsought status of an auxiliary." The "auxiliary" relationship proved to be a good one. It was "an auxiliary organization, working for the same ends" as the General Association "but electing its own officers, making its own plans, taking its own collections and distributing them through the treasurer and agencies of the General Association as it should see fit." Again quoting Lumpkin, "This relationship requires a good measure of autonomy for the WMU. Baptist polity does not know the relationship of superior and inferior bodies. It balances organizational autonomy with organizational inter-dependence."

It would also become evident that Virginia's women accomplished more in joining hearts and hands in a "Union" with other Baptist women across the nation as part of the Woman's Missionary Union, Auxiliary to the Southern Baptist Convention. Reflective of the first words of the national organization's permanent watchword, "laborers together," the women were united in prayer, giving, community missions, and missionary education of their own members and of young people.

Mrs. F.W. Armstrong captured the very essence of WMU's philosophy in her presidential address at the WMU, SBC, annual meeting in 1936: "The record of gifts, activities and all the multiplied things that enter into our life as 'laborers together' combine to form an incentive to renewed effort. But they are more: they are sure evidence that this work of our hands and hearts and minds is His work, that verily we are 'laborers together with God.' But for this fact the work could not survive the mistakes, the failures we have made and the disloyalties of which we have often been guilty. Without Him, we are weak and our labors are futile, but with God we are made strong, we are invincible, we are conquerors. 'If God be for us who can be against us?' His presence and power are ours because the work is His work and because we are fellow-workers with Him."

As "laborers together with God" the women of Virginia have jointly accomplished great works. Gathering up the years into five epochs, this volume highlights the laborers and how they effectively worked together as hearts and hands joined in missions.

Chapter 1

The Founding Years,

1874–1899

They were the "King's daughters," these women with a missions vision. Ever conscious that they "must begin and build with care a holy place," they supported missionaries through prayers and gifts. As they built, other towers were erected of personal service, of education, and of missions in their "own Jerusalem" of Virginia. As each woman sought to perfect herself, she never forgot that God's temple was "chiselled from within."

If an unspoken creed was accepted, it was the belief in the promise of girls, "in the women of a great tomorrow and that whatsoever the girl soweth the woman shall reap." These early leaders soon included in their widening vision their own daughters and then their young sons as well. Missions organizations developed for all ages and for boys as well as girls.

Great missions heroes and heroines emerged from each generation. Susan Broadus Stone, the Moon sisters, Nannie Bland David, Susan Braxton Taylor, May Bagby Rudd, Fannie Russell . . . the women of Virginia sent forth their own daughters.

The founding years called for courage as women asserted themselves into leadership positions and effectively proved that a woman's gentle voice could clearly spread the greatest message ever given. The pioneering sisters perceived that Christ's commission was as much their prerogative and their burden as it was their brother's. Mary Catherine Jeter, Jennie Hatcher, Abby Gwathmey, Juliet Pollard, Anna Elsom, the Ellyson women and the ranks which they represented did not confront the men as much as they led them, gently and wisely, to accept woman's work in its new and bold definition.

These years—setting the course for all to follow—were the times when women learned the power of a penny and a prayer each day. Vision, tenacity, and resolve characterize the founding years, the last quarter of the nineteenth century.

"KING'S DAUGHTERS"

King's daughters!
Wouldst thou be all fair,
Without, within—
Peerless and beautiful,
A Very Queen?
Thou must begin
And build with care
A Holy Place
Watching ever, praying ever,
Keep it fragrant,
    sweet and clean,
So by God's grace
    it be fit place,
His Christ shall enter
    and shall dwell therein
Thy temple face is chiselled
    from within.

John Oxenham

Co-Laborers

" 'Laborers together' are the first words in the permanent watchword of Woman's Missionary Union. Through the years we have developed a wonderful 'togetherness' in our plan of organization. The word 'Union' in our name indicated that we are together in our work—united in a great program of service.

"In Woman's Missionary Union we are laborers together in **prayer**. Surely the praying of thousands in agreement finds a hearing with the Father who is in Heaven. We feel that united praying accounts for much of the success of WMU.

"We are laborers together in **giving**. United giving makes large giving. Few Southern Baptist women can give large sums but many, faithfully paying tithes and giving offerings, brings into the Lord's treasury millions of dollars every year.

"We are laborers together in **community missions**. Members of WMU organizations, united in personal soul-winning and Christian service in their various communities, are a great evangelizing and Christianizing force in our nation.

"We are laborers together in the **missionary education of young people**. By working together for and with the young people, we are training another generation to labor together in the furtherance of the Gospel.

"Laborers together—north, east, south, west; in city, country, town and village; rich and poor, young and old; women, girls, boys and little children, laborers together to tell the world about Jesus—that's the WMU."

Royal Service
May, 1948

"First Call for the Lottie Moon Christmas Offering"

"Baptist women of the south have undertaken to put in the treasury of the Foreign Mission Board money to support all female missionaries. At a meeting of ladies held in connection with the Albemarle Association, it was determined that the Woman's Missionary Societies of that body work for the support of Miss Lottie Moon who went out from the Association. The Fork Union Society was the first to respond to the call, and pledged one-sixth of the $600 required.

"Middle District Societies ask for Mrs. Bartow Rudd whose husband went out from that body. The society of his old church, Skinquarter, in a meeting last Sunday, offered also one-sixth or $100 for Mrs. Rudd's support.

What association will respond next? Let the societies talk over the matter and inform the Central Committee through their Associational President of their purposes."

Mrs. W.E. Hatcher
Religious Herald
September 25, 1890

Auxiliary: *A Good Word*

Webster defines the word, "auxiliary," as one who helps or aids. As an auxiliary, our Woman's Missionary Society strives to be a strong helper, a sympathetic ally of our church as it seeks to obey the Great Commission. Since the organization of the first woman's missionary society—those women who followed Jesus "throughout all the cities and villages of Galilee"—other methods have been introduced. Today individual and united prayer for the spread of the Gospel, individual and united witness to the saving power of Jesus Christ in each community, and the giving of material possessions remain the basic plans of our work. We have added the study of the missionary message of the Bible and other missionary literature, the missionary education of our young people, and efforts to enlist all of the women members of our church in all of these activities.

[*In the 1880s*] Virginia women were so anxious to work closely with the General Association that their desire and request was for the General Association to establish a board (*or department*) for woman's work. The "brethren" disagreed among themselves and controversy raged. Some urged that the General Association establish such a board while others contended that the women should have no separate organization, local, associational or state, but should work only through the churches. In November, 1888 the General Association agreed to a compromise, accepting the Central Committee for Woman's Work, but not as a board or department. It was to be "an *auxiliary* organization working for the same ends [as the General Association], electing its own officers, making its own plans for promoting its activities among the women throughout the state, taking its own collections and distributing them through the treasury and agencies of the General Association as it should see fit, making an annual report to the General Association."

Again in 1898 when both the name and organization of the Central Committee were changed to Woman's Missionary Union, women requested the General Association to establish a board of woman's work. The General Association gave approval to the reorganization but refused to establish a board, thus continuing the relationship as an auxiliary.

In light of almost a century of progress, we believe, the "brethren" were wise, and the "sisters" were nearsighted. The status of auxiliary opened avenues of service to Baptist women which a board could never have given.

Some today continue to oppose Woman's Missionary Union and her auxiliary status as others did in the 19th century. In this day when even Baptists are "compulsively driven to unification of effort," to conformity, and to centralization of authority with "its attendant evils of mechanization and bureaucracy," an auxiliary with a measure of autonomy can be a blessing and a counter-balance. Baptist polity does not know the relationship of superior and inferior bodies. It balances organizational autonomy with organization inter-dependence.

Religious Herald
February 3, 1966

Mary Catherine Jeter

*S*he came into Baptist history as "the Widow Dabbs." Jeremiah Bell Jeter, the pre-eminent leader among Virginia Baptists, was bewitched by her, affectionately referring to her as a "witch" who had charmed him. Having married and buried three wives, he pondered whether it was the better part of good judgment to marry a fourth but marry he did and then penned in his private journal: "A good wife is a treasure to any man who finds her and he shall know true pleasure provided he minds her."

Jeremiah Bell Jeter must not have regretted "minding" Mary Catherine Dabbs Jeter for he soon made her an unofficial advisor for his **Religious Herald** and for more than 20 years she "indirectly or directly" influenced "the editorial conduct of the paper." For years she edited the Woman's Page, which increased circulation, widened the audience, and offered women a platform for their ideas.

She was also the central character in the formation of the Central Committee, which would direct woman's missions work in Virginia and serve as the forerunner of Virginia WMU. From 1874 until shortly before her death in 1887, she was its president and a major influence upon Virginia women.

As wife of the pastor of Grace Street Church, she taught the "Infant Class" which enrolled between 250 and 300 pupils, "the largest in the South." She was also president of the church's Ladies' Aid Society. While accompanying her husband to the SBC meeting in Baltimore, she met Ann Graves and became inspired to organize women for larger missions service. But many things had happened in her life before these dramatic episodes would be played.

Born in Petersburg in 1824, she was "endowed with unusual charms" and attended the "best schools" of the times. At 26 she married a young minister, Christopher Jennett, who was her pastor. He briefly served in Augusta, Georgia; after barely a year of marriage he died. Six years later she married Josiah Dabbs, a wealthy planter and an active Baptist layman. They made their home at High Meadows, which still is known as "the Dabbs House," in Henrico County. He died in 1862 and the young widow, then 38 years of age, spent her time in the city at the residence of the wealthy and influential Mrs. Archibald Thomas. It was there that she met the widowed Jeter, who remarked to a friend that he had been "charmed, won, captured, spell-bound" by the Widow Dabbs.

Contemporaries observed that the two were "sufficiently alike in aim and tastes to be entirely congenial" yet "sufficiently unlike in mental characteristics to be very helpful to one another." The minister was in his sixties and found his "Kate" the real "tower of strength" in his old age. A close friend once commented that Kate Jeter was her husband's "strength, pride, counsellor" in whom "he confided the secrets of his heart."

In 1865, Jeter and Alfred E. Dickinson purchased the **Herald**. From the beginning Mrs. Jeter helped her husband "select and prune articles, scanning [other papers] and calling his attention to such matters as he ought to read, glancing over new books and current *magazines, and editing the Home Circle and the Children's Column."*

In 1872, she accompanied her husband on a European tour to visit missions territory especially in Italy where George Boardman Taylor pioneered Baptist work. During Jeter's service as president of the Foreign Mission Board, she served again as an unofficial advisor, sharing with him information from her broad reading about the needs of people around the world.

She launched the Baptist Home for Aged Women, the earliest effort by Virginia Baptists to aid the elderly. Her concern for others, transcending denominational lines, led her to provide instrumental support for a Richmond shelter for "abandoned women" or "fallen women," the Victorian terms for unwed mothers.

A male of her day once reflected that although Mary Catherine Jeter presided over many gatherings, "she never overstepped the bounds of feminine modesty." The same man commented that she was "an advocate of women's rights to rule only in her own home." That court over which she clearly ruled was at Grace and First Streets in Richmond, where she and "the Doctor" gave a home to adopted children. It was additionally the unofficial headquarters for Virginia WMU for awhile.

In 1880, she again was widowed and in time moved from the large residence to a "cozy little home" on West Grace Street. She continued to direct the affairs of the Central Committee throughout her long illness, a cancer which made her last months an agony of constant pain.

It fell upon her long-time close friend and her husband's cousin, William E. Hatcher, pastor of Grace Street Church, to deliver the funeral address. The platform was crowded with "all the city pastors." Among her pallbearers were four young men from her Infant Class years earlier, among them Frank Crump, later to serve as treasurer of Virginia WMU.

In his funeral remarks Hatcher identified Mrs. Jeter as "the most widely-known" woman in the church and attributed her leadership to several factors including "her culture, queenly manners, intense personality and thorough self-mastery." Hatcher was frank in telling of the trials endured by Mrs. Jeter. She was human, with all the emotions and perplexities that eveyone experiences. Near the end, depression had descended. But even then, there was triumph. He told of a visit near the end: "I asked her if she had ever had fears and she replied, 'Only once. As I lay upon my bed one night, thinking that I would soon see my Saviour, the tempter came. He laughed at my hopes and pointed to the dark catalogue of my sins. But I pointed him to the all-sufficient blood. He told me that fear would come upon me like a strong man at the last. But my reply was the Lord is my light and my salvation: whom shall I fear? And then he fled, and he never returned.'

"I congratulated her on her serenity of spirit. She simply replied, 'It is peace like a river.' Her last prayer was, 'Lord Jesus, come quickly.' "

Mary Catherine "Kate" Jeter was the model of fulfilled Christian womanhood, a worthy model for the Baptist women of Virginia.

Important to the Baptist Women of Virginia

Henry Allen Tupper, corresponding secretary of the Foreign Mission Board, supported women's missions work.

Mrs. M.C. Jeter, President Central Committee for Virginia:
Dear Sister,

Recently I have sent notes to all the Central Committees, seeking information with regard to their work; and an address to the Societies of each state, urging them to report through their Central Committee. I address you, now, more particularly to ask if you think that the Baptist Woman's Missionary Societies of Virginia understand clearly the relation of your Committee to our Board; and if something more might be done to increase the number of these Societies, and to induce those already formed to report more generally and more regularly through your Committee. Your Committee, being an appointee of the Board of Foreign Missions, must not be confounded with any local Society, though officers of the Committee may happen to be officers of such Society. The chief work of the Central Committee is to foster and multiply Woman's Missionary Societies, by diffusion of information, and other appropriate means, and to receive their reports and funds and transmit them to our Board—the former directly and in summary form; the latter, through intermediary channels of State organizations.

Allow me to inquire, also whether your Committee might not be aided by having a Vice-President in each Baptist Association of the state, selected as the Vice-President of our Board for the Southern States are selected, with special reference to ability and willingness to work for the cause we represent? I would suggest that the clerk or the moderator for each Association be requested to send to your Committee the name of some earnest and competent woman-worker, in the bounds of the Association, who would probably accept this position. The nomination of such ladies by your Committee would secure their appointment by our Board. With such a person in each Association, equipped with missionary tracts, and forms of Constitutions for the organization of Societies, and, above all, with a goodly share of womanly tact, and the grace of God, I do not see why Virginia should not have as many and as efficient Woman Societies as any of her Sister States. Last year our Board reported to the Southern Baptist Convention six-hundred and forty-two such Societies, contributing $16,895.58. By pressing your work vigorously and prudently, the Old Dominion would soon report ten times the Societies now on your roll, and ten times the contributions you report to our Board.

Pastors could aid the work by suggesting to the Clerk, or the moderator, of their Association names of ladies adapted to this Vice-Presidency; by sending to your Committee names of their churches who are willing to organize Woman's Missionary Societies; and by encouraging Societies organized to report to your Committee. And why need the ladies wait for any one to send their names or encourage them? I do not wish to excite State pride to carry on the work of the Master; but I am sure that the Baptist women of Virginia, so eminent in works of patriotism and piety, are unwilling to be otherwise than among the foremost in this divine enterprise of developing their own spiritual resources and of giving the bread of life to perishing sister women among the nations.

I am, very respectfully,
Your obedient servant,
H. A. Tupper,
Corresponding Secretary.

We wish that this communication from the Corresponding Secretary of the Foreign Mission Board could meet the eye of every Baptist lady in Virginia. In every household reached by the **Herald**, we take it for granted that it will be read. May we not feel as well assured that every Woman's Missionary Society in the State will comply with the Secretary's request, and send their contributions to the Treasurer of the Central Committee, early in April, that a report may be made to the Southern Baptist

Convention, which meets in May, of what has been done for Foreign Missions by the Baptist women of Virginia? In the past twelve months only eleven Societies have sent their contributions to the Treasurer of the Central Committee. Can we afford, my dear sisters, to let it appear to the Convention that there are but eleven Woman's Missionary Societies in Virginia, and that the comparatively insignificant amount received is all that has been given by the women of our State? We know that the funds from these Societies do not represent what is done by our Virginia sisters, but we can only report the money received through the Central Committee. In every church in the State let a Woman's Missionary Society be formed at once, and if funds cannot be sent by April, at least inform our Corresponding Secretary, Miss Annie G. Tupper, of the organization of the Society, and furnish the names of its officers.

Mrs. M. C. Jeter, President of Central Committee
Mrs. Richard Adam, Treasurer
Miss Annie G. Tupper, Cor. Sec'y
Richmond, Virginia
Religious Herald
March 19, 1885

"Miss Annie"

*O*ne of the central figures in WMU history was Annie Armstrong, who repeatedly visited Virginia. She was in Richmond for the historic organizational meeting of Woman's Missionary Union, SBC in May, 1888. She shared the platform with her Baptist co-equal in missions heritage, Lottie Moon, at the 1903 meeting of Virginia women held in Norfolk. It was in Virginia that she signed the "Peace Treaty" with Fannie E.S. Heck thereby averting division in WMU ranks.

Virginia women loved and admired Miss Annie, who was their "near neighbor" as a native and resident of Maryland and their "co-laborer" for missions. The following paragraphs help illustrate the life and work of this pivotal person in missions history. They were written by the late Josephine C. Norwood, who also served both Virginia and Maryland women.

"Annie Walker Armstrong was born in Baltimore on July 11, 1850. Her parents were prominent citizens, active in church and civic affairs. When she was only eighteen months old, her father, a wealthy tobacconist, suffered financial reverses and died after a short illness. Her mother was a tower of strength . . .

"When Annie was thirteen, the family moved to the gracious home in which she grew up and where she lived most of her life. She received her education in fashionable private schools for girls.

"In December, 1870, Annie went to a regular evening service at her church. Her pastor, Richard Fuller, said, 'What the Christian has is not peace from trouble, but peace in the midst of trouble.' This captured Annie's attention. At the close of the service she accepted Jesus Christ as her Lord and Saviour.

"Annie Armstrong was a worker in her church. She was inspired by her mother who attended Mrs. Ann Graves' 'female missionary prayer meetings.' Every morning during family prayers she poured out her heart for the souls of the women of China and for doors to

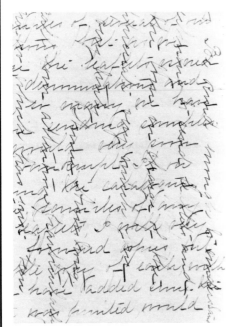

Annie Armstrong conducted heavy correspondence with missions leaders across the country. Practicing economy, she composes her letter on paper previously used. Her distinctive signature, however, remains visible.

open to missionaries.

"Soon she set about her own dedication to the Lord's service. She became superintendent of the 'infant class' in her Sunday school, worked with the Home for the Friendless, and began the Ladies' Bayview Mission.

"When the Woman's Baptist Home Mission Society of Maryland was formed Annie was elected president. She sat in the May, 1884, meeting in Baltimore and listened to the reading of an important resolution which Baltimore women considered a step toward South-wide organization: 'Resolved, that the societies here represented make the union meeting permanent; to meet annually, during the sessions of the SBC, the central committee of the state in which the convention is held having charge of the meeting that year.'

"Annie Armstrong was one of the organizers of the Woman's Missionary Union. She was elected corresponding secretary (now executive secretary). She served without salary in the WMU national office from 1888 to 1906.

"Reading Lottie Moon's appeal for the funds to support a helper, she led the women to begin the Christmas offering for foreign missions in 1888. Seeing the home fields' needs, she led in the development of the Home Missions Offering, first known as the Self-Denial offering in 1895 and renamed after her death as a tribute to her and her love for missions.

"Many of the plans of work today may be traced to the basic program developed by Annie Armstrong—praying, giving, studying, and serving."

"Rosebuds vs. Sunbeams"

"Paul exhorts that we 'consider one another to provoke unto . . . good works.' The Methodists inaugurated the work among the children eight years before our denomination had thought of using this material for advancing the cause of the Master. Verily, 'a little child led them' when, in response from 'Uncle Larry' (Rev. J.B. Laurens) in the *Advocate* that the children would write to him in the children's column, a little girl of seven years wrote: 'We wish to form a child's Missionary Society beginning in our own family. Now won't you tell the little folks and ask them to join?' This little girl was [little Miss] Campbell. She at once received the name of Rosebud Campbell and the pseudonym 'Queen of the Rosebuds.'

"Let us look at the report from this work . . . treasurer's report for year ending November, 1907, $7,632.07. I have been studying these reports in comparison with the Sunbeams who reported last year $3,334.10.

"I have concluded that their success is due to two things:

"1. The cooperation of the pastors. Every pastor is expected to have a Rosebud Society at every church he serves. His church expects it of him, his brethren in the State, and his District and State Conference.

"2. The pastor is desirous to have a good report from that Society. He would as soon think of leaving out the report of the amount raised by his church to Foreign Missions as to fail to report what the Rosebuds gave.

Sunbeam Band, Covington, 1920.

"Some of our pastors realize the responsibility, and do not hesitate to proclaim it from their pulpits. On a recent Sunday, Dr. Ryland Knight, pastor of Calvary Church, Richmond, had this to say, 'I want to call your attention to the crying need of today, that the child should be well and carefully taught the great fundamental truths of the Kingdom of God. The child of today, the man of tomorrow is going out where he will be swept away unless his feet are planted upon the unmoving rock.'"

[Note: The Methodists had their organization for children, called the Rosebuds, before the Baptists sparked the Sunbeams. In the above interesting comparison written in 1908 by Mrs. G.F. Williams, Virginia's Sunbeams Band superintendent, denominational differences and pride are evident.]

"A Sunbeam Lilliputian Wedding" Farmville.

The Value of a Child

"We cannot even approximately estimate the value of a child's life, nor foretell what capacities for good that life may develop. 'He who wins an adult saves a soul; he who wins a child saves a soul plus a life.'

"Upon these little lives our Lord has set a great value. Jesus said, 'Suffer the little children and forbid them not to come unto me . . . ' It has been well said that ever since Jesus used the little lad's five loaves and two fishes to feed the hungry multitude, he has been using children's gifts to bless the world.

"Think how responsive the heart of a child is to any appeal. How many little hearts have grown tender, and how many little hands have dropped their pennies, nickels, aye, their dimes, into the missionary basket . . . What a power lies in the organization known as Sunbeam Bands . . .

"Upon us rests the responsibility of developing in our children all that is needful for the work which will fall upon them, not forgetting that the child of today will be the missionary of the future."

Mrs. L. B. Vaughn, *WMU*
First Church, Richmond, 1907

Christmastide with Gwathmey Sunbeams

"Mrs. G.F. Williams gave to the Gwathmey Sunbeams an instructive talk on China and Sunbeam Mission work there. Her description of child life in China, illustrated by the amusing performance of her manikin, was particularly interesting, and her appeal for Chinese boys and girls who knew no Christmas went straight to the hearts of the children, whose minds were full of happy anticipation of the approaching Christmastide. At the close of the talk, a miniature Christmas stocking to be returned with an offering was presented to each member.

"*[On the day the stockings were returned]* a little Christmas tree, shapely and beautiful, secured by one of the strong young men in the Band, was placed in the chapel. The children formed a line at the chapel entrance, and to the ringing tune, 'We march, we march to victory with the cross of the Lord before us,' marched two by two up the aisle and hung their little stockings jingling with small coins and bulging with large [*coins*], on the tree. When the stockings were emptied they showed the generous offering of $9.75."

Religious Herald
February 6, 1908

Mother of Sunbeams

*I*n 1886 Anna Louisa Elsom was the teacher of the "infant class" in a rural church, Fairmount, in Nelson County. She knew about the Methodists' work for young children called the Rosebuds and felt strongly that the Baptists should promote such work with their children. She began to incorporate missions studies into her classwork and then gave her own group the name of "Sunbeams."

George Braxton Taylor, the son of foreign missionaries to Rome, Italy, and grandson of the first secretary of the Foreign Mission Board, was Mrs. Elsom's pastor. In the 1880s he was a young man—full of enthusiasm, energy, and vision—with more than a passing interest in missions. He caught Mrs. Elsom's spirit and promoted the idea of teaching little children about missions. Thus, thousands of Southern children eventually knew him as "Cousin George."

Though Taylor might be a **cousin**, Anna Louisa Elsom was the only **mother**. In 1898, at the meeting of Virginia WMU held in Lynchburg, someone introduced her to the Virginia Union by the title, "Mother of Sunbeams." The nickname "received hearty and unanimous endorsement by a spontaneous rising of the body and Chautauqua salute." Already she was described as wearing "the snow of many winters" on her head.

Mrs. Elsom expressed "great unworthiness" in the honorific title. She claimed that her small role lay in suggesting the idea to the pastor. Yet she proclaimed: "The Lord can bless the tiniest seed sown in His name and bring fruitage even though the sower be weak and faithless."

In the summer of 1907, George Braxton Taylor returned to lead a meeting in Fairmount, where he was a guest in Mrs. Elsom's home. She recalled: "We greatly enjoyed recounting our labors, hopes, and fears in Sunbeam work. He said, 'Sister Elsom, I believe that work has kept you young.' I told him I have only a small class now and was trying to transfer that to one of our young girls though I get to church whenever it is possible and feel more and more interest as I grow older."

Loving, gentle Jesus,
Hear our happy song,
All the little children
Unto Thee belong.

Pity little children
Knowing not Thy love,
May we help to lead them
To Thy love above.

Fill our hearts with longing
To be more like Thee.
Help us send Thy Gospel
Far across the sea.

Guide each little Sunbeam
As we part today,
Keep our feet from straying
From Thy chosen way.

Royal Service,
January, 1917

MOTHER'S SUNBEAM

Royal Service
February, 1919

My daddy he's a captain,
My brother is a scout,
My sister is a Camp Fire Girl—
But I am just left out,
They each have uniforms to wear
And different things to do.
Oh Dear! I do wish that I
Belonged to something too!
My mother tells me not to mind
She says, 'Why don't you see?
Because you are a Sunbeam
You mean the most to me?'

MENFOLKS:

"Cousin George"

George Braxton Taylor was born for missions! His grandfather, James B. Taylor, was the first corresponding secretary of the Foreign Mission Board. In James B. Taylor's diary of the 1820s through the 1830s, there is an entry recording the birth of his son, George Boardman Taylor, for whom he asks a blessing from God for future usefulness. The son was blessed and used as the first Southern Baptist missionary to Rome, Italy. Taylor and his wife, Susan, opened Baptist work there in 1872. Their son, George Braxton Taylor, had the joy of growing up in Rome; and when time came for college, he returned to Virginia to study at Richmond College. While in the city he lived with his uncle, Alfred E. Dickinson, editor of the **Religious Herald**. His college job was folding the newspapers for mailing.

While in Richmond Taylor experienced the influence of numerous Baptist leaders who took their comrade's son into their homes and confidences. These contacts proved not only invaluable for the young minister in his pastoral career but also extremely helpful in completing the compilation of collective biographical volumes on deceased Virginia Baptist ministers—a task begun by his grandfather.

Taylor knew tragedy. His young wife died and he spent the remainder of his long life without a marital companion. His son, Cabel, died while a young man.

Taylor also knew joys. Someone once remarked that he "sincerely loved children." It was while pastor of rural Fairmount Church near Charlottesville that he responded to the appeal of a female member, Anna Louisa Elsom, for an organization to teach young children about missions. The first meeting was held outside under the spreading limbs of a mighty tree and there Pastor Taylor related stories to the children about people in faraway lands who needed to hear about a Savior. The children were encouraged to pray and to give. And so the first Sunbeam Band was organized. Recalling that the Methodists used the name "Rosebud," he preferred "Sunbeams," declaring that "you must be very near a rosebud to appreciate it but a ray of light travels a very long way and is necessary in darkness."

Taylor wrote the **Religious Herald** about his Sunbeams and suggested others capture the same spirit. One by one, the women formed other Sunbeam Bands and wrote Taylor for ideas. At first he answered with hand-written letters, but soon he penned a special page for the Foreign Mission Board's journal. He used the pen name of "Cousin George" and printed cards with a message to the Sunbeam children from their "cousin." In 1896, Woman's Missionary Union, SBC, took up the challenge of maintaining and enlarging the Sunbeam Bands. But they never forgot "Cousin George."

He became pastor of Enon Church near Roanoke and taught

Founding meeting of the Sunbeams at Fairmount Church, Nelson County. Pastor George Braxton Taylor tells the local children about his parents' missionary service in Italy while Anna Louisa Elsom, who originated the idea of Sunbeam Bands, looks on. (Sidney E. King, artist, VBHS)

George Braxton Taylor, founder of the Sunbeam Bands, visits a Sunbeam group at the Good Will Center, which carried his name.

Bible classes across the road at Hollins College. In 1936, the Jubilee of the Sunbeams, a state-wide celebration was held at First Church, Richmond, and Sunbeams streamed down the aisle to present a floral tribute to their founder. The Good Will Center at St. Charles was erected through gifts from the Sunbeams of Virginia and named in Taylor's honor. He visited it for the dedication and received a salute from the Sunbeams.

What was the measure of the man's life? Most of the WMU adult members were first introduced to missions as little Sunbeams. Many of the candidates over the years for missionary service testified to initial impressions made as Sunbeams. The light of God reflected by the Sunbeams was a great beam which, though names of organizations have changed, has never been extinguished. "Cousin George" had told them to shine.

"Where are you going, my little maid?"
"I'm going to the Sunbeam Band," she said.

"And what might that be, my little maid?"
"We've such good meetings, my friend," she said.

"We sing and pray and study, too,
Of missionaries and what they do,
Of all the needs both near and far,
Of where their stations, and who they are."

"And is that all you do, little maid?"
"Oh, pray you, no, good friend," she said.

"We follow a plan and bring our money
To send to countries cold and sunny.
In this great task we do our part
To gladden and cheer the Master's heart."

Royal Service
October, 1917

THE CAREY CENTENNIAL

In 1892 the Foreign Mission Board sent literature to all the Sunday Schools and Sunbeam Bands, suggesting that funds be raised in commemoration of the Centennial of William Carey's work in India. Major James Gwathmey White, superintendent of the Sunday school at Hebron Church, King William County, received the literature and was impressed with the need for a chapel in Havana, Cuba. The promotional literature called for fifty "bricks" to be sold for ten cents each. Gwathmey gave the challenge to his young granddaughter, Sallie, who described herself as "timid." Yet she could not refuse her grandfather's request. "Looking back," she recalled years later, "I can see myself approaching the members of our Sunday school, card in hand, asking them to buy a brick for the chapel in Cuba. Whenever I sold a brick I made a pinhole in the brick on the card. After the fifty bricks were sold and the five dollars forwarded to the Foreign Mission Board, the Board sent a certificate which [my grandfather] presented to me one Sunday during the Sunday school exercises. This paper [became] a token of my first missionary effort."

"Mother Gwathmey"

*I*n a very unusual and beautiful way she was 'mother' to us all." That's how Douglass McDaniel, wife of the pastor of First Church, Richmond, has explained the effect of Abby Manly Gwathmey on the women of Virginia. "Multitudes of us as individuals leaned upon her, sought her counsel and loved her with a tenderness surpassing affection. The gentle presence of 'Mother Gwathmey' was a benediction to us all."

Abby Manly Gwathmey was president of the Woman's Missionary Union, SBC, for the year of 1894. She was president of the Virginia Central Committee from 1894 to 1896. She helped frame the constitution of Virginia WMU in 1898 and her loving touch was evident in every phase of woman's mission work. She was a member of the Executive Board from its beginning until her death in 1917.

Abby Murray Manly was born into a notable family which made numerous contributions to Baptist life. Her father, Basil Manly, Sr., was president of the University of Alabama and as a South Carolina minister was instrumental in the founding of Furman University. Her brothers were widely known. Basil Manly, Jr., perhaps was best known as a hymn writer or as the head of the Sunday School Board; it was during his tenure as president of the Richmond Female Institute that his sister, Abby, came to Virginia to attend the new school for women. Another brother, Charles, was an effective pastor and served two Virginia churches, the Staunton church and the Lexington church which now bears his name. But Abby Manly never lived in the shadow of the male members of her family. She was a person of accomplishment in her own right!

In Richmond another man entered her life, Dr. William Henry Gwathmey, a prominent physician and member of First Baptist Church. *The Manly Family*, a history of the illustrious clan, states that "her bright vivacious ways and exceptional beauty made an impression on his bachelor heart and he sought her in marriage." The couple married in December, 1858. Gwathmey also became identified with the Foreign Mission Board, serving as its recording secretary.

The couple had nine children including twin daughters, Maria and Alberta. They were nine years old in May, 1888, when their mother brought them along to attend the founding meeting of Woman's Missionary Union, SBC, in the basement of the Broad Street Methodist Church in Richmond. She wanted them to be a part of history. Six years later their mother became president of the national organization for a brief term, and the twins and the rest of the family shared their mother with a much larger family. By now, she truly was "Mother Gwathmey."

The delegates to the 1888 meeting knew they were making history. Some brought their daughters to share in the occasion. Abby Manly Gwathmey, later a president of Southern Union, brought her 10-year-old twin daughters, left to right, *Alberta Gwathmey (Palmore)* and *Maria Gwathmey (Bruner)*, 1895. (Photo courtesy of Ben Bruner)

Report of the Central Committee on Woman's Work

"There is a genuine spirit of enthusiasm among the women of the churches on the subject of missions . . . they only await organization and sympathetic help.

"When we look back and see how many societies have been organized, and how much money has come into the treasuries of our boards . . . we feel encouraged and grateful. When we look forward, with an organization well nigh perfect, we see great possibilities for usefulness; with a missionary society in every church aided by pastor and the male members, with the hearts of all so imbued with zeal for missions that the children of those taking part catch the contagion, and they, too, save their pennies and nickels for the mite box collection—then we will see the fruition of our cherished hopes.

"But, when we look at ourselves—our relations to our environment—the scene changes, we are filled with doubt, disappointment and chagrin. There is an indifference, if not opposition, on the part of some of the pastors that makes it well nigh impossible to accomplish any good results. Another hindrance to the work is found in the fact that this committee is a body without means. It presents the unique spectacle of being a board with no means of running its expenses. Thrown out upon its own resources it made a deathly struggle for self-preservation, and it has survived to the present and grown, but its life has been preserved at the expense of its healthy growth. This failure to provide the committee with funds for expenses we believe to be accidental rather than intentional, and that it is only necessary to have attention called to it. For this committee, instead of desiring means for extending its worth, has had to spend much of its time in raising money for its running expenses, as none of the society's money comes into their hands. This condition of affairs relative to the committee, is an abnormal one, and is without a precedent in the work of this Association. A few of the societies have adopted the Nickel Fund, and have assisted the Richmond ladies in paying the expenses of the work—about $300 has been raised. It would be pleasant for the ladies to have such arrangements made that they could refer all questions of finance to the Cooperation Committee."

Mrs. W.E. Hatcher *and*
Miss Juliett Pollard
BGAV Minutes, 1890

(Note: "In 1891 the Committee on Cooperation furnished the Central Committee $95 for expenses . . . for literature, $10.78; for printing annuals, $22.50; and for stamps, wrappers and writing materials, $48.72. The actual gifts [from the various missionary societies] were over $5,000." From **Light Three Candles.**)

"A Penny a Day and a Prayer"

In 1892, the Baptists celebrated the Centennial of William Carey and the beginning of the modern missionary movement. Virginia Baptists were given a goal of $30,000 as a Centennial offering for Southern Baptist home and foreign missions. The Central Committee for Woman's Work chose as its goal one-sixth of the Virginia goal, or $5,000.

Mary C. Tupper was president of the Virginia Central Committee; and both as president and as the daughter of the secretary of the Foreign Mission Board, she was deeply concerned for the cause of missions. She suggested a simple yet effective way to meet the challenge: "A penny a day and a prayer."

She pleaded with the women: "We would not lay too much stress upon the dollars and cents for which we ask. They are, indeed, needful—without them the work must fall. But we beg that you give also of your precious time; that you use your God-given talents; above all, that your fervent petitions arise for the Holy Spirit's guidance and the Heavenly Father's blessing to rest upon this, the work of our hands—'He loves our importunity, and makes our cause his care.'

"We have asked that the 'Penny a Day and a Prayer' plan be tested. By this we would by no means discourage large contributions, but recognizing the power of mites, and having faith in the efficacy of regular and frequent giving and praying, we submit this plan, hoping that it will find favor in the eyes of our Virginia sisterhood. If the 'little brown penny' be not daily at hand, an earnest prayer each day, and a dime on the Lord's day, will be quite as promotive of good to the cause!"

The plan was adopted but instead of meeting the $5,000 goal, the Baptist women of Virginia doubled the amount!

Homes of the Virginia WMU

In the earliest years the residences of the officers also were the homes of the Union.

1874–78 The Richmond residences of Mrs. H. Theodore Ellyson on Third Street, where contributions were sent, and of Mrs. J.B. Jeter, president of both city and state societies, who lived at 18 E. Grace Street.

1878–89 The Richmond homes of Mrs. Jeter and those of Mrs. Edwin Wortham, 13 E. Franklin Street and Mrs. Richard Adam, 11 S. Twelfth.

1889–91 The State Union was offered weekly use on Tuesday and Thursday mornings of rooms rented by WMU of Richmond at the corner of Fourth and Franklin. With the Ladies' Exchange in the same building, the ladies of the WMU felt comfortable in these quarters.

1891–96 The State Union moved to a room offered by Grace Street Baptist Church, then located at Grace and Foushee Streets.

1896–97 The Central Committee met in the board room of the Foreign Mission Board, SBC, at Eleventh and Main Streets.

1897–1904 The meetings were moved to Second Baptist Church located at Main and Sixth Streets.

1904–06 A room was rented by the State Union at 1505 E. Grace Street and a clerk was employed.

1906–10 The office was moved to 12 E. Main Street.

1910–20 The office was relocated to the home of the first salaried corresponding secretary, Mrs. Julian P. Thomas, at 114 E. Cary Street.

1920–38 The Union offices were moved to the Commercial Building, 216 N. Second Street. Blanche Sydnor White recorded that "this was the first attempt to provide separate offices for the salaried secretaries. The corresponding secretary's office was also the committee and Board room."

1938–44 Again Miss White remembered: "Pride moved us out of very dirty, beloved offices at 216 N. Second to the sixth floor of the Central National Bank Building where we occupied chicken coops and held Board meetings in the director's room of the bank."

1944–62 Miss White attributed the next move to "claustrophobia and the desire to move Virginia Baptists into the lovely panelled and parqueted grandeur of One W. Franklin Street." Virginia WMU occupied the third floor and attic.

1962–86 Virginia Baptists erected a handsome headquarters building on Monument Avenue at Willow Lawn Drive, and Virginia WMU occupied a large suite of offices on the first floor.

1986– Virginia Baptists purchased an office building formerly occupied by Infilcro-Degremont Company in Commerce Center, an office park along West Broad Street near Glenside Drive in Henrico County. The modern facility at 2828 Emerywood Parkway has became the home of Virginia WMU. The Union occupies a suite directly behind the chapel.

"Miss Jennie"

*J*ennie Snead of Fluvanna, born Virginia Oranie Snead, attended the Albemarle Female Institute in Charlottesville, then the female academic equivalent of the University of Virginia. There she learned languages and social graces. And there began lifetime acquaintances with gracious women including Charlotte Digges Moon who as "Lottie" would become the celebrated foreign missionary to China. The young minister William E. Hatcher visited Fluvanna and met his "Miss Jennie." They began to correspond and at Christmastide, 1861, they were married.

"Miss Jennie" was a good wife for the up-and-coming young preacher and served as his helpmate during his long career at Bainbridge Church, Richmond; Franklin Square Church, Baltimore; First Church, Petersburg; and for 26 years at Grace Street Church, Richmond, where the members soon found themselves sharing their pastor with the Baptist Zion across the country. He was frequently absent, fulfilling speaking engagements in the North and South.

"Miss Jennie" kept the homeplace and reared their children. By teaching music and practicing rigid economy she enabled the family to afford their own residence on Grace Street. One room was designated the "preachers' room" and there numerous guests from across the country—new friends made by Dr. Hatcher—were given a place to stay during their Richmond visits.

In 1887, she succeeded Mrs. Jeter as president of the Central Committee. It was her responsibility to welcome the women to Richmond for the May, 1888 founding meeting of WMU, SBC. The very concept of women organizing a separate society was an anathema to many of the Baptist men. Hatcher encouraged his wife to welcome the women from across the South but to persuade Virginia women to refrain from joining the new organization until he and other male leaders could convince the brethren of its worthiness.

As president she turned the dining room of the Hatcher home on Grace Street into the unofficial headquarters of Virginia WMU, enlisting the entire household in stuffing envelopes as she persisted in communications with the numerous societies scattered across Virginia. Her faithful services in organizing and fostering mission societies, in writing and speaking whenever an opportunity permitted became important in the founding of a statewide missions organization.

Jennie Hatcher possessed a fine literary gift, honed in those years at the Institute in Charlottesville, and evident in such works as the biography of the Baptist preacher, A.B. Brown, which carried her husband's by-line so it would sell to a male audience. She even compiled a cookbook to be sold as a promotional for Grace Street Church.

In old age she remained a guiding light to the Virginia women, a mother figure to many and a watchman over the fundamentals of the Union. In 1921, in her late 70s, she attended the Albemarle WMU meeting and offered a resolution which the women adopted. It referred to "materialism and infidelity" as "abroad in the land—the South being so far an exception" and called for the women of the "old Albemarle with its galaxy of noble pastors like Broadus, Flippo, Taylor and others" to "stand by the fundamentals, the articles of faith before which we keep always an open mind, willing to investigate with no hostility to those differing from us."

What were these fundamentals? "The inspiration of the Scriptures" and the various aspects of Christ's divinity and nature. After all these lofty introductory phrases, Miss Jennie got down to real business: "That we try to induce our young people to refrain from immodest dancing." She suggested other activities, such as encouraging "mission work, visiting the poor and needy, Bible reading, and the telling of good stories as an entertainment." A mother of Virginia WMU had become a grandmother for the organization, still encouraging and directing.

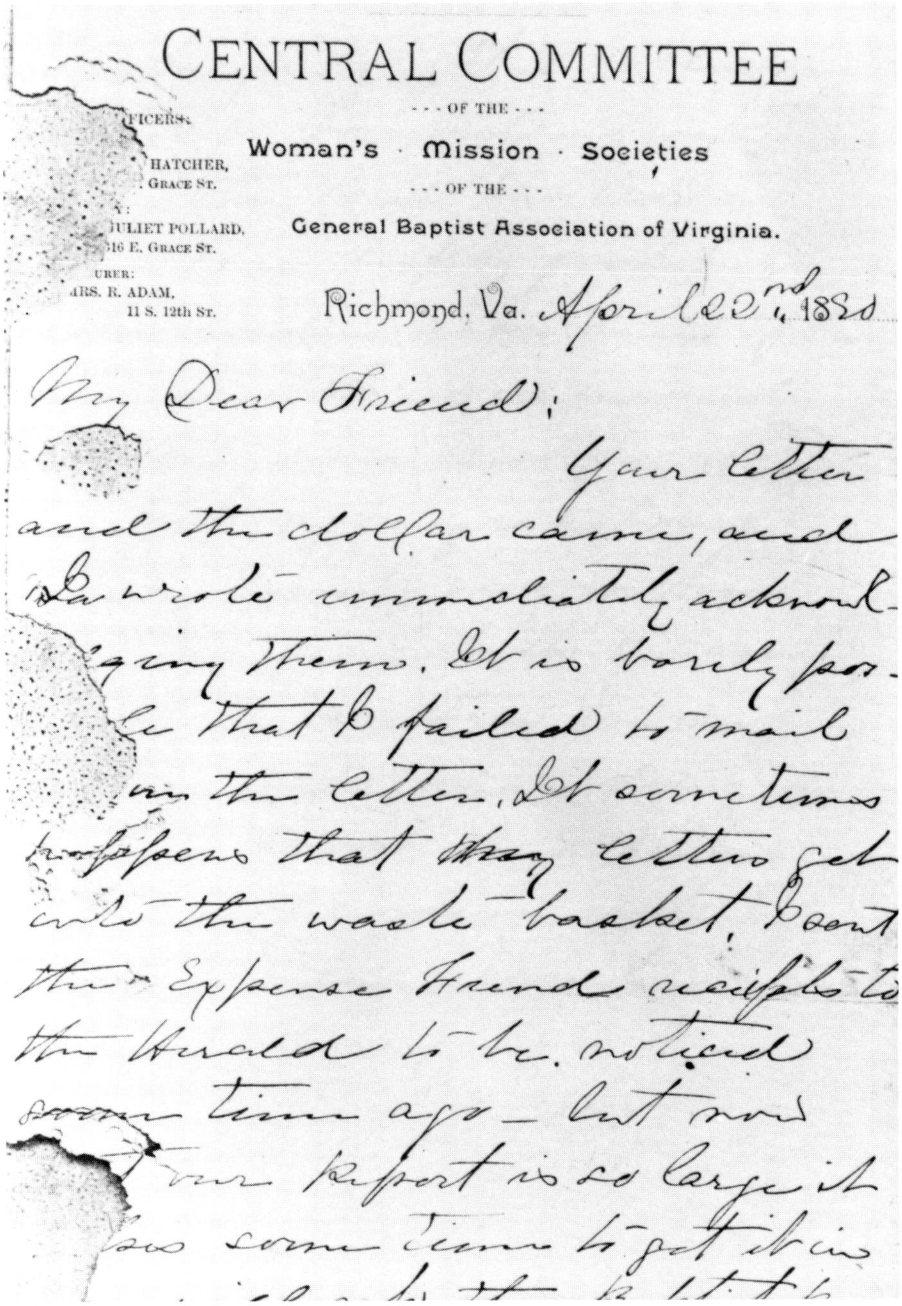

CENTRAL COMMITTEE

--- OF THE ---

Woman's · Mission · Societies

--- OF THE ---

General Baptist Association of Virginia.

OFFICERS:
HATCHER,
GRACE ST.

JULIET POLLARD,
16 E. GRACE ST.

URER:
MRS. R. ADAM,
11 S. 12th St.

Richmond, Va. April 22nd 1880

My Dear Friend;

Your letter and the dollar came, and I wrote immediatly acknowledging them. It is barely possible that I failed to mail the letter. It sometimes happens that stray letters get into the waste-basket. I sent the Expense Fund receipts to the Herald to be noticed some time ago — but now our report is so large it takes some time to get it in

41

BAPTIST WOMAN'S MISSIONARY UNION CONVENTION COURT ST. BAPTIST CHURCH PORTSMOUTH, VA. OCT. 22-29, 1926.

Virginia WMU Annual Meeting, Court Street Church, Portsmouth, 1926.

Chapter 2

The Hopeful Years,
1900–1924

"*Let us go forward, relying upon God, encouraged by the assurance that 'we can do all things through Christ which strengtheneth us.'*" *With those buoyant words Abby Manly Gwathmey, one of the Virginia WMU founders, uplifted the women who carried the organization into the second quarter-century, into years of hopeful plans and programs. The period began with a smoothing of organizational structure as well as general acceptance by the brethren of the distinctiveness and purposefulness of woman's missionary work. The energy expended formerly for establishing the organization could be devoted to enlarging the work itself.*

They indeed were hopeful years. The Training School was launched, the Margaret Home and Fund supported, youth organizations grew, camping experiences were inaugurated, and missions increased. Virginia women felt proud to witness Virginians serving on the mission fields. Lydia and George Green, "Virginia's own," were pioneering medical missions in Africa and "Our Elizabeth" Ellyson Wiley left the Virginia WMU staff for mission service in China. The women responded to "their own" through prayers, correspondence, boxes of supplies, and the beginning of White Cross work to aid medical missions.

The Union itself was efficiently organized with all the trappings of a full-fledged organization including distinctive emblems and a defined headquarters replete with an office's bustling activities. Mrs. Julian P. Thomas became the first paid secretary and she established expectations of professionalism for the position. Dynamic leaders in the period included Verdie Leake, Antoinette Thomas, Lizzie Savage, Minnie James, and Mabel Vines.

The women discovered the renewal which comes with anniversary remembrances. The Jubilate in 1913–14 recognized the twenty-fifth year since Woman's Missionary Union, SBC's founding. All across Virginia went up the cry of "Mundus Christo Jubilate" and the slogan resounded long after the anniversary. "The World for Christ! Hallelujah!" was emblematic of the hopefulness which pervaded Virginia WMU in the first 25 years of the twentieth century.

▶
Nancy Holden Willingham
in ***Royal Service*** July, 1933

LABORERS TOGETHER WITH GOD *(I Cor. 3:9)*

Oh, wondrous plan,
Designed by God above,
That God and man
Should show to man God's love,
"Laborers together"
   —oh, thought sublime—
It humbles me to know this joy
   is mine.
I thank Thee, Lord,
And praise Thy holy name.
Be Thou adored
That Christ, my Savior, came
To dwell on earth—
   a man among all men—
That man might find his way
   back "home" again.
So great the need
That I with God should toil—
Should plant the seed
And till the fertile soil—
God uses me,
   although but humble clay,
To show unto the lost
   His blessed way.
Oh, joy sublime that I
   with God may work—
God grant that I the task
   may never shirk.

Mrs. W. S. Leake

*F*rom 1902 to 1906, Mrs. W.S. Leake served as unsalaried corresponding secretary, planting the seeds of effective organization. During her term a room was rented on Grace Street at $10 a month to house the Virginia WMU office. She managed to secure permission and funds to share a telephone with another party (on another floor of the building) for 50¢ a month! She led the Union to purchase a typewriter and procured a table through a furniture store donation. Things were looking up at the Virginia WMU office.

Verdie French Leake was indefatigable. In fact, after two years of ardorous work, the Executive Board flatly insisted that she take a month's respite. In her last report, she pronounced 1905 through 1906 "the most aggressive and successful [year] in missionary endeavor in the history of the Virginia Union." She observed that "aims are loftier" and specific results were evident: the Christmas Offering for China, as well as state missions gifts, were the largest yet. Virginia had also met its goal for a Chinese hospital and had contributed $200 to furnish the dining room in the Margaret Home.

In 1906, Mrs. Leake's husband, a state missionary pastor, was called to the Moffett Memorial Church in Danville. When she of necessity resigned, she labeled her four years "a genuine labor of love." She commented: "No clouds of dissension appear upon our horizon. We are united, aggressive, successful. Let us be hopeful, courageous, and faithful for the future is rich with promise." When she resigned, the Virginia Union declared, "Wherever she goes we believe she will be a power for good." How prophetic!

In 1907, Mrs. Leake was again pressed into service as the first YWA leader for Virginia. Fannie E.S. Heck once recalled that after much success with the girls, she received an appeal from a boy in Lynchburg: "Mrs. Leake, if you would give up the girls of Virginia and take the boys, we could do anything." With such pulls on her heart, she added the responsibility for the boys of Virginia Baptists in 1909. In her first year with Royal Ambassadors (RAs) she reported that 30 RA chapters gave nearly $150 to missions. In 1911 she was asked to lead an RA conference at the annual meeting of WMU, SBC, because of her Virginia success.

Mrs. Leake believed in education for missions work. In 1906, she stood on the floor of the annual meeting of WMU, SBC, in Chattanooga and introduced a resolution "that the Union establish in Louisville a thoroughly equipped Woman's Missionary Training School." While "the vote of the body scored a victory" for the Training School, the parliamentarian ended Mrs. Leake's moment of glory because of a technicality requiring a three-month notice for a Constitutional change. Another delegate reworded the motion and the original intent was approved. Mrs. Leake became the Virginia member of a committee to study such a training method and how to effect the change. She served as the Virginia representative among the trustees and was the first agent to receive funds for the school during its planning stage.

"Mrs. G. F. Williams: Leader of Sunbeams"

*I*n 1897, shortly after missions work with children was turned over to the Union by its originators, Anna Louisa Elsom and George Braxton Taylor, Mrs. George Frank Williams became the loving custodian of Sunbeam work as the official State Leader or Band Superintendent, a post she held until her death in 1910. She promoted the work admirably. "A woman of lofty aims, high ideals, noble character, and charming personality," wrote Mrs. W.S. Leake, leader of YWAs, "she won her way to a multitude of hearts."

A native of Richmond, Emma Virginia Woodfin was the daughter of Mrs. and Mrs. George Woodfin, active Baptists; at the tender age of 10 she became a Christian and was baptized into the fellowship of Leigh Street Church. In 1872, she married a minister and followed him to his pastorate in Mobile, Alabama. In 1888, the couple returned to Richmond. She soon joined the local missions organizations and became increasingly active in their work. For 14 years she served as secretary of the Missionary Circle of Richmond and Manchester, when the area across the James River was a separate city. She was a member of the first Central Committee in Virginia, formed in 1889 to enlist the Virginia Baptist women. It evolved into the Executive Committee of WMU of Virginia and she remained a member until her death.

Her name was literally a "household name" among Baptists of Virginia and even beyond. She corresponded with the local Sunbeam leaders, designed creative program material, and frequently wrote for the woman's page in the Herald. In August, 1910, she performed her last work by helping at the WMU's meeting of the James River Association at Scottsville. She was not well when she left for Scottsville, and she died within a month after her return to Richmond.

Her passing sent "a wave of grief and sorrow" across Virginia. The Sunbeam leader had departed.

A Turning Point

Virginia women had endured a cumbersome and confusing system with two organizations—the Board of Woman's Work and the Woman's Missionary Union. In a sense the Board was just a device established by the brethren so they could exercise some control over women's missions work. Virginia women devised a plan "analogous to that which exists between the Southern Baptist Convention and the Woman's Missionary Union of the SBC." They appointed a committee-of-one, Mrs. Lillian (*John A.*) Barker, to meet with the General Association's powerful Committee on Co-operation. The brethren met with Mrs. Barker in the Foreign Mission Board offices on the eve of the state Baptist meeting. On Thursday, November 14, 1901, the men gave "the most courteous and earnest attention" to Mrs. Barker and "readily undertook to present the matter to the General Association."

Unlike past vigorous struggles and debates, this time the women got exactly what they wanted—posthaste. Following is the agreement passed by the BGAV on Saturday, November 16, at Grace Street Church, Richmond:

"1. That the Woman's Missionary Union be recognized and considered as auxiliary to the General Association.

"2. That the action of the Association which requires the nomination of a Board for Woman's Work by the Union and its election by this body be rescinded, and in place of this board the Union be permitted to choose its own Executive Committee.

"3. That this Executive Committee, or a majority of the same (as was ordered by the Association in the case of the board), shall reside in Richmond; that the members composing it shall be determined by the Union, but shall always include in its number the Corresponding Secretary and Treasurer of the Union, and that the names of the committee shall be sent to this body in the annual report of the Union.

"4. That the Executive Committee herein contemplated shall not be expected to report to the General Association, but to the Union, and the Union to this body.

"5. That the Union shall submit an estimate of necessary expenses each year to the General Association, which, if approved, shall be paid by the Treasurer of the Association to the Treasurer of the Union in such amounts from time to time as may be agreed upon by them, provided that the Union continues to send its collections into the treasury of the General Association as heretofore."

The male friends of Virginia WMU who presented the report were I.M. Mercer, Charles H. Ryland, M. Ashby Jones, and Walter Sydnor. The report was discussed by no fewer than six delegates and passed. A significant turning point had occurred in the history of WMU and in its relationship with the General Association and its financial support.

Straight Talk:

"Giving or Raising"

"May it not be that the great lack of spirituality in our churches today is because we are trying to do God's work in our own way? God says Give; our aim is to Raise. Now there is no harm done in raising money, but it is not God's way for us to do His work. How, then, are we to work? Just as God taught, by precept and experience. When He wished them to build the Tabernacle, how was it done? They gave—gave of their finest and best—more than was needed. Shall we 'rob God' by refusing to bring in the tithes?

"Some may say festivals, etc., is the only way we can ever get money for anything in our church; the men won't give; tell them what is wanted and they shrug their shoulders and say, 'Oh, well, the ladies will have to have a festival.' Now don't let us be too hard on the men. Are they not doing just what we have taught them to do? Now let us teach the better way. . . God's way. Let us 'make all things according to the pattern,' claiming God's blessing upon our work."

"Our Women's Work" page
Religious Herald
January 24, 1907

The above letter generated reaction, including the following message from Bennie Russell, superintendent of the Peninsula WMU:

"It has been an unwritten law in our circle [in Hampton] never to have an entertainment for getting money to send 'the glad tidings of great joy' into regions beyond. I believe that each member has learned the blessedness of giving cheerfully unto the Lord, remembering that the Lord loveth a cheerful (hilarious) giver."

"Every Woman With Her Own Royal Service"

For decades upon decades Virginia women have received a friendly regular visitor to their homes. It comes from Woman's Missionary Union, SBC, and communicates the organization's purposes and programs and informs everyone of missions. It is *Royal Service*, a magazine familiar to WMU members.

In 1906, the publication began as a quarterly entitled *Our Mission Fields*. A free copy was sent to each woman's missionary society across the SBC. In 1913, Fannie E.S. Heck suggested that the monthly magazine be offered as a subscription. The name *Royal Service* was adopted and the first issue was printed in 1914. In 1956, the fiftieth anniversary of the publication carried an ambitious subscription campaign with the apt slogan, "Every Woman With Her Own Royal Service." Through the years *Royal Service* has been favorite reading of Virginia Baptist women. It has been used for program material, inspiration for mission projects and even clipped by Baptist children and young people for school projects and scrapbooks. Every woman still needs "her own *Royal Service*"—the magazine which has stood the test of time.

Mrs. Julian P. Thomas
"Saved to Serve"

Maria Antoinette Pleasants always had "presence." Even as little "Net" in the family circle she had "presence"; and throughout her adult life as Mrs. Julian P. Thomas, as she was known, she radiated a sense of "presence." In fact, "presence" is the one word Blanche Sydnor White chose to describe her predecessor, the corresponding secretary of Virginia WMU from 1906 to 1921.

Miss White never forgot the initial impression made by the striking woman, in 1913, at the Jubilate celebration held at First Church, Richmond. As Miss White recalled: "Long before the opening of the service, the unreserved section of the lovely and spacious sanctuary was filled. The organist sounded the first notes of the Jubilate processional and up the center aisle came leaders of Virginia women. The guest speaker was the renowned president of the Southern Union, Miss Fannie E.S. Heck. I am sorry to report that I took away from that meeting only one abiding impression. It was of a lady of medium height and weight who was dressed in quiet, exquisite taste. Her features could not be described as beautiful; what she said and did that evening were not extraordinary. It was her 'bearing,' her 'presence,' that marked her as the outstanding person in that brilliant assemblage of prominent women. That lady, an aristocrat of great presence, was Mrs. Julian P. Thomas."

The development and refinement as well as the spiritual growth of Antoinette began at an early age. She was only nine when she was baptized by Dr. J. Lansing Burrows of First Church, Richmond. He was so struck by her tender age that he noted in his journal that

she was the youngest person he had ever baptized during his long Richmond church ministry. In her teens she won a prize for bringing the most new pupils into the Sunday school at her church. At an early age she taught in the Sunday school.

About 1875, she and her sister organized the Young Ladies' Missionary Society of the church, an endeavor more than just social or perfunctory. Among accounts written by Blanche Sydnor White which testify to Antoinette's tenacity and judgment, one regarded the salary of Alfred Bagby, then a young missionary stationed at the new Baptist mission at West Point in King William County. The state Board had seemingly promised him a salary of $150 for a year's labor and then had reneged, offering $100 instead. Miss White paints a vibrant scene in describing the confrontation between two strong personalities, Henry Keeling Ellyson, secretary of the State Mission Board, and the young president of the missionary society. "His salary is to be $100 a year," said Ellyson. "We will pay him $150," the young president declared. "A smaller salary is not commensurate with his needs and our resources." The secretary warned: "If you pay the young man more than $100, the Board will move him from West Point." Miss White declares there was "a temporary compromise."

The Young Ladies' Missionary Society later transferred their support to another missionary in the Virginia mountains. In 1878, they also adopted Miss Sallie Stein of China, paying her salary for her entire career.

Further training awaited Antoinette at Richmond Female Institute, a Baptist school where young ladies learned the graciousness of the Old South as well as academic material. In 1891, she married Julian P. Thomas, principal of the public high school in Richmond later named after Chief Justice John Marshall. She was henceforth identified by her husband's name in all WMU materials and in her weekly *Religious Herald* page.

In 1906, Virginia WMU was without a corresponding secretary. Mrs. W.S. Leake had resigned, but in considering her replacement, the ladies were considering someone who could devote herself full time to the organization's growing demands. They also wanted to "be led to the woman of God's own choosing." Mrs. Thomas was in her early fifties and ready to give her life over to some great work.

It was Mrs. William Ellyson, former treasurer of the Union and, at the time, member of the Executive Board, who suggested the idea. She had been at home busy at work when the name of Mrs. Thomas "came into her thoughts with such peculiar force that it seemed to her almost as though a voice had spoken the name." She sought Mrs. Thomas and asked her to give prayerful consideration to the work. In April, 1906, the Executive Board unanimously elected Mrs. Thomas.

From 1906 to 1920, she directed the work from her home. She traveled widely, cultivated relationships, led conferences and encouraged the many societies within the state. During her first year in office, 101 new woman's missionary societies were organized. During her 15 years of service she helped the number of active societies to increase from 531 to 836. Young people's societies flourished, increasing from 536 to 1,369. In 1906, money gifts amounted to

*E*arliest photo of the Virginia WMU office shows Corresponding Secretary Mrs. Julian P. Thomas (1906–21), in swivel chair, at her rolltop desk.

$24,504, but in the last year of her service, in 1921, the total reached $379,324.

When she shocked the Union by resigning in 1921, the President, Mrs. John F. Vines, declared: "It is needless to speak of the growth of the WMU of Virginia during this period. Those who have journeyed to such heights can recall with the retiring secretary the days when the work was small. With keen admiration you have watched the growth to dimensions almost beyond fondest expectations. The successes of today bespeak the foundations of yesterday!"

For years before women were appointed to the Foreign Mission Board, Mrs. Thomas "represented the women of the South at the Board meetings, especially when there were new missionaries to be appointed." In 1924, she became a member of the Foreign Mission Board and gave special help in the educational department, serving as a "critic of mission study books and in the selection and preparation of manuscripts." Jessie Ruth Ford of the Board said: "Her gracious tact and courtesy, her clear-thinking and broad vision were always evident. She was courageous in her views but ever thoughtful and considerate of the feelings of others." Even when illness prevented her from attending a meeting, she would telephone afterwards to inquire what had transpired. "She carried the world in her heart," stated Ford, "and the deep, abiding interest of her life was for missions."

One of Mrs. Thomas' tangible credits is the editorship of the woman's page in the *Religious Herald* from 1913 until her resignation. This became a forum for presenting women's work, new methods and news from across the state. "If my own feelings are any indication," she stated to her readers in her final page, "we have had a good time together. You have been so patient, so forbearing, so sympathetic. [You] told me that you opened the *Herald* at 'our page' and read that first."

The women wanted a permanent memorial for Mrs. Thomas and so they proposed to furnish a room in the yet-to-be-built Virginia Baptist Hospital. When she died in 1936, the editor of the *Herald*, R.H. Pitt, added another tribute: "Of gentle birth, finely educated, with large and successful experience as a teacher, with glowing missionary passion and marvelous capacity for work, she has made an ideal leader and her fine intelligence and unselfish spirit have earned for her the high regard not only of Virginia women but of the forward-looking women throughout the South." She was a lady of presence and a large part of that presence was her sense of having been at a tender age "saved to serve."

The Training School

"The minds that must serve the gift of the Spirit must be informed to understand and trained to do and direct. The order of Jesus in planning a Kingdom ministry was—call, training, commission, empowering by the filling of the Holy Spirit with His varied gifts. Preparation precedes Pentecost." Those words of W. O. Carver expressed the Baptist belief in proper training for ministry. It was years, however, before Southern Baptists recognized the need to train women for missions work.

In 1889, when Southern Union was only a year old, E.Z. Simmons,

VISION of SERVICE

CALLS TO

PREPARATION

AT THE

W. M. U.

TRAINING SCHOOL

Virginia women at the WMU Training School in 1940 included Helen Falls, at extreme right front, *who became professor of missions at New Orleans Baptist Theological Seminary, and*, second row center from left, *Cornelia Leavell, missionary to the Orient and Frances Copenhaver DeFoe, who worked as a Good Will Center director in Virginia.*

Virginia students at the WMU Training School. Among these pictured above is Frances Hudgins (second row, extreme right) who served as missionary to Thailand.

a missionary to China, challenged Baptist women to educate women for missions service. The idea took hold and finally in 1907, the WMU Training School was established in Louisville, Kentucky, "to train women for efficient service in foreign and home missions and all departments of denominational work."

One review of the school's history credits five women as most instrumental in the institution's founding and early success—Eliza Broadus, Mrs. S.E. Woody, Mrs. George B. Eager, Fannie E. S. Heck, and Maud Reynolds McLure. A later significant figure was Carrie U. Littlejohn, who served as principal.

In 1942, the school occupied a handsome new facility located along Lexington Road in Louisville, "a spacious red brick structure of southern colonial design." Located within walking distance of the Southern Seminary campus, there were opportunities for cooperation between the two schools.

The Training School produced well over two-thousand trained women who entered every area of service. Some were pastors' wives, denominational servants, teachers, leaders of Good Will Centers and missionaries.

Mrs. Ryland Knight, who served as a trustee of the school, summed up the nature of the Training School in the following remarks: "God's spirit has permeated the School. It is this Spirit which goes with the young women who live in its inspiring atmosphere and then go out to inspire others to follow Christ. Even upon entering the new building for the first time, one is conscious that God is in this place."

Elsie Gilliam of Lynchburg was Virginia's first student. Upon her graduation in 1909, she went under appointment of the Foreign Mission Board to Shanghai, China. Sula Thomas of the Blue Ridge Association, the second Virginian to enter the Training School, served from the time of her graduation until her death as missionary of the Home Mission Board in an Oklahoma mining town. Her salary was paid by the YWAs of Virginia. Others of equal stature followed these two splendid pioneers. They include the following: Marian Terrell, Alice Taylor, Marie Snow, Melvah English, Parolee Livesay, Mildred Thorne, Emmeline Thornbill, Nannie West, Margie Shumate, Olive Bagby, Sallie Vann, Mattie Thomas, Eva Gravatt, Lillian Williams, Ruth Kersey, Martha Dabney, and Ethel Winfield.

"Missionary boxes, so long a loved and important part of our WMU work, go largely to our Southwest territory. As the Frontier church becomes self-supporting, giving its pastor an adequate salary, the number of boxes will naturally decrease. The time when they will not be needed is however far distant. In the meantime, we wish to make the boxes still more valuable than in the past, to put into them more love, more thought, more comfort. The Golden Rule is the measure of a box. The Union advises only those societies who can send boxes of good, substantial clothing and other supplies, whose value would be fully $50 to them if they were the receivers rather than the senders."

Our Mission Fields
July, 1907

"HOMING THOUGHTS"

"I am thinking tonight of a place that I love,
The WMU Training School,
Where the girls are the closest in all the world,
Where love and loving doth rule.

How I wish I was there for just one sweet day,
I'd walk again in those halls,
To hear the sweet laughter and voices of mirth,
Which memory ever recalls.

I can see the girls gaily trooping to school,
So merry a down the street,
With arms full of books and lessons all learned,
Those great professors to meet.

I just think I can hear those same girls tonight,
When in the chapel they meet
With worship and praise; and the songs that *they* sing,
Sing in my heart, fresh and sweet.

And again my eyes see our faculty dear,
These women so helpful and strong,
Their lives are our standard, and surely for them
All praise and honor belong.

But most loved of all is our good principal—
Oh, for a touch of her hand!
What would I not give for her counsel tonight,
In far-away China-land!

The lessons I learned at the dear Training School
With me still ever abide,
For they give to me hope and guide me with strength
To serve and follow my Guide."

Margie Shumate
Royal Service
May, 1918

MENFOLKS:
Robert Healy Pitt

Anyone could recognize him: he was the small musta-chioed man with a boutonniere in his lapel. He car-ried a notepad so he wouldn't miss a word for the **Religious Herald**, which had been his life so long that the name Pitt and the **Herald** were interchangeable. He was the genial, thoughtful, provocative editor who reflected, shaped, and eloquently defined the "Virginia Baptist temper."

Robert Healy Pitt, dean of religious newspaper editors with 49 years of association with the **Religious Herald**, was a fierce defender and interpreter of religious freedom, who did not mind battling the well-meaning but sadly-misguided folks of his

day, people who thoughtlessly advocated compulsory Bible reading in the public schools; he was a visionary in supporting Baptist fraternal cooperation, sounding the first clarion calls through his editorial pen for the creation of the Baptist World Alliance; and he was a staunch friend and supporter of Baptist women and their peculiar mission. Early in his association with the **Herald**, he devoted free column space to the women, leaving the content to the discretion of WMU's corresponding secretary. When some of the vocal brethren besmirched the women's cause, R.H. Pitt boldly came to their defense.

He expected little, if anything, in return. The **Herald** has always existed to serve, "independent in its views of denominational life." A WMU tribute once extolled its "traditions of courtesy and kindness maintained in its columns . . . its clear, wholesome, useful and entertaining qualities found in its pages."

But there was an occasion when he devoted a full-page cover appeal to the Baptist women of Virginia, pointedly to the WMU, to help increase the number of subscriptions. Then there were times when the women took the initiative, launching a subscription campaign in 1933 to coincide with Pitt's eightieth birthday. He was still editor-in-chief and one WMU, the women of Freemason Street Church, Norfolk suggested their church add 80 new subscribers, one for each year in Pitt's life. They prompted Virginia WMU to take up the challenge and Blanche Sydnor White encouraged the women to follow suit. She urged that the circulation be more than doubled!

After service as a pastor, Pitt had joined the small staff of the **Herald** in 1888, and found his life's work with the religious press. Printer's ink was in his bloodstream and the pages in Pitt's long tenure are filled with stirring editorials, whimsical Baptist folklore, articles for women and children, interpretation of national news, and invaluable church histories and biographical treatments of laity and clergy. Miss White once summarized the editor's position as "evangelical in doctrine, standing in the old paths, but not willing to stand still."

Pitt's involvements—almost all requisite to his position— touched all phases of Baptist life. He was president of the General Association, long-time trustee of his alma mater—the University of Richmond—and a member of the Foreign Mission Board for over 40 years. Where Pitt went the extra mile was in outstretching his hand to the half (and more) of the population of the Baptist churches—the traditionally disenfranchised women. He gave them due justice, attention, exposure and they knew he was their friend.

In gathering up the years it is evident that all of the editors of the **Religious Herald** from Jeter to Pentecost have been aware of the significance of woman's work for missions and have been active voices of support, through pen, spoken word and behind-the-scenes efforts, for Woman's Missionary Union of Virginia.

The Religious Herald *was helpful to Baptist women, regularly putting aside space for a column by and about women. In 1910, Editor R. H. Pitt in turn appealed to WMU members to mount an ambitious subscription drive to help the Baptist newspaper.*

"To the Baptist Women of Virginia . . . "

*"For the first time in the long history of the **Religious Herald** an appeal is made to the Baptist women of the State to help the **Religious Herald** in its efforts to reach the homes of all the people. The **Religious Herald** has steadily and enthusiastically supported the organized work of our women. We are proud of the fact that we took this position when scarcely another Baptist paper in the entire South was willing to speak a good, honest word of encouragement for this work, and when quite a group of our influential papers were discouraging the organization of our women.*

*"We have lived to see this work grow by leaps and bounds until it is now regarded as one of our chief agencies in spreading missionary intelligence and promoting missionary activity. The Baptist women of no State in the South have been more efficient and progressive and devoted than those of Virginia. For a long time past these women have had the right of way in the columns of the **Religious Herald**. A full page is given over to them every week, and this page has always been controlled by some representative of our women's work. We have been fortunate, and our readers have been fortunate, in having the page committed to women of rare intelligence.*

*"Now, for the first time in all its history, the **Herald** is asking these ladies to turn their attention for just a few days to the work of increasing its circulation, particularly among the Baptist women. The WMU has kindly sent to some representative of every society . . . a letter asking that an effort be made, serious, earnest, determined, to secure [more] Baptist women as subscribers."*

R. H. Pitt, Editor
Religious Herald
March 31, 1910.

THE AMBASSADOR ACROSTIC

If we would truly be Royal Ambassadors
for the King, we must be—
Righteous, always true and just;
Obedient to His commands,
Yielding to His will,
Active in His service,
Loyal to His standard.

Achieving for His honor.
Manly, as He was manly.
Bold, standing for the right.
Acquainted with His law.
Strong in His strength.
Steady, serving Him unceasingly.
Attentive to His business
Docile, being led by Him.
Opposed to all that is wrong.
Restrictive, being temperate in all things.
Sincere, true to ourselves, our King, and our followers.

Fred Blivens, Ambassador-in-Chief
Yates Chapter, RAs
First Church, Bristol, Va., 1910

Sula Thomas, home missionary from Franklin County, Virginia, c. 1912. (Photo courtesy of Beulah Church, Franklin County.)

"Missie Tweedie"

WMU played an important role in reaching the immigrants arriving at Virginia seaports. In 1909, it was estimated that there were 3,000 Italians, 2,000 Greeks, 100 Chinese, 50 Japanese, 200 Syrians, and many "Bohemians, Bulgarians, Poles, and Jews" in Norfolk and Portsmouth. In 1910 the WMU ladies of Portsmouth Association reported: "It is a joy that the work . . . is soon to be opened . . . the work among the Foreigners . . . It would be unfair to go farther without presenting the work of our valiant women . . . for it was among them that the successful idea arose and every society is arising to shoulder their part of the undertaking." To begin their endeavor, Norfolk women raised $500 and Virginia women agreed to raise $1,500 annually.

In March, 1911, Margaret Tweedy of Georgia, a recent WMU Training School graduate, arrived in Norfolk to begin the work under sponsorship of the Home Mission Board. A building was secured on Bermuda Street in Norfolk for $15 monthly, and a Sunday school and week-day industrial school were established. Many individuals and churches helped with the project. A Sunday school class at First Church, Norfolk provided a table for a classroom. The Ladies' Working Society of Park Place Church, Norfolk sent $10 towards the cost of floor linoleum. Freemason Street Church bought 150 volumes for the library. Some contributed towards window screens. One loyal friend sent a mite box filled with money.

At the close of her first year, Miss Tweedy reported: "The work is for foreign children especially. Every effort however is made to interest and reach the neglected American child. The Sunday school is a very interesting feature of the work. There are 65 on the roll, the attendance having doubled during the past year. . . . The industrial school is a very effective phase of the work. Through it we are able to reach some we cannot get into the Sunday school. Here part of the time is given to religious teaching, such as Bible stories, memo-

rizing Scripture verses. The children are taught the plain, practical methods of sewing. They are soon able to make their own clothes. There are 50 children on the roll of the Industrial School. We have also a Sunbeam Band."

Clearly Miss Tweedy loved her charges, and the children loved her back. They called her "Missie Tweedie"; at the summer encampment at Virginia Beach in 1913, about 56 of her children presented a demonstration of their work before the WMU. They sang hymns, repeated the Twenty-third Psalm, and presented a recitation in which one child carried a lighted candle representing the light of the gospel while others lighted torches of faith and hope. "Many eyes were filled with tears as they looked upon this sight," reported Mrs. Julian P. Thomas, "and the Norfolk immigrant work will be a real thing to many who learned of it here for the first time."

Before day's end at Virginia Beach, the immigrant children were treated to a picnic with Bettie Ellyson of Second Church, Richmond, providing ice cream for all. Miss Ellyson also gave the children a ride on the merry-go-round at the seaside amusement park.

In 1919, Miss Tweedy married H.E. Hood of Norfolk and Ella Wixon became director of the immigrant work. In 1920, she was followed by Nonie Gravett. In time the immigrants became more assimilated into the native population; as each group gained a greater degree of prosperity, it relocated in the city. In time, there was no longer one neighborhood exclusively foreign in nature. In 1923, the immigrant work was closed but at the same time Portsmouth women opened a Good Will Center which responded to other needs.

Miss Tweedy's Good Will Center.

Bureaus for Buchanan

"That the loving interest of our women and girls is centered in our Mountain Mission School in Buchanan County has been indicated by their liberal gifts. . . . Soon after Mr. and Mrs. R.A. Henderson went over to Buchanan to take charge of the school [in 1911], the writer was at the Woman's Meeting of the New Lebanon Association [at] Honaker. Mrs. Henderson was present and gave a wonderfully inter-

esting description of the school. . . . The most pressing need of the moment seemed to be for window shades and wastewater jars for the dormitories . . . there was not a window shade in the house, no outside or inside blinds, and there were no slop-jars. The good women of the New Lebanon decided to come to the rescue . . . [and] with equal celerity and remarkable liberality raised about $40 in cash. The morning following the meeting a sufficient number of substantial window shades for the dormitory and good quality jars of blue and white enameled granite ware, one for each room, were ordered . . .

"Seldom have I witnessed a more joyous, enthusiastic scene than was presented in the Honaker church when that offering was taken. A cash offering of those proportions was unprecedented in a Woman's meeting of that Association. They had done a really great, generous deed. They realized it, and their joy was an inspiration.

"The next most urgent need was for bureaus. There are no closets built in the house, many of the students walk to the school miles over the mountains, bringing their clothing in suitcases, so there are few, if any, trunks. Mrs. Henderson requires the occupants to care for the bed linens, the towels and table napkins and to keep the room neat and attractive. The dressers seemed a necessity. Later, when I returned home, it was suggested by officers of the Union that I secure gifts at several associational meetings to purchase the needed dressers. Offerings were taken in the Woman's Meetings of the Petersburg, Augusta and Piedmont Associations. . . . In the Piedmont, one of our smallest, the societies gave as follows: WMS, Amherst, $5.50; WMS, Emmanuel, $4; WMS, Prospect, $1.50. The grand total was $124.35 and twelve substantial, solid oak dressers, with good mirrors, were purchased. The price paid for each was $9.50. Mrs. Henderson says, 'The dressers are beautiful.'

"The possibilities of work done in this school are great beyond our power of conception."

Mrs. W. S. Leake

Lottie Moon Monument

On December 24, 1914, the Woman's Missionary Union of Virginia placed a simple monument on the burial site of Lotte Moon's ashes—exactly two years after her death. It was "plain but handsome, in keeping with the taste of the one to whom it was erected."

Lottie Moon had requested for her remains to be placed beside her brother in the Crewe Cemetery; Mrs. J.M. Kidd of Crewe called the spot "holy ground." She and other WMU members had led the campaign to erect the monument. Individuals gave modest sums of $.25 or $.50 or $1 until the needed amount was raised.

In July, 1915, the women of the Concord Association gathered at the cemetery for a wreath-laying ceremony. Mrs. Collins of Crewe, a life-long friend of Lottie Moon, gave a talk and hymns were sung.

A Royal Ambassador stands beside the tombstone erected by Virginia women for Lottie Moon's gravesite in Crewe.

"More Than Book Learning"

*W*hen Mrs. F.L. Cox joined her husband as his assistant, overseeing the work at Oak Hill, a mountain school affiliated with the Baptists, she was shocked. The knives and forks in the dining room were "rust-eaten." She begged: "How we would appreciate sets of plated silverware from different Woman's Missionary Societies over Virginia. We need some more table linens. When we came here there was not a scrap of table linen of any description; all that was used last year was worn out. We do want to have our school attractive to the boys and girls so that they will love it; and we want them to learn how to conduct themselves in a well-kept home and in good society. A good education means so much more than just book learning. When we are so handicapped by lack of the necessities we cannot do our best. We need stewpans and boilers for the kitchen and dishes for the dining room and . . . "

Within a month of her appeal Mrs. Cox was supplied by Virginia women. "I have purchased one dozen quadrupled Rogers' silver knives," she reported, adding that dozens of other pieces were purchased with cash sent by women. Other women sent their own tableware. Several women at Rockfish, Virginia, sent lace curtains as well as teaspoons.

"Now we have a sufficient supply of table linens and knives and spoons. That is, we will have enough knives and forks when the Hampton WMS sends us what they had pledged. I am so thankful. But you know our wants are never satisfied . . . we need a new large range for our kitchen. I have $12 in cash to start a fund for a stove. What WMS will send me checks to add to the fund?" There always were needs ("shades for the girls' dormitory, a dining table in the parlor, rugs") but Mrs. Cox knew Virginia women would help her "climb over the mountains we cannot remove."

In 1916, Mrs. Cox reported that "every student of Oak Hill Academy is a Christian." Her husband had led a two-week revival at the school and 50 professed conversion. "Isn't that glorious," she declared, reminding the women anew that from kitchen to chapel the school was for more than book learning.

*O*ak Hill Academy was one of several mountain schools supported by Virginia WMU, 1938.

Recollections of Miss Moon

"My recollections of Miss Lottie Moon are vivid and have with them a sense of deep gratitude. I had heard of Miss Moon, it seems to me, all my life and she embodied for me the whole subject of foreign missions. I am not sure of the date of my first meeting her, but it must have been on her last furlough and several years previous to my coming to China in 1908. The place was Fork Church in Fluvanna County, Virginia. The occasion was our association or protracted meeting. I do not remember which. Miss Moon made an address on missions in China which deeply impressed all. My mother, Mrs. B.B. Gay, was an ardent missionary spirit, ever carrying joyfully upon her heart the work of the Woman's Missionary Society. A day or two after the meeting Miss Moon, with her hostess, Mrs. William E. Hatcher, called at our home. I was at that time living in Atlanta and only at home in Virginia for a visit. I am deeply interested and active in support of a Traveler's Aid work in Atlanta and talked to Miss Moon at some length about this work. I remember what a good listener she was, drawing me

Miss Lottie Moon

out upon this comparatively small subject when she might have been using the time to tell of her much greater work in China.

"When we arrived in China Miss Moon greeted us with a most cordial letter of welcome and later invited us to visit her the following summer. This we did and every impression of that visit was pleasant—the good Virginia cooking taught to her Chinese cook, the way she laughed at herself when she found her precious cook book, which she thought had been stolen but which eventually "turned up" just where she had put it for safe keeping "during the whitewashing." Later this book came into my possession and is prized especially for this association.

"Perhaps that which most impressed me, a newcomer to China, was Miss Moon's oneness with the Chinese, her respect for them and love, even when in some cases they disappointed her, yet a love that could be severe when it was for the good of the individual.

"Two summers later I was in ill health and Miss Moon insisted that we spend the whole summer with her. A hospital experience in Tsingtao took up most of the summer, but we were able to return home by way of Tongschow in September. Miss Moon was very busy with her school by that time but not too busy to think of many things for my comfort. She seemed to us there in her home quite normal in every way, but later we realized that even then anxiety for the Board and its work was heavy upon her heart. By the time winter set in the strong mind and body were failing and when brought to our home to be under Dr. Gaston's care, she was but a shadow of her former self. We need not dwell upon those last days. Better to remember her when she was at her best, or better still to think of her in the fair beyond where every faculty will have been perfected and every charm of heart and life will have reached its fullest flower."

Annie B. Gay Gaston
Religious Herald
November 24, 1927

How the Lottie Moon Offering Began

"Dr. H.A. Tupper, secretary of the Foreign Mission Board, placed with Miss Armstrong letters from Lottie Moon of China. In one letter she showed particularly her longing for the missions involvement of more women. She wrote, 'Picture it yourselves. Here are women with hearts as warm and tender as yours, with little children so sweet and dear to them as yours are to you. In each home is a kitchen God; in many as well is a God of wealth. Yonder hangs the female Buddha put up to worship by hands of devotees. . . . ' When Dr. Tupper sent this letter to Miss Armstrong, he included one of his own: 'There is force [in this letter] that must be felt by every appreciative reader. Her proposition to send several women of the right sort to Pingtu is important, wise and practicable. It has occurred to me that your Executive Committee might give special attention to this matter. . . . What do you think? Here is a clear work of Woman's Mission to Woman. The only hope of China is through the women. Might this not be successfully pressed?'

"Miss Armstrong brought Miss Moon's and Dr. Tupper's request to the Executive Committee on October 11, 1888. Plans were approved for a Christmas offering for China, with a goal of $2,000, the amount necessary for two women to go to Pingtu. Prayer gave strength to their plans. Miss Armstrong prepared programs and offering envelopes and sent them to the women's societies in cities, towns, and villages, urging the women to study, to pray and to give to the

Christmas offering for China. In sacrifice and love, devoted women brought their offerings - $3,315.26, enough to send three missionaries to Pingtu!

"From this small beginning, spurred by a letter from a weary, lonely young missionary, the Week of Prayer for Foreign Missions came into being.

"Not until 1918, six years after her death, was the Christmas offering named for Lottie Moon. It was done in the annual meeting by a simple voice vote. She would not have approved but a more worthy name could not have been found."

Religious Herald
October 29, 1981

"The Marvelous Miss Emma"

*S*he was a breath of fresh air for Woman's Missionary Union. She was in all ways talented, a creative force, a bolt of energy, the consummate artist. She saw beauty in everything and added touches of beauty to everything.

Emma Morehead Whitfield was identified with the WMU practically all of her life. Her mother, Annie Morehead Whitfield, was the presiding officer when Woman's Missionary Union, SBC held its founding meeting in Richmond in May, 1888. In time Emma herself became active. For 16 years she served on the Executive Board of Virginia WMU and became "the artist of our Southern Union."

Born in Greensboro, North Carolina, into a pastor's family she learned about missions at an early age from her mother and her father, the Rev. Theodore Whitfield. In 1887, the family moved to Richmond where her father was pastor of Fulton Baptist Church. Emma attended the Baptist school, the Richmond Female Institute; as the school dissolved and Westhampton College eventually evolved, Emma remained a friend of Baptist higher education for women. She was active in women's organizations, especially in the WMU of Grove Avenue Church in Richmond where she was a member.

But it was her artistic talent which claimed most of her time for WMU. She designed the pin and seal for WMU, SBC, "its alabaster box, its tithing box and the challenging pictures which carried the messages of the seasons of prayer." For Virginia, she served as historian and prepared a history for the twenty-fifth anniversary. She designed Virginia's seal. She did everything expected of a member of the Executive Board and more.

"God endowed her with gifts of mind and personality varied and unusual," wrote a Virginia WMU leader, "and she deliberately chose to use them in His service, to be a servant of God. Her connection with this Board was characterized by devotion to missions, constructive ability, loyal cooperation, strength of character, never-failing cheerfulness, and abiding spirituality."

When she compiled a Book of Remembrances for the Virginia Union, some of her fellow members—unbeknownst to her—slipped in a tribute for the compiler. It read: "Fitted by ancestry, training, consecrations, personal magnetism, keen sense of humor, whole-

hearted devotion to the cause of Christ and His missionary program to be one of our greatest and best-beloved leaders."

Miss Emma used her talent as a portrait painter and taught art at Richmond's Collegiate School. When she died on May 6, 1932, the women had lost their artist but the marvelous Miss Emma continued to shine through her works.

WMU EMBLEM

uring the Jubilee Year (1913) Woman's Missionary Union adopted its pin, the design of which has become the official emblem of Woman's Missionary Union. The shape is the double fish head, a symbol precious because of its use in the early days of Christianity. Fearing persecution if discovered, the followers of Christ did not needlessly disclose their faith to their enemies. It was their custom to make the sign of the fish head when they met anyone whose attitude toward Christianity was not known. If the person were an enemy of Christianity, the sign would mean nothing to him. If he were a believer, he would recognize the sign and so be discovered as a friend.

The fish symbol was used by the Christians because in the Greek the first letters of Jesus Christ, Son of God, Saviour spell the word fish. The symbol thus became precious to the early Christians as a brief profession of their faith in the deity of Christ.

Around the border of the pin is engraved: Woman's Missionary Union SBC 1888. In the center is pictured a Bible, opened at First Corinthians 3:9—*"Laborers together with God,"* the WMU watchword.

Above the open Bible is a lighted torch, a symbol of our Saviour who said: "I am the light of the world: he that followeth after me shall not walk in darkness but have the light of life." The staff of the torch, extending behind and below the globe, suggests the wonderful strengthening, keeping, and saving power of God, our Father, whose love is above, below, and back of us as we follow the Light of life. The globe suggests that there is no boundary line for the gospel.

In the early years of Woman's Missionary Union it was not considered proper in times of sorrow to wear any color unless it were lavender. Accordingly WMU leaders adopted lavender as the Union's official color, feeling that women in mourning would not mind wearing a lavender bow as a badge at a WMU meeting. Subsequently, notably during the Jubilate, white was combined with the lavender. These colors suggest the purity and fragrance of Christlike living which seeks to penetrate the darkness of sin with the sweetness and light of the Gospel message.

The emblem with necessary language adaptations is used by Woman's Missionary Unions in many lands and the pin is worn by women the world around. All wear it proudly for it speaks of the One they serve.

WMU, SBC Literature

JUBILATE!

"Mundus Christo Jubilate: The World for Christ! Hallelujah!" That was the stirring cry of the Jubilate year, which ran from May, 1913, to May, 1914, in celebration of the twenty-fifth year since the founding meeting of 1888. The cry of the Jubilate remained Virginia's official motto.

What a celebration! Individual societies planned observances along a suggested outline. Official colors were lavender and white. The Scripture selection was the 100th Psalm.

Virginia women participated in the Southwide meeting held in St. Louis in May, 1913. Alice Taylor, Virginia's young people's leader, remembered the excitement: "From the very time we boarded the train in Richmond, we began to feel that this was to be the great meeting which it has indeed proven. The trip out was fine. The weather was ideal, the company delightful; we had the honor of having our president, Miss Heck, with us from the start. The Maryland delegation joined us at Charlottesville. We enjoyed a short stop in Louisville where the coaches from several states made up the special train." Virginia women on the platform in the St. Louis meeting included Lizzie Savage and Mrs. Kate Hinkle, the delegate chosen to respond to the welcome from St. Louis women. Again from Alice Taylor are these memories: "In the roster of States our own Virginia president, Miss Lizzie Savage, made us feel proud of our State in naming the victories of the past year. She could not tell, however, that Virginia made her apportionment."

Alice Taylor was present in the Odeon, a large, beautiful theatre, for the Jubilate Sunday sessions. She wrote: "This was the real Jubilate. The great theatre was filled. The processional surpassed that of the morning. Besides their Sunbeam hymn, the Royal Ambassadors hymn, the Young Woman's Auxiliary hymn, and the Woman's hymn, written by Miss Heck for the occasion, all sung by Sunbeams, Royal Ambassadors and young women, groups of girls dressed in the costumes of heathen and papal nations followed, singing to the Children of Light the plea from heathenism and darkness—a touching sight. . . . Our own Corresponding Secretary, Mrs. Julian P. Thomas presented the Jubilate offering. A woman from Georgia gave $5,000; numbers gave $1,000 each. We had one $1,000 gift from Virginia and several $100 gifts. The total from all the states was over $38,000. One woman gave her diamond ring. It was a time of rejoicing. The recessional, 'Lift up your voices, ye children of light,' closed the real Jubilate."

During the mid-summer Virginia Beach encampment, a Jubilate celebration featured an eloquent address by Mrs. W.C. James. Lizzie Savage explained that Virginia's gifts would go to the Judson Centennial for Foreign Missions and the Church Building Loan Fund for Home Missions. Fannie E.S. Heck spoke on "The Religion of the Women of Tomorrow." Someone present summarized her message: "She traced the evolution of woman from her position as the capable but unpaid worker in the home to the present day, when woman has followed her former occupations of weaving and sewing out of the home into the factory and store. She showed how this affected the status of woman, not only financially, but in every way. Then she followed this with a plan for so planning our society work as that the

VIRGINIA WMU EMBLEM

he Virginia WMU Emblem was designed for the Jubilate Celebration in 1913, by Miss Emma Whitfield who knew the laws of heraldry as well as the Christian symbols. For the Virginia emblem she chose the cross as the "*coat of arms*." In the Middle Ages a woman of royalty, not being permitted to use a shield, placed her coat of arms on a diamond-shaped background, a "*lozenge*." Around the cross a circle carries the Latin motto, "*Mundus Christo Jubilate*"—The World for Christ, Hallelujah! At the upper point of the lozenge Miss Whitfield entwined the "*V*" and "*A*" for Virginia, and at the lower point the initials WMU and the date of organization.

Virginia WMU Literature

busy, occupied woman, and the young woman especially, might have a part in it, and that it might fill the lives of our leisure women with something worthwhile. She sorrowed over the fact that our societies were not doing work big enough to arrest and engage the interest of all our women, and pleaded that we work and pray for a large vision that will develop a future for our work, adequate and satisfying to all."

The highlight of the Jubilate year for Virginia women came at the annual state meeting held in November at First Church, Roanoke. A choral processional opened a session with Sunbeams, Royal Ambassadors, and YWAs singing their hymns. The last group to pass in review were young women clad in white, representing each district association, and each woman was accompanied by an orphan girl. The RAs escorted orphanage boys into the meeting. T.B. Ray of the Foreign Mission Board urged the Virginia Union to help as Baptists raised $1,250,000 for equipment needed on the mission field. Of the $425,000 asked of WMU, SBC, Virginia women were urged to give $75,000 of the amount.

Across Virginia many local WMS Jubilate celebrations followed the same general format. At Bacon's Castle Church the women found it more convenient to meet at their president's home than at the church. The president, Mrs. W.L. Ward, wrote Mrs. Julian Thomas about their Jubilate: "We followed the program for the morning service exactly, only we had some extra music. All members wore the colors—lavender and white. We have all felt a spiritual uplift from our meeting." Mrs. R.D. Bates of Upper King and Queen Church wrote: "The bazaar and oyster supper at Thanksgiving were a greater success than last year. We cleared nearly $80 for missions." Mrs. L.N. Fox of the Ashland Church reported that their Jubilate was held near Thanksgiving so they decided to have a "pounding for missions" and Sunbeam children brought "onions, potatoes, toys, cakes and money." The gifts were "auctioned off" and the WMU realized $5.73 from the children for missions. Dover women gathered at Cool Spring Church where they heard reports on their successful project to furnish the infirmary at the Buchanan Mountain Mission School. The Dover women had come in "carriages, buggies and automobiles until the capacity of the church was taxed."

Several Virginia cities played host to local Jubilate celebrations. Hampton women met in the snow and pledged $400 to the Jubilate fund. They heard reports on their own personal service work among the immigrants.

Franklin's Jubilate had the sweet smell of violets. The YWAs would pin a posey tied with white ribbon on each guest. Staunton women copied the "Children of Light" pageant from the Southern Union. Clifton Forge women offered a "daintly served luncheon" to visitors which promised "an opportunity to meet the women socially." Culpeper women attended despite snow and "felt that the meeting was a great success." Richmond women heard Miss Heck as she "urged each individual woman to search her own heart to the end that she might consecrate her life, her thoughts, her time, her money as a Jubilate praise to God." In Danville, George Braxton Taylor, founder of the Sunbeams, talked on "Our Blessing a Trust for the World." In Virginia's far corner "in spite of the snow-covered earth and gloomy skies," Bristol was ready for the Jubilate with large audiences for the three services.

Down by the sea Norfolk experienced "a zero temperature, a blinding snowstorm, ice and sleet" yet it was like springtime inside Freemason Street Church for the Jubilate. "Hundreds of clusters of lavender and purple wisteria (made by the decorating committee themselves), hung from the green bower of spruce pine which lined the walls behind the rostrum and the gallery railing." Mrs. Sparks Melton served as hostess at the luncheon. When the Sunbeams entered the processional they were dressed in white and each one carried a yellow jonquil.

The Jubilate was a time for rejoicing over the Lord's leadership in the past and for pressing forward for increased missions work. The good created by the Jubilate lasted for years.

"My Dear Sister: So much is being said about the Jubilate Offering that I feel that something ought to be said on how we may all have a part in this extra gift. Many of us would be glad to give to it, but how may we get [money] to give? The rich give of their abundance, and many, though not rich, give one-tenth of their salary to the Lord's work, but we whose husbands can only give us money for the necessities must make every dollar do its utmost; how can we give of that which is not our own? I am writing this to suggest a way by which almost every woman can give to this great cause, the Jubilate fund; it is this: Instead of getting a new hat for spring or summer, give the money you would spend for it to the Jubilate Fund and wear last summer's hat. Think of the enormous amount of money spent for millinery every season! How much good the same amount would do if used for the needs of the work in our various mission fields! I cannot help thinking of it every time the seasons change and the ladies purchase new hats and I cannot buy one often for the reason that my conscience will not let me. Most frequently I go bareheaded in summer. If there is any woman who had (as I had) intended spending $5 on her new hat for the coming summer, and who will do without one and join me in giving the amount to the Jubilate Fund, please write Mrs. Thomas. Let your gift go through your society. There are hundreds of women who would do this if they could only realize the needs of the work on our mission fields. May God open the hearts of our women!"

A Pastor's Wife

Hat Money for Missions

THE WORD OF THE WATER

In the early years of the twentieth century when the mighty Rappahannock River was really a highway, large steamers plied the waters. About 1912, the women of Hermitage Church in Middlesex County came up with a plan to place copies of the New Testament in each stateroom and the Bible in the saloon of each of the three Rappahannock steamers—the Middlesex, Potomac and Lancaster. The largest steamer, the Middlesex, had 67 staterooms.

They shared their idea and soon the women of the Rappahannock promoted the cause. Quickly the missionary societies at Harmony Grove, Glebe Landing, Olivet, Wares, Clark's Neck, and others in the association's bounds had joined this "labor of love."

The project became part of WMU Personal Service Work. Mrs. W.B. Haislip of Church View inspired the women with her pleas: "The precious word of God will be made easily accessible to all who travel up and down the broad highway of the beautiful Rappahannock. What if only one life were touched and uplifted—only one soul saved to righteous living! Would this not be worth unspeakably more than it has cost us in effort and time! Eternity alone can reveal the harvest of this wide seed-sowing!"

The WMU of the Rappahannock gave so generously that the steamboats were supplied with Scriptures, with enough money left over in July, 1914, to give a purse to Olive Bagby, a Rappahannock daughter bound for the mission field of China. The purse was money to purchase Bibles for the Chinese. And so the Rappahannock women placed the word on the waters at home and across the world.

MENFOLKS:
R. J. Willingham

When Robert Josiah Willingham died in December, 1914, the "Baptist Women's Work" page in the **Religious Herald** felt "impelled" to pay an added tribute to the life of the Foreign Mission Board leader from the women's perspective. Virginia WMU considered him "their kind and helpful friend, their good counsellor." Mrs. Julian Thomas wrote: "Never did they come to him for help, whether [for] advice [or] information, to speak in their meetings, to work out their plans, but he was ready to give fully and freely of the great resources of this noble mind. Virginia Baptist women have lost a friend whose place cannot be filled."

His life's journey had begun in Beaufort, South Carolina, in 1854; at his birth his father prayed that his son might become a preacher of the Gospel. As a boy attending Sunday school, he once had to memorize the great missions hymn, "From Greenland's Icy Mountains." There the heartthrob of missions began. In time, he began his service as pastor of small town churches in Georgia and then came pastorates at First Church, Chattanooga, and First Church, Memphis. It was from Memphis that Willingham came to Richmond in 1893 to assume the executive leadership role at the Foreign Mission Board, devoting to that work his last 21 years.

The names of Willingham and the Foreign Mission Board became synonymous. A contemporary reflected: "His public addresses for missions were powerful chiefly perhaps because those who heard him believed so fully in the sincerity and earnestness of the man. It was not an uncommon thing to see him and his audience with tears flowing down their faces as they planned and pledged for greater things for God and His Kingdom. Dr. Willingham devoted every atom of strength at his command and hardly ever did he make an address without portraying the divine origin of missions."

The statistics of the period of his secretaryship show that annual gifts rose from $106,000 to over a half-million. Virginia's gifts alone rose from $22,800 to over $80,000. But there were other signs of success as a report in 1914 stated: "[At the beginning of his service] there were only a few day schools; now there are schools ranging from the kindergarten to the college and the theological seminary. Then there were no hospitals or printing plants; now there are eight hospital buildings where eleven medical missionaries treated 74,839 patients [in 1913], and a number of printing plants which send out millions of pages of literature. One of the greatest achievements of Dr. Willingham's administration was the remarkable increase of interest and growth in contributions from the churches . . . often with a supreme effort he increased the contributions of a church many-fold for world-wide missions."

Perhaps Bob Willingham deserved the Nobel Peace Prize because he was among the inner circle of SBC leaders who effected the "peace treaty" between Annie Armstrong and Fannie Heck in 1898. He brought the two women with their divergent views together to forge a "peace" agreement at a private meeting in Norfolk in the summer of 1898. The friction it ended had grown out of disagreement over a Bible Fund but also reflected a fundamental power question between the executive office and the president of the WMU, SBC.

It was Bob Willingham who graciously allowed Virginia WMU's Central Committee to use the offices of the Foreign Mission Board as their meeting place. For awhile he was their benevolent "landlord" so to speak and Virginia women knew they had a friend in "Dr. Willingham."

Virginia—The Banner State

"Look out for the banner state" was the slogan of the subscription drive for the new *Royal Service*, successor to *Our Mission Fields*, the official organ of WMU, SBC. Which state would be pictured carrying the banner representing the most subscriptions? WMU cautioned, of course, that "since ours is a Union the victory of one means the triumph of all" yet when the banner was revealed it read "Virginia." The women of Virginia had placed 766 subscriptions. They yet were urged for still further victory: "There are more than 1,400 societies in Virginia and every one of these should have at least one copy of *Royal Service*. Suppose all our women and girls subscribed to it and read it. Think what we could do! We should never need to ask for money for any object. Let's urge everyone to participate!"

Virginia held the Royal Service *banner, 1914.*

"Can Country Women Tithe?"

That was Mrs. G.W. Bedell's topic before a meeting of the Dover WMU in 1914. As president of the Four Mile Creek (Church) Aid and Missionary Society, she knew all about country women since her listeners were all women living several miles from the city and even up to five miles from the church in the Henrico countryside. "We were holding socials, ice-cream sales, bazaars, entertainments to raise our missionary money," she said, "and at our last oyster supper the weather was bad and after hard work and much worry we cleared five dollars! I have always been thankful for that oyster supper on that stormy night for it was the first real object lesson I could present to our ladies to show them how infinitely better would be a 'voluntary contribution' than an oyster supper!"

Mrs. Bedell then introduced the method of tithing pledges, whereby each woman was encouraged to give one-tenth of all the money "under her control."

She observed: "The country women may have the money from sale of certain farm products like butter, eggs, and vegetables, and this is to tithe. But now let us suppose she does not have the sale of any of those things but she does have the butter, eggs, and vegetables for family use; then let her just quietly but with firmness propose in her heart that one-tenth of those products shall be given to the Lord; that she will save out one-tenth of the eggs and butter and dispose of them as best she can, using the money for church work. Let her take one-tenth of the vegetables and give them wherever she thinks will do the most good, possibly to some sick person, whom ill health has kept from making a garden. Let her gladly, willingly, cheerfully, and systematically give one-tenth of what is given to her, and she will, I am sure, soon be surprised to hear the comments the other members of the family will make about it, and ere he knows it the husband will say, 'Well, if you are going to divide, I will,' and then will they know, for the first time, the real pleasure and worship there is in giving. The country woman who tithes religiously need never be ashamed of the little money she has to give if she conscientiously gives of the good things which she has in abundance."

"Why I Like the Woman's Missionary Union"
By
Dr. W.C. James

"There are so many things about the WMU which I like— [including] the fine business sense which is shown in the conduct of its affairs. The Baptist women of the South, judging from the WMU are not only spiritually minded but they are also worldly wise and in the finest sense of the phrase. . . . The WMU craves the privilege of helping every cause fostered by the Convention. While the WMU supports all phases of our organized work, yet its preeminent business is that of missions. . . . The women have done well to make it the heart of all their efforts. Another feature of the WMU which appeals to me is its insistence upon prayer as fundamental to all its efforts and successes. The main characteristic of the work of the WMU is educational. . . . The women are great givers. They believe, however, that the right kind of giving must have a basis which is both intelligent and spiritual. Appeals based on mere emotion and the employment of 'hurrah' methods do not carry much weight with the women of the WMU. They are building rather on a foundation of fact. One great contributing factor to the success, zeal and consecration of the women is their acquaintance with the needs almost everywhere.

"Another reason why I like the WMU is because it gives the women something to do which challenges the best there is in them. Were it not for the WMU many of the

women whom it has enlisted would be living lives of household drudgery, of unrelieved daily toil, or they would belong to that class of women who, while not guilty of positive harm, are at the same time doing absolutely no good in the world. . . . But the WMU has gotten hold of all kinds of women giving them a vision of the worldwide Kingdom of God and along with it a vision of the contribution they can make toward the realization of that kingdom.

"Another thing I like about the WMU is that it is succeeding in the work it has undertaken, each year setting its stakes further ahead, thus making the goal of one year the starting point for the next.

"One of the most impressive sights is going into a state WMU meeting. The women are there representing all walks of life, all degrees of wealth, culture and social position, but united in one common purpose. Their faces are lighted up with the fires of a holy reserve."

Mrs. W.C. James

"*W*hen the hour for the election of officers for 1915–16 arrived, there was a hush of sacred silence presiding over the entire congregation. Each woman's heart knew the hand of God would be laid upon the right member of the Union to take up the burden laid down by Miss Heck. Not a shadow of doubt rested on any soul; and prayers were silently ascending to Him that His own anointed would hear Him speaking through the voice of his sisters, when she was named as President of the Union.

"In all respects it seemed most appropriate that Mrs. W.C. James should wear the mantle of her illustrious predecessor. It was she who had conceived and carried out the wonderful conception of our Jubilate celebration. It was her consecrated intellect that had made possible numerous forward movements of the WMU. As the years have sped along the Baptist women of the Southland have realized more and more that she was God's chosen. She has indeed come to the kingdom for such a time as this."
Margaret McRae Lackey in
Decade of WMU Service, 1913–1923.

Lydia Williams Green

"*I*t is not possible to think or speak of the Greens separately for they were a team," wrote Rees Watkins in January, 1967 when she penned the memorial tribute to Lydia Williams Green. And Miss Watkins was correct. The two were a team from their marriage in 1905, through 31 years of unparalleled medical missions work in Nigeria until only death separated Lydia Green from her husband in 1962. On January 2, 1967, within days of what would have been the sixtieth anniversary of their wedding, Mrs. Green joined George Green in death.

Lydia Barnes Williams was born and reared in Norfolk and was educated at Mary Washington College. In the summer of 1905, George Green, a young intern at DePaul Hospital and a Baptist minister, was asked to supply the pulpit of Park Avenue Church, Norfolk, and there he met and subsequently asked for the hand of a young woman in the congregation, Lydia Williams.

Within a month after marriage Lydia and George Green were bound for Africa, their home for nearly four decades. Rees Watkins, who years later also served in the same missions field, heard from others the stories of Lydia's journey "by boat, steamship, 'mammy chair,' and hammock" to Ogbomosho. Lydia would tell about the pouring rains on their arrival. The natives said such rain was "a good omen" and meant the strangers would remain a long time.

At first the Greens used their own house as a clinic and Lydia's kitchen table served as an early operating table. She was the nurse-anesthetist. Although she lacked formal training, her husband taught her and for many years she assisted with operations.

When their daughter, Virginia, was born the clinic was moved to sheds in the backyard. A large tree in the front yard served as "a waiting room, consulting room and visiting room" for 15 years. When the crowds gathered they also heard Bible readings and prayers "for the Greens insisted always that medical work was an aid for evangelism."

Lydia was active in local church work, helping to teach the children and women. She called the children her "Stars" and spent Sunday afternoons teaching them the Scriptures and Christian hymns. In a little mud hut used as a church, she organized the first WMU in Ogbomosho.

In 1935, during the twenty-fifth anniversary of the reign of King George V and Queen Mary, Lydia and George Green were recognized for their services with Jubilee medals. Of course Virginia women had already honored their beloved daughter through their support with prayers and gifts.

Dr. George Green:
A Missions Legend

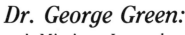

Virginia women felt a special kinship with Dr. George Green, the first Southern Baptist medical missionary to Africa. Born in London and involved, at first, with the home missions work of Canadian Baptists, he became a Virginian. He was educated in the Commonwealth at its acclaimed Medical College in Richmond where he enrolled in 1901. He became a Southern Baptist and preached while at MCV. He married a Virginian. In 1905 he served as a supply pastor at Park Avenue Church, Norfolk, and there he met Lydia Barnes Williams. They were married in 1907. He trained in Virginia, serving a year's internship in Norfolk. As the missionary doctor at Ogbomosho, Nigeria, he was supported by Virginia, WMU. The women of Virginia furnished a building and medical supplies. Through the years George and Lydia Green were featured frequently in missions articles and on the WMU page in the Religious Herald. Numerous missions circles chose to carry Lydia's name and associational unions claimed them as their own missionaries. When retirement came, it was Virginia which became George Green's home as he moved to Danville to live with a daughter.

From 1959 until his death in 1962, George Green was associated with the life of First Church, Danville. The pastor, Robert L. McCan, once presented a sketch of the missions legend. In part, he said:

"When the Greens arrived in Ogbomosho, he was the only trained medical doctor in the city of 80,000 persons. They opened a clinic in the basement of their house. Practice began with some good medical instruments, medicines and $50 in money. With the money they put in a concrete floor, whitewashed the walls and had an operating table carved from native wood. Under those conditions Dr. Green treated more than 2,000 patients during the first year.

"The first real hospital came in 1921. A number of doctors joined Dr. Green and Lydia Green turned her attention to being school teacher for their four daughters and to working in missionary society work."

In 1935, the Greens were given Jubilee medals in recognition of their service within the British Empire. In the 1940s the local leaders presented George Green with a robe and insignia, recognizing him as "Chief of the Medicine Men."

WMU children present dolls to Dr. George Green for his little patients in the Ogbomosho Hospital, 1919.

A Bell for Ogbomosho

"We had a very interesting service in connection with the laying of a panel in the front wall of our new hospital building. The hospital is to be named 'The Virginia Baptist Hospital.' You will remember that at the time of the jubilate of WMU, the YWA's of Virginia agreed to raise $3,500 for the hospital at Ogbomosho. This they did, and I thought it would be very fitting if this could be commemorated in some way in the building, so I made a stone of concrete and cemented the face of it and cut the following letters on it:

Y.W.A.

Va.

U.S.A.

"A Yoruba Bible, a copy of the **Religious Herald**, **Home and Foreign Fields**, **Royal Service**, and a copy of Kind Words containing the life story of M.L. Stone, an Ogbomosho boy, who became the Spurgeon of Yoruba preachers, were placed and sealed in the stone box. The President of the Oyo Province very kindly graced the occasion by his presence, also the Bale (the King) of Ogbomosho and all the chiefs of the town were present at the service. The influence of this service means great promise for the future Baptist work in Ogbomosho. "By the way, we are going to need a good bell for the hospital compound. Dr. MacLean could bring the bell with him when he returns. You see I have faith sufficient to send shipping instructions along with the expressed desire for the bell. Dr. Love thought of making the appeal for this bell through **Home and Foreign Fields**, but we felt sure that inasmuch as the bell was to be used on 'The Virginia Hospital' our Virginia women would want to supply this need. Who will be the first to let us know about a bell? Dr. MacLean will probably sail in March. It will be very much cheaper for him to take it as excess baggage."

Dr. George Green

Within two weeks a bell for Ogbomosho was offered by the Norton Church. Mrs. W.A. Surface was the WMU member who led the Norton Church to devote its "good, sweet-toned bell."

Armless Nigerian turned to the Ogbomosho Hospital for help. The cornerstone reads "YWA, VA, USA".

War Time and the Women

"If you have bought a government Liberty Loan Bond you have proved your patriotism.

"If you will give your Liberty Loan Bonds to the Church Building Loan Fund it will prove your consecration.

"The government pays you 4 per cent on your bonds. The Church Building Loan Fund will pay you the same and the bonds will be credited on the WMU Church Building Loan Fund apportionment."

Religious Herald
Nov. 1, 1917

"In talking with an associational superintendent, I learned that her own Society was meeting its apportionment, but that it was becoming increasingly hard to get the members to maintain the other missionary activities of the Society because they were busy with the Red Cross work. There can be no question as to the necessity for the Red Cross work, but neither can there be any excuse for neglecting the missionary study and enlistment. Christian leaders unite in believing that after the war there will be almost limitless missionary opportunities. We must prepare to meet them."

Kathleen Mallory, 1918.

"Last year soon after war was declared the Charter Home Demonstration Club was organized, and we began at once to form plans for doing our bit.

"We helped and encouraged each other to conserve our food supply, and I am sure there was very little if any waste of food in our little corner of the world. [We planted tomatoes on the school grounds and] when August came and the tomatoes were ready, the women went over to the school and canned 100 quarts, and after paying for the cans, we turned into the Civic League treasury $17 to be used for the benefit of the school. These women were putting more food on the market to help feed more people and the money back into the school to help build the character of the future citizens."

Mrs. R.H. Bruce

Ruth Kersey

"*S*hould the Board see fit to send me, I shall try to serve faithfully for a lifetime. I am accustomed to hard work, and I don't mind a hard place. I am not afraid, and I don't mind a dangerous place. I am strong and I would like to go where healthy, strong people can best go and the more unhealthy cannot go."

These words—from a young woman's application to the Foreign Mission Board—embody the spirit guiding Ruth May Kersey, Virginia-born missionary to Africa. The spirit resided in a heart knowing Christ since the age of nine. Born in Hanover in 1889, she attended the public schools of her county and joined the Ashland church. Later she went to Richmond's John Marshall High School and the

Woman's College. She was graduated from the WMU Training School in 1916.

It was in the Training School that Ruth Kersey first heard Dr. George Green, the pioneer medical missionary of Ogbomosho, speak of the pressing need for more medical workers. Although she had previously prayed that the Lord would not send her to Africa, she surrendered to the need. She entered Retreat for the Sick Hospital in Richmond for nursing training and was graduated in 1920. On June 10, 1920, she was appointed by the Board and sailed for Africa in December. Ruth Kersey, the self-described "strong" woman, would need every ounce of strength for what awaited the pioneer Southern Baptist nurse to Nigeria.

One simple incident occurred which set a new direction in her service. Mrs. George Green once recounted that: "Ruth had lived in our home when she first came to Nigeria and I could almost tell what she was thinking as she looked at a little black baby whose mother had died and at the father with such pleading eyes. Somehow he had managed to keep the baby alive for nearly two weeks and the loving heart of the missionary nurse was touched. She told the father to leave the baby and she would do what she could. She had a crib taken from the hospital to her house, named the baby Emma for her own mother and started a determined program to keep her alive! Every two hours the baby had to be fed, thus interfering with much needed rest, for Ruth was still the only missionary nurse in the hospital. Soon the baby began to gain [weight] and became a healthy, happy child. She became quite an object of curiosity for such a thing had never been known in that section of the country. As time went on, other babies whose mothers died at, or soon after childbirth, were brought to the hospital. In fact, so many were brought that a whole room in the hospital had to be set aside for them."

Virginia WMU launched the building of a special facility for the babies next to the hospital. Mrs. W.E. Morris of Petersburg, Virginia's White Cross chairman, led the women to give some $5,300 for the infants' hospital. Eva Sanders, a fellow Virginian and co-worker, recalled: "Many babies were brought who had little or no chance to live, but she spent the same untiring care for them. Each time a starved or sick baby was brought and did not live, she wept as if it were her own. She found it so hard to return three-year-olds to their Moslem or heathen families when they were considered old enough to eat Yoruba food—and so she filled the little house in her back yard with the bigger boys and kept the girls in any extra space in the baby building." Miss Sanders believes that the missionary nurse still lives in hundreds of African lives today. "The fruit of her labors is seen as pastors' wives and other Christian workers proudly acclaim Miss Kersey as the one who rescued them in infancy." As a tribute the Home for Motherless Babies was named the Kersey Children's Home.

On furlough in 1939, she shared with Virginia women and others the news of her life's work. In a letter to one of her hostesses she confessed: "Have thought often of the pleasant night spent in your home. It is such a sweet, quiet place. I kept in a whirl all the time home. There never was time to read or write. Hope all the 'much talking' will be for His Glory." ➤

W*omen raised funds to build and equip a building for "motherless children."*

Everything Ruth May Kersey did was for His Glory. She died in November, 1958, as an emeritus missionary but her works continued.

Elizabeth Ellyson Wiley

*E*lizabeth first heard about missions as a small child when her mother explained that girls her own age in China had never heard of the Saviour. Another time her father spoke at the supper table about some thrilling experience from the mission field so far away. Every morning at family prayers, petitions were offered for foreign missions. Her parents were missions personified; her mother was a state WMU leader, serving as treasurer of the Virginia Central Committee, and her father was the state Baptist executive for 30 years. He had followed his father in the post and also served as president of the Foreign Mission Board. For generations the name Ellyson was associated with Baptist work.

At nine she was converted and joined her parents' church, Second Baptist Church of Richmond. She was educated at Westhampton College and the WMU Training School and for six glorious months in 1920 she served as young people's secretary for Virginia WMU. Mrs. Julian Thomas liked to boast that the Virginia Union had no finer secretary than "Lizzie" Ellyson but Elizabeth soon was engaged to a prospective foreign missionary. While mother and aunts fretted about a wedding trousseau, Elizabeth Ellyson continued "enlisting and training" the young people of Virginia. She especially worked among the college students.

On June 30, 1921, Elizabeth and James Hundley Wiley were married in a home wedding. "Hun," the son of a preacher, had surrendered to God's call to the ministry during his senior year at Richmond College.

In August, 1921, Wiley and his bride headed for China and a teaching career at the University of Shanghai. Wiley became a leading professor at the school, which had a large enrollment. In a quieter, more intimate way he also influenced others through his Fellowship Bible Class. While he taught sociology, Mrs. Wiley taught religion.

In 1923, Elizabeth's sister, Louise, volunteered to direct girls' athletics at the University of Shanghai. The next year she married a missionary, C. Hart Westbrook, who was dean of the university.

In 1927, Elizabeth Wiley returned home for her first furlough. When travelling about the state, renewing old acquaintances with Virginia's young people and women, she stumbled upon the very special idea of Christmas-in-August.

Elizabeth found her special calling in China by working with the women servants or amahs. Wednesday afternoons were set aside for the amahs for prayer meetings in her home. She interested Virginia women in sending funds to establish a community center for the amahs similar to the House of Happiness in Richmond.

In the 1920s Virginia WMU designated associations as sponsors of particular missionaries. Shenandoah women sponsored Elizabeth

Wiley and Goshen women sponsored her husband. The promotional literature stated that each one's services could be sponsored for nine cents an hour or an $800 salary a year.

In the 1930s the world of old China missions began to fall apart. Mrs. Wiley remembered: "The real war with Japan began in 1937. It made my husband very nervous. I was not nervous. Several times we had to leave the college and go into the city to find a place to live. My husband had to stand guard at night on campus with a flare gun. He was supposed to fire it if any Japanese soldiers came into the campus and U.S. gunboats would shell the Japanese."

The Wileys left China in 1937 and stayed in the Philippines until they were allowed to re-enter. "We left again at Thanksgiving in 1940. All American women and children had to leave."

Back in Virginia, Hun Wiley found a useful place of service at his alma mater where he taught sociology. After Wiley's death, Elizabeth Wiley continued to live in the West End of Richmond and remained active at Second Baptist Church. She remained forever the dutiful daughter of Virginia Baptists.

Christmas-in-August

The idea was born and developed in Virginia by a genuine Virginia missionary, "our Elizabeth Ellyson," as the women insisted upon calling her long after she was Mrs. J. Hundley Wiley, missionary to China.

In 1927, renewing old friendships on her first furlough, Elizabeth Wiley fell into a conversation with a Sunbeam Band leader, Mrs. Guy Via, of First Church, Charlottesville, who asked if the Sunbeams could help with the missions cause. Elizabeth replied that the servant's children at the university would appreciate Christmas presents. These would teach that Christians cared just as God did. This conversation sparked the highly successful Christmas-in-August program. Gifts gathered in August and placed under summertime Christmas trees in Virginia churches could be shipped to reach China for the winter celebration. The idea took hold and other missionaries benefited from the program.

There were 100 gifts from Virginia that first year and they were varied ones—sewing needles and soap for the women, small toys and crayons for children. These gifts indicated to the Chinese women that

Christmas-in-August program for the George Braxton Taylor Sunbeam Band at Liberty Church, Appomattox, c. 1950s.

others, Christian friends, half-a-world away cared about them just as God had cared on that first Christmas.

There were many Chinese children and mothers. Around 400 lived in the village around the university's gates. Mrs. Wiley wrote letters home, telling of the joy generated from the simple gifts. More Sunbeam Bands joined in the annual project. Gifts were shipped to the Virginia WMU office in Richmond and then re-shipped to China.

In 1937, the Christmas box from Virginia containing 1,000 gifts was permanently lost, traced only to the Philippines. World conditions closed China but Virginia women could not close Christmas-in-August. They re-directed their gifts to other mission centers in Virginia and to the Indians in Oklahoma, New Mexico and Arizona.

In 1953, Woman's Missionary Union, SBC adopted Virginia's project. A labor begun by "our Elizabeth" and Virginia's Sunbeams spread to give Christmas blessings to countless people.

Annual Meeting
Petersburg 1921

"The unprecedented number of 566 delegates enrolled at noon on Thursday for the 23rd annual session of WMU. Miss Shumate, of China, brought the heart message; and Virginia's Training School girls presented an impressive pageant—'United for Service.'

"A strong plea was made for permanent quarters of the GA and RA camps at Virginia Beach.

"The Training School trustees reported the number of Virginia girls to be the largest number WMU has ever sent to the school. Twenty two are already there.

"At [Mrs. W.E. Hatcher's] suggestion, the body instructed the corresponding secretary to send a telegram to President Harding, expressing the Union's prayerful interest in the ultimate success of the Limitation of Armaments Conference.

"One of the most timely and forceful messages ever brought to the Union was the address of Mrs. Henry Schmelz on the 'Christian Approach to our Colored Neighbors.' She pled for no dual standard of one for white and another for black; no distinction in the application of the golden rule; and that social gradations within the Negro race might be recognized, thereby giving the individual the benefit of individual character and attainments. At the close of her address the Union passed a resolution of cooperation with the Interracial Commission."

Mrs. J. L. McCutcheon

"To Russia, With Love"

In 1921, Southern Baptists were sending food and clothing to help Russia's destitute. Everett Gill of the Foreign Mission Board was approached as the person to arrange for the distribution. Virginia women were asked to send their gifts to New York with labels from the WMU office in Richmond. Virginia WMU was sending "knitted garments, stout warm suits, simple cotton dresses, underwear, stockings, sensible shoes with low heels and broad toes, hats, yarns, leather, cloth, baby clothing," and, most of all, love. And they were sending it quickly, before winter.

The One and Only

Bessie Trevvett Lewis was the one and only educational secretary for Virginia WMU. Compared to her lengthy life of nearly a century, her four-year position, from 1922 to 1926, was a brief but pivotal episode. For Virginia women those four years were important ones as she pioneered mission study among Virginia women. She laid foundations in beginning mission study classes and promoting the work by awarding diplomas and seals. She shared her ideas broadly.

Helen T. Henderson

"Love—the Greatest Thing in the World." That was the theme Mae Maynard of the New Lebanon WMU chose to characterize the extraordinary life of Helen Timmons Henderson who with her husband, Robert, led the work at the Buchanan Mission School. She served as *"school mother, teacher, disciplinarian, housekeeper, dietitian, nurse, and public relations representative."*

Carrie S. Vaughan described the striking woman, a tall erect blue-eyed, white-haired figure, as full of grace. *"If she but turned her head to speak or reached out her hand to touch something the movement was with unassumed grace. She was endowed with enthusiasm, initiative, and a fiery spirit. She used to say that except for the grace of God she would have been on the stage. She was the one who planned the recreation and entertainment and holiday festivals. She demanded the greatest respect of the students who stood in fear and awe of her but also loved her devotedly."*

Once, when she was prostrated from illness on a train journey, the mountain boys made a litter of limbs and a mattress and carried her eight miles from the railroad depot to the school.

Buchanan Mission School was always struggling. Virginia WMU embraced the school and many individual societies supplied clothing and student expenses. From 1906 to 1913, *"those years in which the women struggled for the existence of the school,"* WMU gifts *"multiplied threefold."* One Virginia WMU member declared: *"No enterprise our Union has ever fostered has been dearer to our hearts than Buchanan Mission School."* The person who kept the state and local organizations informed was Helen Henderson.

In 1923, she was elected as a representative to the Virginia House of Delegates, the first woman elected to the Virginia legislature. She took a firm stand for the improvement of the mountain roads. When she died in 1925, Governor Trinkle ordered the flags at the state capitol to be flown at half-mast. Her legacy included the changed *lives of boys and girls who had come through the school and now were merchants and professionals and farmers and ministers and housewives.*

In 1911, Helen T. Henderson and her husband, Robert, became head of the Buchanan Mountain Mission School, devoting themselves to the school's mission. She became a vice-president of Virginia WMU and in 1923 became the first woman elected to the Virginia legislature.

Chapter 3

The Expanding Years,
1925–1949

*U*nparalleled in expansion of the missions spirit and action, the third epoch opened and closed with the executive leadership of an individual who gave creative and indefatigable service to the Virginia Union and its allied women's organizations. Blanche Sydnor White took a small but promising organization and developed it into a formidable missions force.

In her first New Year's greeting as secretary, Miss White sounded the high notes of self-sacrifice and service which characterized her life, her entire career, and the era she launched. In 1925, when she wrote of the unspoiled, unspotted leaf upon which the new year's events would be written, she specified three things she wanted on her own page: gratitude, determination, and the desire to be used.

In her words: "Gratitude to God and to you [for] the privilege of serving Him. . . . Gratitude, too, to those who have handed down to us the splendid organization of women and young people who study about, pray for and support our Lord's work 'round the world. Determination to serve more loyally, more unselfishly, more efficiently. . . . Forgetting the things of self and keeping in mind and heart the things of the Kingdom, surely the leaf will bear fewer blots of disappointment and spots of sin at the close of the year." She implored her Virginia women to help the secretary: "If you will allow her to slip into your local and associational work, letting her feel your work is [her] work, your burdens her burdens, your triumphs her joys—then the year 1925 will be the sweetest, loveliest page of all the pages she has given back to the Heavenly Father."

And the women did just that . . . they opened meetings, homes, and hearts to their beloved secretary and she was greatly used in missions work. If the years were like pages, Blanche Sydnor White filled volumes in resourceful living.

> "Help me to build a new
>   Virginia,
> After the pattern of the
>   Kingdom of our Lord,
> Create within her the
>   Spirit of our Master,
> Make old Virginia the place
>   of this abode.
> Seek out Thy children
>   who live in her cities,
> Call out her youth from the
>   farms and from the towns;
> Bless all her hosts from the
>   sea unto the hilltops.
> In old Virginia Thy tender
>   mercies crown."
>
> Blanche Sydnor White

Early in her career with Virginia WMU Miss White surmised correctly that "Virginia Baptist women are 'special workers' with the dictionary definition of 'special' as 'chief in excellence' " and that "they will face the many problems and appeals and difficulties in a 'special' way." From 1925 to 1950, as corresponding secretary, she witnessed the women of Virginia do extraordinary, "special" work in such areas as missions education, camping, Good Will Center activities, interracial cooperation, to name but a few.

There were many "special workers" besides Blanche Sydnor White. There were superlative presidents—Mrs. George R. Martin, Mrs. Howard C. Gilmer, Mrs. A.S. Downes, and Mrs. Lester L. Knight. There were co-workers in the office including Bessie Trevvett, Katherine Harris, Bessie McGahey, Ellen Douglas Oliver, Rees Watkins, and Phyllis Wills. There was a bevy of young women ready to help as represented by persons like Carrie Vaughan or Josephine Norwood. There was a host of capable leaders across the state including "the Soops" as Miss White called her capable superintendents and chairmen such as Mrs. Ralph McDanel, Mrs. J. M. Kidd, Mrs. O. L. Jones, Mrs. Herbert Lewis, Mrs. Kenneth E. Burke, Mary Barksdale, Alta Foster, Mrs. J. H. Meek, Mrs. J. M. Bloxom, Mrs. E. D. Poe, Mrs. Nellie Copenhaver, Mrs. W. E. Morrison, Mrs. Amy C. Hickerson, Elsie Gilliam, and Mrs. G. Paul LaRoque.

It was a "golden age" of missions at home and abroad with women who were living legends— Louise Fletcher, Elizabeth Hale, Eva Sanders, Olive Riddell, Margie Shumate, Mary Ellen Dozier, and Ruth Walden. Each woman became personally known and loved by Virginia women. Good Will Centers across the state became focal points of practical missions opportunities. Following the vast destruction of World War II, Virginia WMU performed practical missions, sending tons of raisins, rice, and sugar so Europeans could have Christmas puddings and tons of clothing, blankets, and bedding as well as shipments of sewing machines for German women. It was a time of great strides, truly pioneering work in race relations. Nannie Helen Burroughs, leader among black Baptist women, became a frequent guest of Virginia WMU. Fletcher Mae Howell became WMU's first black employee, and she directed cooperative projects between white and black Baptist women. Camp Carey was opened for young black girls.

It was the worst and best of times economically. The denomination was sorely crippled by crushing debts during an unparalleled financial depression. Yet it was the best of times as Virginia WMU rallied the Baptists to give for debt removal.

It was an era of celebration and no one could upstage Miss White in regards to anniversaries. The Shuck Centennial of 1936 sparked new pride in Virginia's earliest female missionary, Henrietta Hall Shuck, and commitment for the very heartbeat of missions. The era closed with the highest drama, the Diamond Jubilee, celebrating 75 years of heritage. Enabled through Diamond Jubilee scholarships to study in America, several foreign students shared their own experiences with Virginia WMU and returned to their native lands with new skills and ways to help. These students were a married couple, the Adegbites from Nigeria and Irene Ma of China. Later other students would receive Diamond Jubilee scholarships for study.

In 75 years of vigorous executive leadership, WMU had experienced an expansion of mission activities beyond its founders' dreams. Substituting the word "woman" for "man," Fannie Crosby's verses stated: "To every woman there openeth a high way and a low and the high soul climbs the high way and the low soul gropes the low and in between on the misty flats, the rest drift to and fro. Every woman decideth the way her soul shall go." For the women of Virginia WMU, from their leaders to their members and to their youth, the high way, the expanding way would be theirs.

Precious Thoughts

*I*n 1926, Virginia women missed the presence of Lizzie Savage in their midst. She had served as corresponding secretary from 1921, until declining health necessitated her 1924 resignation. Only a big-spirited woman like Blanche Sydnor White, her successor, could have found a way to involve this ailing former leader. Miss White knew that Miss Savage had "no more 'given up' Virginia WMU than Virginia WMU had 'given her up.'" Miss White revealed that "down in Franklin, fighting the persistent disease which fastened itself upon her while she served us, Miss Savage is thinking of every department of the work."

Miss White's idea to keep Virginia women and their beloved former secretary still in touch was for Miss Savage to supply a weekly thought for the Woman's Page in the *Religious Herald*. They were not original but they were genuine pearls of wisdom: "You can never raise men higher than you have raised yourself" (August 27, 1925). "The world is too sweet and fair to darken it with the clouds of anger. Forgive and forget, if you can, but forgive anyway" (April 30, 1925). "Life is a struggle but not a warfare; it is a day's labor, but on earth's earth, under the sun and stars, with other laborers, where we may think, and sing, and rejoice as we work" (April 9, 1925). The wise quotes were headlined "Miss Savage's Message for the Week."

Early in the summer of 1925, the following notice in the Woman's Page read, "We believe the doctors have made a great mistake in thinking her work is over here in Virginia. She is able to come downstairs for the evening meal, is keenly interested in the work, complains of very little pain and drives over to Norfolk to visit her brother." By late summer there were more encouraging signs and someone observed: "Her sense of humor is as keen as her interest in WMU work. She laughs at herself, in spite of the weariness of body and mind which she must feel during these days of strain and pain."

Virginia WMU annual meeting, Freemason Street Church, Norfolk, 1929.

"B.S.W."

$\mathcal{N}$o one associated with Baptist work in Virginia during the half-century of the 1920s to the 1970s, whether male or female, clergy or laity, could have failed to have known the dynamic executive leader of Woman's Missionary Union of Virginia, Blanche Sydnor White. On her worn briefcase—now in the artifacts collection of the Virginia Baptist Historical Society—are embossed three initials: "B.S.W." On countless historical notes and manuscripts in the Virginia Baptist Historical Society collections, one finds the initials "B.S.W." affixed to several humorous, tongue-in-cheek resolutions promising to slow down, to have "no more bright ideas" are the initials "B.S.W."

For two years Blanche Sydnor White was a field worker for the Southern Union; then on January 1, 1925, she was elected corresponding secretary of Virginia WMU. The Dinwiddie County native had returned home. Her first words to the Virginia women expressed gratitude. "I appreciate Virginia's confidence in me. I love the work there and those who have carried it forward. I do pray most earnestly that the Lord will enable me to 'carry on.' I am happy to be coming to you."

Her leadership produced an abundant harvest. She further developed programs and secured a competent staff. She enhanced and

Blanche Sydnor White, in center, departs for BWA meeting in London, 1947.

*enlarged camping and training activities. She encouraged Virginia women to give, even sacrificially, to debt removal and new work. She preached missions and missionaries with a zeal. She reached out to black Baptist women and added a black woman to the WMU staff. She established Good Will Centers across the state. She studied Baptist history, producing some 50 volumes on missions and history, indexing the issues of the **Religious Herald** from the 1820s to the 1870s, and supporting the Virginia Baptist Historical Society in their quest for a library building. In her retirement she focused on the Historical Society and upon the reorganization and expansion of the Women's Department of the Baptist World Alliance. She developed personally and professionally and became a recognized "missionary statesman."*

Olive B. Martin knew her as few others. They were co-laborers, Mrs. Martin as the elected official and Miss White as the executive. They were frequent travelling companions and together provided dynamic leadership and a lasting influence upon the state, national, and world bodies of women's mission work. Mrs. Martin expressed the following about "B.S.W.": "No scales can weigh the worth of her many-sided, far-reaching service. No figures can compute the sterling worth of her fidelity. No measuring rod can compass the reach of her influence. . . . No telescope is powerful enough to indicate the extent of her service. No microscope is minute enough to reveal its details. No pen is facile enough to record its true value. No lips are eloquent enough to properly appraise her value."

Committed Unto Us

"We are the carpenters of a new and better America. When we have expended upon this task the best we have to give, if we find that it is still not large enough to fit the place He has given us to fill, then let us ask Him to take hold on one side of our material while we take hold on the other. Together, our Lord and we can make our gift adequate."

Blanche Sydnor White

Goals For the Ruby Year

The Union was divided into districts and each contained several associations. The associations would set goals to start new organizations. For example, in the Western District the Powell River Association set a goal of eight and reached it! In the Eastern District the early reports for 1928 showed the Albemarle—with a goal of 25—had originated 14 new organizations; the Concord claimed 11 from its lofty goal of 60; the James River—with a goal of 21—reported no new societies "but hope to put on special programs in each church." Mrs. O.L. Jones, of First Church, Bristol and chairman of the Western District's Ruby Anniversary, set about a plan for her church. She sent to all eight circles within the church the names of all women who were not WMU members and requested that each circle try to enlist those on the list; and by the time the women had said "no" eight times, the WMU leaders were "convinced that they cannot be won into the WMU."

"As our women pray, work and love, let us remember that these are the unseen wires that stretch from the heart of man to the heart of God and thus we will accomplish the seemingly impossible."

Mrs. L.B. Allen
Ruby Anniversary Chairman

81

"*The Soops (Superintendents) Gather.*"

"WMU of Virginia will pledge anew its utmost to bring in 1928 a perfect jewel—our ruby—fit for His use."

Mrs. L. B. Allen

RUBY ANNIVERSARY ENLISTMENT SONG

"There's a woman next to you.
She should be a member, too.
Who will seek her to enlist?
Listen then, our plan is this:

If you'll bring the woman next to you,
And I'll bring the one next to me,
In all kinds of weather,
We'll all work together

And see what can be done.
If you'll bring the woman next to you,
And I'll bring the one next to me,
In no time at all
We'll have them all:

So win them, win them, one by one."

Camp Carey

In 1940, in a pioneering project for the South, Virginia WMU established a camp for black girls to be led and taught by black and white Baptist women. Facilities in rural Chesterfield County were rented and the camp was named for two pioneer missionaries, William Carey, the white missionary from England to India, and Lott Cary, the Virginia-born black missionary to Liberia. The *Herald* of May 30, 1940, carried the following: "Because we are anxious that our young people shall hear the call of God, the Inter-Racial Missionary Department of WMU of Virginia offers to fifty Negro Baptist girls and young women from 12 to 25 years of age the privileges of Camp Carey, June 22–29." Forty-eight girls filled the camp in the Swift Creek Recreational Area nearly to capacity. The cost of the week's activities was $3.50, but those unable to pay the full amount were eligible for a $2 camp scholarship; the balance, the $1.50, was to be earned or saved. The camp offered mission study, Bible study, "Red Circle and Young Woman's League methods," handcrafts, recreation, games, and swimming. By the second summer the camp had doubled, offering two weeks for 48 girls each. In 1941, the campers heard the dynamic Nannie Helen Burroughs of Washington, D.C.

In August, 1942, a "Crusaders Camp" was offered for 50 Negro boys, ages 12 to 16, at Virginia Union University in Richmond. The university gave free dormitory space and the only WMU expense was the food, which was provided "at cost." The boys missionary camp cost each participant only $5. Again local societies were asked to provide camp scholarships. "Select a worthy Negro boy in your community," the women were told, "who has the capacity for religious leadership, tell him about this camp, give him a camp scholarship of $2.50 and urge him to save the other $2.50." Many missionary and WMU leaders participated in the camp including Fletcher Mae Howell, the interracial coordinator in the WMU office and Lena Smith, a black woman who served as camp director for Camp Carey for 27 years.

Having fun at Camp Carey.

Good Will Centers

"The Baptists of Virginia are doing settlement work through the Good Will Centers at Richmond, Danville and Petersburg. The Center in Petersburg known as the 'Sunshine House' opened last March [1924] under the auspices of the YWA. There is a Bluebird Club for girls, Story Hour for the small children and woodwork for the boys. Miss Kathleen Hagood is the director. The Richmond Center, the 'House of Happiness,' was started ten years ago with Miss Nannie West as director. In October, 1923, it moved into its spacious quarters, which were formally dedicated and opened to the public in February, 1924. The building when completed will provide facilities for clubs and classes for all ages, gymnasium, showers, library, woodwork shops and living quarters for workers. The primary aim of all our settlement work is to lead others to Christ. Evangelistic services were conducted at the House of Happiness and resulted in a number of conversions. The summer camp conducted each year for six weeks at Millboro Springs in the Allegheny Mountains is one of the outstanding features. Here in the morning worship hour many have

found Christ and signified their intention of love for Him. One of the girls said: 'I've learned so much—I've learned to darn stockings, work buttonholes, to swim, to take long walks without getting tired and to sleep out under the stars and not be afraid.' Another said: 'The Camp has drawn us closer to God and these beautiful mountains make us realize what He means to us.' "

Eva Gravatt
Royal Service
February, 1925

Mabola Ayorinde came to America with her husband, Tanimola, in 1938 to celebrate the Golden Jubilee and to study at Miss Burroughs' school in Washington, D.C., Hampton Institute and Virginia Union University. A frequent guest at Virginia WMU events, she became president of Women's Department, BWA, for Africa.

"I know of but one thing that can cause us to fail and that is to lose the vision of the Saviour. I have been talking to you about the Woman's Missionary Union, the Union, the Union! But I plead with you in my last word as your president that before the Union, in the Union, and above the Union you place the Saviour, the Saviour of the world, whose we are, whom we serve and whose witnesses we must be."

Mrs. W. C. James

Diamond Jubilee

"Preparation for the Diamond Jubilee Year began in 1948, when the last three months of the year were set aside as a time of spiritual preparation. Goals were set up in each department of our work. It was decided to go back to Richmond, the birthplace of the Union, for the celebration. A Jubilee Offering of $50,000 was included in the plans, objects to be the Cooperative Program, State, Home, and Foreign Missions, and a share in the new headquarters building of the Southern Union to be erected in Birmingham. The form of the offering was one [used in] 1892, 'A Penny-A-Day and A-Prayer.'

"In March, 1949, 1301 delegates gathered. . . . The first session was a commemorative service and the Pageant, 'A Diamond Jubilee,' was given at the Mosque. . . . The entire meeting was on a high plane and brought a challenge for greater loyalty and endeavor for years to come.

"After the close of 1949, when all gifts to the Jubilee Offering had come in, it was found that the goal of $50,000 had been exceeded by over $20,000. [*Virginia WMU brought*] to this country for further study and training three young women from China and a young couple from Nigeria, products of our Baptist mission work. Two of the young women, Dr. Wei Mei Chen and Mrs. Irene Ma, have returned to their country, and already are making their contribution to the cause of Christ there.

"The $10,000 of the Jubilee Offering designated for use 'in the needy places of Virginia' was turned over to the executive secretary of the General Association. This sum has been spent in the establishment of a mission center at Dungannon in Scott County and in the development of churches in New Lebanon Association.

"As we look over the records of 1949, we can say in humility, that it was a good year, and that the Diamond Jubilee Celebration gave impetus and enthusiasm to all phases of the work. To Him we would give our praise and gratitude."

Annual Report of Virginia WMU to BGAV.

►
Sunbeam Band episode in the Diamond Jubilee pageant, 1949. The children are singing "We are but a band of children; we are few, weak and small. But we all can work for Jesus and there's room enough for all."

Virginia delegation at YWA Camp, Ridgecrest, 1950.

Alta Foster

or Alta Foster, recording secretary from 1908 to 1941, the task was "more than a mere recital of motions, resolutions and names of speakers." The minutes became "a moving record of spiritual power and conquest" and she lovingly and carefully penned them "with marvelous clarity, brevity and sympathy."

Sister Jo

hat's how her real sisters knew her, but through Woman's Missionary Union Josephine Carroll Norwood had many spiritual sisters; some of those chose to call her "Miss Jo." She responded to God's call at the age of 15 and entered full-time Christian service. She became an educational and church secretary at her own church, Barton Heights (now Northminster), and at Grove Avenue Church, both in Richmond; and during these periods of church employment, she did outstanding work as a leader in associational WMU work.

In October, 1950, the invitation came to join the Virginia WMU staff as associate secretary under the leadership of Ellen Douglas Oliver. "Sister Jo" would find new sisters in Christ among the Virginia black women as she guided interracial work. Other responsibilities included the Business Women's Circles and Federations and the camps for young people.

Everywhere one looked there was evidence of Sister Jo's magic touch. Camp Viewmont was built near Charlottesville; and WMU camp attendance hit 2,147 in the summer of 1954, the highest figure in the state WMU's history. The number of Business Women's Circles had expanded. And the building of White Hall at Virginia Union was largely directed by the busy associate secretary. The beloved Blanche Sydnor White, a busy worker herself, recognized Jo Norwood's worth and industry when she said, "She simply cannot touch a piece of work without expanding it."

In the fall of 1954, Maryland women " 'stole' her away" from Virginia and she became executive secretary for Woman's Missionary Union of Maryland. Now the whirlwind could really spin! For 24 years she led Maryland women with "a saga of service, commitment without compromise and devotion far beyond the call of duty."

Camping

The great camp movement sponsored by Virginia WMU began in a modest way when, in the summer of 1917, Mrs. John F. Vines, president of the Union, promoted the first Royal Ambassadors camp at Virginia Beach. Twelve boys came that first summer and lived in cramped quarters over a borrowed drug store. In 1922, the GA building was completed, but the RA building was delayed until 1926, after Virginia women raised the construction funds.

Katherine Harris, young people's secretary, reported on the summer of 1925: "The boys and girls were put on a point system which worked beautifully. For each room there were leaders responsible for the work and behavior of that room. In the girls' camp we had somewhat of an honor council which met each day."

The girl campers of 1925 reported on their experiences. Virginia Greene stated: "This camp has shown me how GAs can 'make girls over' and help them get another outlook on the life of a Christian." Jane Love Little reported: "During these twelve days I have gained in health and happiness, advanced in knowledge, learned what true discipline and friendship are, and have had some of the best times imaginable."

In 1925 The YWAs of Virginia began their camping program in a beach cottage and later moved to the GA building. Through the first decade many opportunities arose for mission study and for meeting missionaries.

At the RA Camp of 1936, R.H. Downey, the camp pastor, had a wonderful experience. During the week he discovered that nine of the boys had never made a profession of faith. The following was reported in the *Religious Herald:* "As he talked with them and played with them and lounged on the beach with them, Pastor Downey discovered those boys. On the last day of camp he announced to them that he was going to bring an evangelistic message that night, and at the close of the vesper hour an opportunity would be given for confessions of faith. In that service the nine boys came!" The WMU Page in an August issue of the *Herald* announced: "Nine times the bells of Heaven must have rang with joy as these nine young men came so quietly, yet so firmly." ▶

Mrs. G. Paul LaRoque of Richmond is surrounded by "her girls" at YWA camp, Virginia Beach.

GA camp with Elizabeth Hale in front of the new center.
(Photo courtesy of Helen Butler George.)

Wilton Atkinson remembered camping days: "When anyone speaks to me of RA Camp, I can see in my imagination a happy group of boys playing on the beach, ascend the stairs and walk down the street to the camp where the mid-day meal awaited. The whistle blows and all are seated and the Director returns thanks for our many blessings. . . . There is plenty for everyone and a very large variety. The meal is over and the boys scatter about the camp for a short free period. Later you can see them playing volleyball or baseball, playing horseshoes, playing pingpong and that old favorite, checkers."

He had warm words for all involved in the RA Camp. Paul Decker, the director, was remembered as one who "knows boys, knows what boys like, and mingles with the boys first as a real true camper would do." He was especially grateful for the housekeeper, Mrs. H.E. Hood. "When you come to think of it," Atkinson reflected, "the Royal Ambassadors Camp is a good place to spend a part of your vacation, for here one grows in wisdom, in stature, and in favor with God and man."

YWA camp counselors.

Early GA camp, Virginia Beach. (Photo courtesy of Helen Butler George.)

The Vaughan Twins

*T*hey were an answer to a prayer for Miss Bennie Russell of Hampton. After she went to Newport News to keep house for her half-brother, Edwin Vaughan, whose wife had died, the women in her church, the Hampton Baptist Church, missed her so much that they prayed that Edwin might find a wife—but not just any wife. At Miss Bennie's behest, they prayed for "a fine, Christian wife" and included "[her] request for children." Miss Bennie and the Baptist women of Hampton had their prayers answered! Edgar married Carrie Sinton and children came, first Molly Wrenn, followed two years later, in 1910, by twin girls. While expectant, Mrs. Vaughan had promised to name her baby, if a girl, after her closest friend, Florence Jones. When twin girls were born someone suggested that since these good friends, Florence Jones and Carrie Sinton, were always together, the mother might as well name the babies after both women.

Before the twins were born, their father died and Mrs. Vaughan had sole responsibility for rearing the three girls. Of course there was still Aunt Bennie's good influence. Her love for missions and Christian service provided a positive example for the twins. Miss Bennie Russell was superintendent of the Peninsula WMU.

The girls were inseparable. At age 10 they were baptized by Harry Jeter Goodwin into the fellowship of the Orcutt Avenue Church in Newport News. There they grew to young womanhood, involved in the church's every activity. They were members of Sunbeams, GAs, YWAs. They listened carefully to their pastor, J.L. Carrick, with his many messages about the Bible and Baptist doctrine. He also in-

volved them in church work, and they would—as teenagers—teach the Sunday school children.

Aunt Bennie took them on their first trips to the GA Camp at Virginia Beach (in about 1925). Thus began their summer tradition of attending WMU camps; and thus began the lasting friendships with contemporaries, with whom they would continue their love of missions into adulthood, and with older women who became role models, women like Blanche Sydnor White, Ida Paterson Storm, Mrs. George R. Martin.

The girls excelled in scholastics; in 1929, Florence and Carrie were salutatorian and valedictorian, respectively. Together they planned for careers while attending the Fredericksburg State Teachers College, now Mary Washington College. On graduation in 1931, teaching opportunities required that they separate for the first time. Carrie, who had majored in domestic science, began teaching in Fauquier County while Florence taught elementary school in Henrico County. After four years they were reunited in Newport News, employed by the school system there and involved in the ministry of First Baptist Church—notably in the activities of the Woman's Missionary Union.

In 1937, the Vaughan twins were among the first group of young WMU women to pioneer Vacation Bible School work in the coal mining camps of Southwest Virginia around Stonega. Florence became principal of the first school at Slaughter Pen Hollow, which would become the Baptist Center of Appalachia.

For Florence Vaughan the summer of 1942 was spent as head counsellor at The Cedars, the WMU camp near Marion, but after unexpected surgery she died. Eight years later the chapel at Baptist Lodge, the WMU camp at Virginia Beach, was dedicated to the memory of Florence Vaughan.

The surviving twin, Carrie, continued her work in education until called in 1957 to become executive secretary for Woman's Missionary Union of Virginia starting in 1958. The first great love for the young Vaughan twins, the women and fellowship surrounding Virginia WMU, became the final life's work for Carrie. She carried the responsibility with grace and effectiveness for 18 years until her retirement in 1975.

Business Women

"In March, 1943, during the annual state meeting in Roanoke, a group met in a private dining room of the Patrick Henry Hotel to consider the organization of a state federation of Business Woman's Circles (BWC). As a result, a committee was appointed to work out plans. The Virginia WMU Executive Board asked one of its members, Mrs. Thomas J. Starke, to be adviser and approved plans recommended by the special committee. Thus the next summer the Federation of Business Woman's Circles of Virginia 'came alive' with Carrie Sinton Vaughan of Newport News as president. Mrs. George Long of Roanoke and Clarice McKnight of Richmond were vice-presidents, with Mrs. Sue Moore of Charlottesville serving as recording secretary. This organization gave new impetus to the city and associational BWC federations, and by 1944 their number had increased from three to seven. By 1949, twenty associational federations had been formed, and Business Woman's Circles in the state numbered 495."

from *Light Three Candles*

Elizabeth Neal Hale
"Not to Be Ministered Unto, But to Minister"

Elizabeth Hale, of course, belonged to the world. Because of her missions service in China and Malaysia, she belonged to all the Baptist people who love and support missions. But she belonged peculiarly and particularly to Virginia Baptists. Never mind that she was born in North Carolina for she came to South Boston at the age of 12 and has been claimed by the people of Halifax County and of all Virginia. She was the daughter of a Baptist minister who died soon after Elizabeth's younger sister, Ruth, was born. Her mother moved to South Boston to keep house for a bachelor brother who was a merchant.

Her matriculation at a Virginia Baptist school, Westhampton College of the University of Richmond, from where she was graduated in 1929, establishes her Virginia roots with even more certainty.

In 1934, Elizabeth was one of several Virginia women to be appointed for missions work—Ruth Walden of Norfolk for Africa; Helen Yates of Augusta Association for China; Elizabeth Jackson Johnson for Brazil; Elizabeth Neal Hale herself to China. Before their departure Ruth Walden and Elizabeth Hale attended the WMU, SBC, annual meeting in New Orleans. Blanche Sydnor White was there too, and she reported "Oh, my friends, if you whose loving interest in the training of these dear ones could have been here! I wept for joy as they expressed their gratitude to you who led in missionary organizations which had contributed to this glad hour."

When the time came to depart for China, Elizabeth Hale penned a "farewell message" to the Virginia women. She said: "One day in my reading [of the Bible] five new words stood out before me—words which I love to think about. In the first part of that wonderful letter Paul wrote to the Colossians we find him speaking of 'the dispensation of God which is given to me for you.' Don't you love that—'given to me for you'? With the help of His Spirit some of the meaning of that has become a part of me. Everything God has given to me— the heritage that comes to one born here in the United States of Christian parents, the privileges of all sorts in school and town and church, in work and play, the blessings of ennobling friendships, everything that has gone into my life was given to me for you— whoever you are. With this in mind a study of the life of the Master shows how we can pass on to others what He has entrusted to us— for 'even the Son of Man came not to be ministered unto but to minister and to give His life in ransom for many.'"

She recalled "a bit of verse" learned as a child: "Though friends may weep and bid you stay and point you to an easier way, Heed not their plea, your way pursue, For God, the Father, calleth you." Her closing thoughts were to seek "a will to know and to do," learning as Christians the necessity to "take up our crosses and follow Him."

Elizabeth Hale and her Chinese children. She once wrote to Blanche Sydnor White: "I know so little. Then when I think too much about little me, I remember that you saw something in me somewhere that you thought He could use if I'd let him . . ."

Elizabeth carried her spirit of sacrificial service to China, where she quickly learned the language and found a place of ministry. Her sacrificial nature bloomed most fully when she chose to remain behind in China rather than escape during the war. She gave her own place to another when she realized the boat she would be travelling on was crowded. Roberta P. Johnson declared: "Elizabeth Hale made her decision, even after great effort to make her change it, more firm to stay, it seemed. She seemed to feel that the Lord was very clearly leading her to stay. She seemed in perfect health and kept busy with camp duties."

For two-and-a-half years she was interred in a Japanese concentration camp. James A. Dunachil, an English missionary, wrote comforting words to Elizabeth's mother: "You need not be the slightest bit anxious concerning her. You have every reason to be proud of her. I was Floor Monitor in the same building in which she lived . . . [and] on the infirmary staff in which she worked . . . your dear Elizabeth's sweet, Christlike life of unselfish service was a constant source of wonder to many of us."

Later in the same letter, he added the most convincing testimony to Elizabeth's effect on others: "I heard non-Christians say, again and again, that they did not know what real Christianity was until they met Elizabeth Hale!"

In 1946, she finally returned home where she cared for her elderly mother and uncle. In 1952, she returned to the foreign mission field, serving in Malaysia. Even in retirement she wanted to serve and so promoted an old-folks home, Bethel Hill, in Kedah, Malaysia. At last she returned to Virginia to reside at the Culpeper Home. Still she continued to minister, cheering up other residents, sending greetings to many, and attending Baptist meetings. She chose to decorate her corner bedroom with nature's beauty—a seashell, a leaf, a pretty rock. And in the window, a crystal, catching the rays of the sun and letting them dance about the room. That crystal was just like Elizabeth Hale of Virginia, a woman who caught God's love and reflected it for others to see.

Ruth Walden: Waiting to Serve

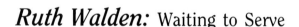

"*A*n Intermediate GA, only thirteen, tall, slender, with big soft brown eyes, made her way down the aisle of the church where the district WMU meeting was being held, and surrendered her life to foreign service. When Ruth Walden gave her heart to the Lord the year before, she also gave him her life, and now she was publicly confessing her willingness to heed the call wherever the voice might direct. It was quite natural that she should think of China for her interest in missions began with the Chinese Sunday school which the Baptists of Norfolk conducted each Sunday afternoon in the church of which she was a member.

"When the family moved from Roanoke to Norfolk, when Ruth was eleven, she attended the Park Avenue Church which was near her home. Immediately her childish fancy was attracted to the group of Chinese immigrants who were being taught English and

the gospel each Lord's Day. The childish fancy grew into a deep concern and love for the Chinese people which manifested itself in five years of teaching the children's class and in acting as secretary of the missions Sunday school.

"When high school days were over, Ruth entered Averett College. It was here, while in the study and prayer groups of the Student Volunteer Board, that she was brought face to face with the fact that she had chosen China and that she was not resigned to go anywhere the Master might lead. Sweet surrender came in that hour when her heart said, 'Yes, I'm ready to go to the hardest field.' And to her that field was Africa. She has never doubted from that moment until this that Africa was where God wanted her to invest her life.

"Ruth suffered keen disappointment when she did not receive an appointment to Africa at the time of her graduation from the Training School. Very few missionaries were being sent out in 1929 and the years immediately following. Ruth resolved to give herself to any task the Lord might open for her. In 1929, she was elected young people's secretary of the Tennessee WMU. She held this position until the summer of 1934, the year of her appointment to Africa.

"The period of waiting was a difficult one for Ruth. People did not always understand the high-spirited, yet reserved, independent, somewhat moody young woman who could have explained it all if she had wished in the one sentence, 'I'm waiting to go to Africa.'

"Those who were closest to Ruth saw the great change that came over her when she knew she was going to the mission field of God's choice. What motive, unity of thought, and action were now hers! The dreams that had dominated her life for fifteen years were to become a reality. Africa was hers at last!"

Mildred Dodson McMurry
Constraining Love
1939

"Our Margie"

*S*he was born in March, 1890, and when she came of age, Margie Shumate wanted to be a missionary more than anything else in the world. She studied at Virginia Intermont College and in 1914 completed the preparation at the Training School. In June, 1914 she was appointed for mission work in China. Following a special service in Pearisburg Church, she left in February of the following year for Shiu Hing, Kwang Tung Province in South China. She found in Shiu Hing one Baptist church and a boarding school for females where she could work.

She devoted her energies to teaching at the school, yet she also was deeply concerned for the vast number of Chinese who had never heard of Christ. Working alongside Chinese "Bible women," she traveled widely to reach the unsaved. "Crowded in small boats, climbing steep mountains, and risking pirates," the report for 1917 stated, "she spends much time in native villages, sleeping on hard bed boards and faring on the best the kind villagers can offer."

For 37 years "Our Margie," as the Virginia women loved to call her, labored among the Chinese. When China began its long isola-

*M*argie Shumate, left, and an important visitor, Mrs. Charles E. Maddry.

tion, she worked for seven additional years in Thailand. All the while, in a steady correspondence and on infrequent furloughs, she maintained close ties with both Virginia women and those in the wide bounds of the SBC. Probably no other missionary's work was as published in the WMU pages of the Herald *as that of Miss Shumate.*

Virginia women loved her. "She is 'Margie' to many of us, 'Our Margie' to a few, and 'Margie Shumate' to the rest of us," explained a 1933 entry in Royal Service. *"She holds the hearts of this generation as surely as Lottie Moon held the affection of the past generation."*

On October 1, 1958, Margie Shumate became an emeritus missionary yet she had set her sights on new work among the Chinese of New York City. Within two weeks of her "retirement," "Our Margie" died at the Virginia Baptist Hospital in Lynchburg.

In 1963, the Margie Shumate Memorial Publication Building for Baptists in Thailand was dedicated in Bangkok. It had been made possible through gifts from Virginia WMU to honor "Our Margie" and came "from Margie Shumate circles, from friends of Miss Shumate, from ones who dared try to match her spirit of sacrifice."

Margie Shumate and her "Bible Women."

MENFOLKS:
Frank T. Crump

Frank T. Crump married into that leading Virginia Baptist family, the Ellysons, but he earned his own distinction from his years as executive secretary and treasurer of the State Baptist Board. He served 30 years as treasurer of the BGAV and in 1920 took on the WMU treasurership, which he carried for 29 years without any additional salary. During those years he received and disbursed $13,028,422.42 of missionary money from hundreds of WMU organizations across the state and never lost track of a single dollar! "It was in the handling of these funds," Blanche Sydnor White once observed, "in his attitude toward our Union and her officers, in his courtesy and consideration that we saw Mr. Crump at his greatest and best."

Balancing the Books

"When Phyllis Wills, bookkeeper for WMU of Virginia during the past eighteen years, announced that she would 'step up' into Mr. Crump's General Association office, we were all but hopeless. What would we do without her? We knew that she was unusually accurate, unusually devoted to her task, unusually conversant with WMU 'peculiarities' in remitting funds for missions. The goodness of her heart led her to take over the February, 1945, books and we breathed easily for another month. But her own duties demanded her undivided attention in March.

Virginia WMU occupied the third floor of the Baptist Building at 1 West Franklin Street, Richmond, formerly an elegant private mansion.

"Now, March brings many other duties to your corresponding secretary's hands and mind . . . annual reports and the annual meeting of the Executive Board and the planning of missionary itineraries to many, many group meetings, and annual associational meetings which would continue in April.

"So it was late in March when your corresponding secretary, with a fearful heart, opened Miss Wills' immaculate books and began to set down the remittances from four-thousand missionary societies.

"It is an interesting task, this recording of WMU gifts. Two penny items, several 2 cent items, a number of 5 cent items and all the way up to the fifteen-hundred dollar remittance.

"March brings to us the Home Mission Thank Offering. Centennial Birthday Gifts are beginning to come in. . . . Late remittances through the Christmas Offering for Foreign Missions prove that societies are gleaning diligently, even as late in the year as March.

"Early in the morning and late at night the untried bookkeeper-secretary labored. Visitors were denied admittance to the room, correspondence was pushed aside until the secretary's desk resembled nothing so much as a junk pile. On the afternoon of April 13th—a Friday by the way—the last Associational Record was added, and the State Total was torn from the patient adding machine. The figures did not conform to the record. Moans of anguish could not be indulged in at this moment for the members of the State Interracial

An invincible team: the Virginia WMU staff in the 1930s and 1940s included, left to right, *Blanche Sydnor White, executive secretary; Phyllis Wills, bookkeeper; Ellen Douglas Oliver, young people's secretary and associate secretary and later, executive secretary; Emma Yates, Miss Oliver's secretary; and Bessie McGahey, Miss White's secretary, 1942.*

Administrative Board were already assembling in the secretary's room. Just a moment was left to think about the unbalanced books. 'Phyllis, what do you do under circumstances like this?' she asked. Miss Wills replied so calmly. 'Why, Miss White, you just made two mistakes instead of one.' So, with that doubtful reassurance of a double error, the secretary went to the meeting, leaving her mind and heart in the Bookkeeping Room. After two-and-one-half hours of conference, she returned to the books. Miss Wills and Mrs. McGahey were hovering over them. They had discovered the double error of $1.40—a Forward Movement gift from the Dover. There was still a mistake of 56 cents in Cooperative Program columns and of $20.00 in Designations, but the secretary had the honor of taking Margie Shumate to dinner so the procession descended to the first floor of the Virginia Baptist Building.

"About 7:15 that evening the weary secretary returned to her office. She heard the typewriter sounding forth gallantly. Mrs. McGahey was on the Third Floor. As the elevator landed at the WMU office level, Miss Wills stepped to the door of the Bookkeeping Room. 'The books are balanced, Miss White,' she announced. Those blessed girls, without any dinner at all, had worked for two hours and had discovered all of the errors.

"Then came the balancing of the 'Specials'. That required Friday evening and most of Saturday. An elusive five cents had to be chased down and then a ten cents error consumed about two hours of hard work. But by Saturday evening, April 14th, the March books were copied for Mr. Crump's careful study.

"Was it worthwhile, all of the work which had to be done in order to capture those gifts from Sunbeams, Girls' Auxiliary members, Royal Ambassadors, Young Woman's Auxiliary ladies? Oh, yes, it was

worth all that it cost. Because behind those figures—large or small—
there were many thrilling stories of consecrated, loving zeal.

"There were some special joys. Lawrenceville gave $900 for the
salary of one of the new missionaries. Bainbridge began the salary of
a missionary. Blue Ridge and Dover are investing into the University
of Richmond Memorial Library Campaign in a great way. In all,
twenty of the thirty associational Woman's Missionary Unions went
beyond their gifts during the first quarter of 1944.

"Someone else will 'keep' the WMU books for April, May and June.
What dramatic scenes will she share as she works behind the scenes
to keep your gifts in the proper columns . . ."

Religious Herald
April 19, 1945

ROYAL AMBASSADORS ON THE AIR

In November, 1936 an exciting project was born when a Virginia
pastor asked a WMU worker, "Why doesn't our WMU have an RA
hour on the radio?" "Impossible!" replied the WMU worker. "But the
idea became leaven," confessed Blanche Sydnor White, "that swelled
so rapidly that the WMU worker found other ideas being jostled very
rudely by the RA Broadcast suggestion." She elaborated: "So it came
to pass that on April Fool's Day [1937] she went to WRVA [in Rich-
mond] to ask whether or not such a plan would be entirely out of
the reach of a missionary organization. The friends there were interested, sympathetic, intrigued with this new idea, and offered such
reasonable rates that the WMU worker dared to bring the matter to
the attention of the State Executive Board."

*Royal Ambassadors huddle
around a radio for the great RA radio
broadcasts.*

A newly appointed committee thus sought the advice of the men,
and several agreed to serve as a committee. Douglas Southall Free-
man, the noted Richmond newspaper editor and member of Second
Church, Richmond, helped pave the way with necessary radio contacts. Ellen Graves was employed to write and direct the broadcasts.
Arrangements were made for radio hook-ups with Richmond,
Roanoke, Bristol, Danville, and Norfolk. A Radio Club was formed
and boys who "listen[ed] in" could write for a membership button for
the RA Radio Club. Five-thousand buttons were ordered so Virginia
WMU expected a good audience! The first RA program was heard over
WRVA, Richmond, at 5:45 p.m. on Saturday, January 8, 1938.

Following the first broadcast, the WMU Page reported: "Good
work, Royal Ambassadors! Your audience was delighted with the first
broadcast of 'Cavaliers at Camp.' The presentation of the Judsons in
Burma was sympathetic and forceful. We expect to be glued to the
radio on next Sunday afternoon. But, Royal Ambassadors, please do
something about your song. You can do better than that."

On January 20, 1939, 11 radio stations across the state broadcast
an evening program to reach members of the 722 RA chapters as
well as all interested persons within range of the broadcast. Afterwards over 4,000 Virginia boys in 11 cities gathered to eat supper
together and to participate in a missions rally. About 500 Richmond-
area RA boys attended a supper at First Baptist Church where the
meals were provided for a quarter each.

Across the state boys were involved. The WMU declared, "If ever
our women rallied to an opportunity, this should be the time!"

Traveling in Style

"Hearken to us and hear a story which will challenge our Virginia hospitality. It came to pass that 11 of the Virginians attending the Oklahoma meeting of the WMU [in 1944] discovered that bus schedules would not lend themselves to an adequate visit to our Indian Mission Fields. The Greyhound Bus Line was consulted; but because of war restrictions, they could not rent to us. The 'Drive It Yourself' Car Companies were besought for two cars but war restrictions prevented their cooperation with us.

"In desperation one of the party telephoned Dr. Andrew Potter, executive secretary of the Oklahoma Baptist Convention, who had graciously offered to the Union officers every courtesy within his power. 'Please, sir,' she timidly said, 'the Virginia group wants to rent a station wagon. Could you help us to get one?' 'Ma'am!' the good secretary gasped, 'I'll do my best!'

"Within an hour or two he produced his best. The Governor of Oklahoma, His Excellency Governor Robert S. Kerr, is a Baptist and, moreover, is the President of the Oklahoma Baptist Convention. Governor Kerr was in Washington on official business, but Dr. Potter reached him by telephone. 'We have 11 Virginia ladies here in Oklahoma City who want to visit the Indian Mission Fields,' we know he said. 'Of course,' said the gracious Baptist Governor, 'I shall be glad for those ladies to use my car. My chauffeur will take them wherever they want to go.'

"Then because all 11 of us—some of us a little overweight—could not be squeezed into one car, Secretary Haskins of the Oklahoma Baptist Convention, volunteered to drive his car and take the 'leftovers.' The 11 Virginians left Oklahoma City at seven o'clock on the morning of September 22 for one of the most thrilling experiences of our lives.

"Mrs. George R. Martin, our efficient President, weighed us in and divided our weight according to the strength of the eight tires on the cars. Miss Olive Bagby of Rappahannock Association; Mrs. C.B. Clements of Pittsylvania; Mrs. L.L. Knight of Portsmouth; and Mrs. Harry Mundy of Valley, being the smallest in the group sat on the back seat of the Governor's car. Miss Oliver, Mrs. G. Paul LaRoque of Dover; Mrs. George F. Murdock of Middle District; Mrs. Ashton Jones of Potomac; Mrs. S.L. Mitchell of Blue Ridge rode in the official car of the Assistant Secretary of the Oklahoma Baptist Convention. Mrs. Martin and I—your corresponding secretary—rode on the front seat of the Governor's car with the very gallant and thoughtful general manager, Tracy Robinson, who takes care of the Governor of Oklahoma and his guests.

"The trip included the Cherokee Indian Baptist Association and the Pawnee Baptist Church . . . [and all the while] the Virginia party traveled in perfect ease and comfort and happiness."

Blanche Sydnor White
Religious Herald
October 28, 1944

Wartime Opportunities

"As World War II progressed people poured into the Norfolk-Portsmouth area to work in defense industries and the Norfolk Navy Yard. With funds from the 1942 State Missions Offering, WMU sent Louise Fletcher and Allie Lee Arendall to the two cities. Miss Fletcher's field was Broad Creek Village of Norfolk, where new houses were set up complete in seventy minutes each. Miss Arendall's work was in a housing development, Alexander Park, of Portsmouth. In addition to establishing religious services and rendering a spiritual ministry, these two experienced missionaries helped women find housing for their families, befriended the lonely, and guided the bewildered in adjusting to a new mode of living."

from *Light Three Candles*

"Our Work in the Defense Areas"

"If you have ever visited Portsmouth, you will remember it as a quiet, peaceful city, rich in treasured traditions. If you should return today you would find a boom town; our public buildings are crowded; our streets are alive day and night with the hustle and bustle of workers; we are beset by all the problems engendered by war conditions. Daily expansion in every line of government activity has filled our city to overflowing with defense workers and their families.

"Perhaps I can give you a clearer picture if I tell you that we have sixteen new residential defense areas. The largest is 'victory village' which has 4,250 demountable homes. That means from three to five as many persons because there are nearly always children in the homes.

"There are also two large trailer camps which [soon] will number 2,500 trailers. These trailers are now coming into Portsmouth at the rate of eighty per day.

"Already there are more than 22,000 new persons living in the vicinity of Portsmouth. Many of these persons are earnest Christians coming from active church relationships. They wish to continue their relationships but are required to forego them because of inadequate transportation. Our public conveyances are crowded even on Sunday almost beyond endurance.

"Then, of course, there are many of these new inhabitants who are indifferent to religion and unaffiliated with any church. But we believe that many of these could be won and enlisted now, today.

"Our WMU of Virginia has rallied to the emergency and supplied us with a full time worker in the person of Allie Lee Arendall of Richmond. A grand person she is! A tireless, experienced, consecrated worker whose plans unfold as quietly—and as regularly—as the coming of dawn."

Religious Herald
April 15, 1943

"There must be no missing link in the chain of faith that reaches across Virginia. We will supply the loaves and fishes. God will work the miracle."

Mrs. Norwood B. Richardson

European Relief

Following the destruction of World War II, Virginia WMU gave evidence of their worldwide vision and love through gifts to European women. Christmas gifts in 1949 included such items as 758 pounds of bedding and washcloths (and five boxes of candy!) to Norway; 530 pounds of bedding, clothing, soap, meat, and shortening to England; 270 pounds of candy, sugar, and coffee to France; 782 pounds of similar supplies to Italy; and over 700 pounds of supplies to Sweden. There were packages to Denmark, Germany, Finland, Austria, and Spain.

Expressions of gratitude similar to the following letter from Berlin flooded the Virginia WMU office:

"Very Dear Sisters in our Lord!

Quite happily my sisters surrounded me yesterday, when they saw all the beautiful things, which your Love had given to us. Before the sisters had come, I spread the dresses out upon the tables and chairs so they could oversee all the fine things, which are till today very rare in our Russian sector. And every sister found just that she was in distress for. A sister said quite happily 'You see, I would sew a nightdress for me and for it I need just as much material as there is in this long white bag.' Another sister said 'Oh, look here, that jacket fits perfectly to my little boy!' . . . and so on.

And now we wish with all our hearts that the Lord, who had turned your hearts to this friendly service, may bless you and that he may help you in your difficulties as he had helped us by you. We shall think of you in prayer!

Once more many thanks and good wishes with Matt. 25:40."

Yours very affectionately
Sisters from the 'women-group'
Mrs. Auguste Meister
Adlershof Teldhevrenstrape 27

Lady of the Cedars

*M*rs. O.L. Jones of Bristol embodied everything The Cedars represented: lofty dreams, missions commitment, youthful spirit. From 1938 until her tragic death in the summer of 1944 she was chairman of Virginia WMU's committee to establish a camp in Southwest Virginia. Under her direction a mountain campsite was chosen and the buildings erected. For $15,000 she placed on the mountaintop in the midst of the great cedar trees, a camp that within six years was valued at over three times that amount. As a contemporary expressed: "It was her dream that there would come here not only the young people of Southwest Virginia but also from every section of Virginia, to keep on the mountaintop a rendezvous with Christ and to go down from there with His personal world-wide Commission in their hearts. To this dream she was faithful."*

Mrs. Jones had already built her Lebanon WMU into a forceful organization. When she was elected superintendent of the Lebanon

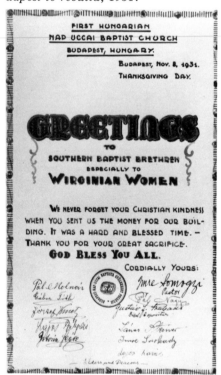

Virginia WMU helped the members of First Hungarian Church, Budapest to rebuild, 1931.

A grateful congregation sent a tribute to the Virginia women.

in 1929, there were only 19 Woman's Missionary Societies and 44 young people's organizations in the association. When she resigned in 1935, there were 30 Woman's Missionary Societies and a total of 111 missionary organizations. She directed her region's Ruby Anniversary celebration and served from 1931 to 1935 as vice-president of the Virginia Union.

It was on a Friday in June, 1944 that she suffered an accident "while on missionary duty." She had gone to The Cedars to meet Ellen Douglas Oliver, the state young people's secretary, and to help prepare the buildings and grounds for the new season. There she fell and injured her spine. At first the prospects of full recovery were hopeful, but within 10 days her condition took a turn for the worse. To all who would listen, she spent her last day relating her dreams for the camp. One of the WMU workers who shared those last hours with her in the hospital in Abingdon recalled: "She reviewed with joy and satisfaction her experience in building the camp and especially, the latest triumph, securing plans and materials for the new swimming pool. She outlined some dreams for the future promotion of 'The Cedars,' looking toward that day when the camp would mean more and more to the young people of Virginia."

Coming Together

"One cold January day in 1932, Ora Brown Stokes visited Blanche Sydnor White in WMU headquarters in Richmond. 'I am a Baptist,' she said, 'and proud of my denomination, but I do not know my white sisters of that faith. Other white women have extended the hand of Christian fellowship. Why have you failed to extend yours?' Miss White was aroused by the indictment. What could she do? What could Virginia Baptist women do in a united effort?" The visit from the black woman proved to be a turning point in race relations. It is thus recorded in Juliette Mather's **Light Three Candles**.

Una Roberts Lawrence, a leader in WMU, SBC, interracial efforts, introduced Miss White to Nannie Helen Burroughs, the corresponding secretary of the black Women's Auxiliary of the National Baptist Convention and a noted educator. In 1934 Miss Burroughs, in an annual meeting of Virginia WMU, challenged the two races to work cooperatively.

With the groundwork laid, in 1934 Virginia women opened an office, the Interracial Missionary Department, operated by Virginia WMU. The project was co-sponsored by four state missionary organizations of Baptist women of both races. "After prayer and conference," read the official news story, "Fletcher Mae Howell was chosen to lead us in this interracial work as field missionary." The conferences surely must have included words of approval from Dr. W.T. Clark, president of Virginia Union University in Richmond. Dr. Clark's wife was a member of the administration committee responsible for securing the first field worker.

For nearly a decade, the capable Fletcher Mae Howell represented the spirit and work of the interracial effort. A native of Suffolk, she graduated from Hartshorn Memorial College, later a part of Virginia Union, the Law Department of Freylinghausen University, and the Social Service Community School of Chicago. She taught in the Virginia public schools and pioneered in social work during World War I.

Fletcher Mae Howell, interracial worker for Virginia WMU.

In her greeting to Virginia women, Fletcher Mae described the interracial work as "Cooperating in Our Father's Business." In practical missions experiences "the white and colored women of Virginia joined hands and hearts in Christlike fellowship and missionary responsibility." The work included "teaching mission study classes, conducting roundtables and panel discussions on missions," Missionary Institutes, hundreds of local Vacation Bible Schools, and interracial missionary conferences and rallies. Among the projects was a Baptist missionary camp for young black girls. The camp, led by black and white Baptist women, was "the first of its kind in the Southland."

When she retired in 1943 in ill health, Fletcher Mae left her post having earned the deep appreciation of Virginia Baptist women, black and white. "She has proven herself," expressed the Virginia WMU, "diligent, conscientious, consecrated, cooperative, persevering and loyal." One of her abiding interests was the education of young black women. With her own funds, she established a scholarship in her name enabling young women to attend the department of Christian leadership and missions at Virginia Union University.

Fletcher Mae Howell, kneeling at left, surrounded by some of the women involved in interracial work through WMU.

The Queen of Baptist Women

*T*hat's what an American Baptist Convention publication once called Nannie Helen Burroughs, the highly-effective leader among black Baptist women. Born in Orange County, Virginia, "sometime in the 1880s," she wanted to be a teacher in the public schools. Although denied the opportunity, she pursued a greater outlet for her interest in education. She founded a school, the National Training School for Women and Girls, in Washington, D.C. "Common sense and high idealism" comprised a major portion of her curriculum as well as the "three Bs"—"Bible, Bathtub and Broom— emblems of clean lives and clean homes."

Miss Burroughs was a leader within the black organization, the National Baptist Convention. Elected corresponding secretary of the

NBC's Woman's Auxiliary, she held the position for more than 40 years. She was also a member of the Executive Committee of the Baptist World Alliance and was a favorite speaker at Baptist gatherings.

She first came to international attention in 1905 at the tender age of 19, when she addressed the delegates at the first gathering of the Baptist World Alliance in London. When she spoke in Hyde Park near Marble Arch, the London press termed her "sensational." In order to be audible to a crowd numbered at 10,000 or over, speakers mounted a wagon equipped with a soundboard. Miss Burroughs—the final speaker that Sunday afternoon—addressed the large crowd on "The Triumph of Truth," declaring that Christianity was conquering everything. She praised the first BWA Congress as proof of the song, "From Greenland's Icy Mountains." She said: "We have been making noise during the Congress and our only apology might be expressed in the words of a Baptist sister whose church had been conducting a revival. One morning her employer asked her what all the noise was about down at the Baptist church. She replied, 'We are having a revival.' Her boss said, 'But Solomon built a temple and one could not hear so much as the noise of a hammer.' The woman replied, 'Yes, Boss, I know all about that temple; but don't you see, we are not ready to build a temple; we are only blasting rocks!' "

Miss Burroughs became a friend of Blanche Sydnor White and other leaders within Virginia WMU; in 1933, speaking before the annual meeting of Woman's Missionary Union at Richmond, she gave her perspective on "How White and Colored Women Can Cooperate in Building a Christian Civilization." In her address she declared: "The women of the two races should unite in a common effort to defeat all common enemies to Christian growth—ignorance, selfishness, indifference, antagonism or race prejudice. The forces of Christianity should unite for better habits, better health, better homes and better hearts."

Virginia WMU supported the work of Rev. and Mrs. Sandor B. Kovacs among the Czechoslovakians in Prince George County, Virginia, 1935.

The Slavs

Through the State Missions Offering, Virginia WMU supported the pastor of the Czecho-Slovak Baptist Church in Prince George County. Sandor B. Kovacs, the pastor, had come to the United States from Hungary where his father was the pastor of one of the country's largest churches. In America he served the Czecho-Slovak Baptist Church in New York City and performed ministries among the Slovak people entering America at Perth Amboy, New Jersey. In April, 1930, the church's clerk, John Mierka, reported: "Although quite a young man, he has experience in the ministry that enables him to be a real friend of the people. Since his coming, we have grown spiritually, as he leads us into a closer relationship with God."

Dr. Everett Gill, European representative for the Foreign Mission Board, introduced "these Slovak people" in the following excerpt from a piece written for the WMU page in 1935: "The Slavs are the most numerous race of Europe. The World War was the last act in the Balkan Slavic drama of some fourteen countries—a veritable and long drawn out Gethsemane and Calvary, that ended with a resurrection. The world is just beginning to realize that a new situation has been created in Europe, that the Slavs have come on the stage of

First group of Bible School workers sent to Southwest Virginia mining camps, Summer of 1937.

history. Today the Slavic family, numbering two hundred million, extends from the Baltic Sea on the north, to the Black Sea on the south, and from the Adriatic on the west to the Pacific in the Far East. That great block of human beings, with their undreamed potentialities, constitutes one of the arresting and outstanding facts of the world situation today." The Slavic people also made their home in Virginia, where Blanche Sydnor White and the Virginia WMU opened the doors to their "undreamed potentialities."

Vacation Bible Schools

In 1938, Virginia WMU sponsored Daily Vacation Bible Schools in Southwest Virginia. Pictured are the children at Clinchco, where 124 pupils had perfect attendance. Mrs. G. Paul LaRoque of Richmond, far left, led the project.

Bible School site, Haw Orchard, 1941.

Beginners Class, Daily Vacation Bible School, Norton, 1937.

Boys at Vacation Bible School, Clinchco, 1938.

White Cross Department, Virginia WMU

Virginia's White Cross work began sometime between 1920 and 1921, under the leadership of Lizzie Savage, corresponding secretary, and Mrs. W. P. Mathews, chairman. In May, 1921, a large box of supplies, valued at $468, was shipped directly from WMU headquarters to Ogbomosho, Africa, to Dr. George Green's hospital. Exactly 102 Virginia societies participated in the first project.

At the close of World War I, Virginia women were ready to turn from "Red Cross" work for soldiers to "White Cross" work for "missionary soldiers." Virginia WMU turned quite naturally to the Ogbomosho Hospital, built by their own Dr. and Mrs. George Green. It was also the place of service of another Virginia daughter, Ruth Kersey.

From 1922 to 1924, Mrs. G. Paul LaRoque served as White Cross chairman. She led the women to provide hospital beds for Ogbomosho in place of grass mats and pallets. A Virginian visiting the Nigerian hospital in 1947 glimpsed brass plates on the sturdy beds, acknowledging the gifts of Virginia women in the 1920s. The beds were intended to last!

The third chairman, Mrs. Herbert Lewis, served from 1924 to 1927. It was reported to Mrs. Lewis that serums which would save many lives could not be stored by the hospital of Nigeria due to lack of refrigeration. Also, surgical operations performed at night required an attendant to hold a lantern. Within two years White Cross money was raised for a generating plant.

For 36 years, from 1927 to 1963, Grace Morrison of Petersburg led the White Cross Department. Through economic depression, world war and financial retrenchment at the Foreign Mission Board, Mrs. Morrison called upon Virginia women to help. The adult women provided the funds for hospital operational expenses and equipment, while the young people's organizations would furnish medical supplies. Virginia women also provided furlough expenses and "out-going expenses" for doctors who replaced those leaving the staff.

From 1928 to 1929, the call was heard to erect a "home for the motherless babies" saved by Ruth Kersey. The Camp of Hope for lepers was established, and the Department of Dispensaries and Clinics, under Eva M. Sanders of Virginia, was added to the medical department of the Nigerian Mission "because the White Cross Department of WMU led in providing funds for those forward movements."

Grace Morrison thoroughly enjoyed the work of acquiring and sending needed medical supplies. Her brother operated a business which supplied the necessary shipping boxes. Rees Watkins remembered Mrs. Morrison as "a direct and rather abrupt" person engaging less in small talk and more on getting the job done. She also recalled the chairman's fondness for large "picture hats"; one accompanying her to an annual meeting would discover—reserved for the hats—the entire backseat of the automobile.

From 1963 to 1977, Mrs. Stone Landess was chairman. She and her husband, who also participated in the work, had a vacant garage in the rear of the house where they did the yeoman work of packing boxes of supplies.

In later years other places besides "Dr. Green's Hospital" would benefit from Virginia's White Cross work, including the nurses' homes at Gaza, Paraguay, and Yemen; and as Miss Watkins laughingly observed, "diapers were sent everywhere." White Cross chairmen in recent years have been Martha Hudgins from 1977 to 1982; Elizabeth Axselle from 1982 to 1987; and Mildred Jenkins, 1987 to 1989.

Shuck Centennial

In September, 1835 Jehu Lewis and Henrietta Hall Shuck departed America for the China missions field. In September, 1836, they arrived in China. From 1935 to 1936, Baptists of two continents celebrated the twin anniversaries—both the Shucks' departure and their arrival—thus, the origins of Baptist work in China.

Across Virginia, celebrations were held. In Kilmarnock, the birthplace of Henrietta in October, 1817, and in First Baptist Church, Richmond, where the missionary couple were "set apart for missions" in 1835, there were special observances. Morattico Church near Kilmarnock held commemorative services for Henrietta's baptism and nurturing from the country congregation. A bronze tablet was erected in her honor. A highway marker was erected in Kilmarnock at her birth site.

Virginia WMU organizations studied Henrietta's life through the Centennial year and designated substantial sums of the Lottie Moon Christmas Offering for China missions in remembrance of their "fairest flower." Rappahannock Association pledged funds towards a chapel to be erected in South China bearing Henrietta's name.

In Richmond, Virginia, women staged an epic drama on Henrietta's life at the Mosque, an auditorium seating 5,000 persons. Hundreds were turned away. In the midst of the Great Depression, in Henrietta's home state, the Shuck Pageant was, in the opinion of the WMU constituency, "the biggest thing that ever happened in Richmond."

Girls vied for the honor of playing the role of Henrietta. The pageant traveled across the state, and local Baptists in several Virginia cities staged it.

Shuck Pageants were staged in several Virginia cities. Here is one of the girls who portrayed Henrietta Hall Shuck.

Virginia WMU supplied the keynote speaker, Blanche Sydnor White, for a meeting with American Baptists as they, too, paid remembrance to Henrietta's work. In China a more encompassing celebration recalled the dedication of a host of men and women "whom God used in this century in building up Baptist work." The WMU of South China focused upon Henrietta. One Chinese WMU commemorated the event by sending forth six "Bible women" to serve in areas yet to know Christ. There were pilgrimages to Henrietta's grave in Happy Valley Cemetery, Hong Kong.

The Shuck Centennial was perhaps Virginia WMU's finest hour. They placed before the Southern Union—indeed the world—the name and deeds of one of their noblest daughters. They celebrated, yes, but they also committed themselves anew to the cause of missions.

Mrs. F. Y. O. Ling, secretary of All-China WMU, was a guest of Virginia WMU for the Shuck Centennial (1935–36). (Photo courtesy of Helen Butler George.)

American women pay respects at Henrietta Shuck's grave in Happy Valley Cemetery, Hong Kong, during the Shuck Centennial.

Mrs. George R. Martin
"To serve our present age"

*O*live Martin served two separate tenures as president of Virginia WMU, from 1925 to 1929 and from 1934 to 1946. In addition she served 11 years as a highly effective president of WMU, SBC. And then there was her superlative leadership of the Women's Department, BWA. Olive Martin, usually known as Mrs. George R. Martin, was clearly a leader. Yet merely listing the offices she held fails to flesh out the form of a woman who led with quiet dignity and a touch of elegance. ➤

After practical preparation as president of her church's WMU and as superintendent of the Portsmouth WMU, Olive Brinson Martin was elected president of the state Union when barely into her thirties. Despite her experience she, too, felt in awe of the job, expressing a natural feeling of inadequacy for her task. "Amid the responsibilities which are before me," she declared in 1925, "my courage almost falters, and I ask, 'Who is sufficient?' Paul answers and says, 'Your sufficiency is not in yourself, but in God.' " She carried a verse with her as she entered the office—"Sunrise and morning star, and one clear call for me. And may no wilful disobedience mar the life Thou'st given me."

The women of Virginia quickly placed their earnest confidence in their young leader. In time the confidence grew to respect, even adulation. They discerned the qualities observed by one Portsmouth woman: "She is a woman of rare good judgment. She is never hasty in her judgments but takes time to think things through. She is very fair-minded, always endeavoring to get the other person's viewpoint." Her local friend also gave expression to another important quality: "She is at all times open to convictions, but when once has decided upon the right course, follows that with an unfaltering purpose."

Olive Martin and Blanche Sydnor White were a team! Always respecting the other, the two were loyal co-laborers. Miss White played a key role in the behind-the-scenes activities which led to Mrs. Martin's election in 1945 by the WMU Executive Committee, SBC, which met to select a successor to Mrs. F. W. Armstrong who had died in office. Out of the 20 vice-presidents no one was constitutionally identified to assume the office and Miss White pressed the case of Mrs. Martin's lengthy tenure of 17 years in office.

Olive Martin was forward looking. In her presidential address of May, 1946, she asserted " 'To serve the present age' is our responsibility and our privilege. The glorious and timely service of the past will not excuse us for failure in discerning the signs of our times or having discerned them, for failure to serve fully our generation."

In the post-war era, Olive Martin inspired Southern women to help in European relief endeavors. She also possessed a wider view than perhaps some of her contemporaries. She once challenged the women: "What of the spirit of selfish isolationism within our own Southern Baptist Convention? Someone has said, 'There are many small minds who have never taken in the wide world or felt any obligation for all of it. They have repeated, "God so loved the world that He gave," but it never occurred to them to give themselves. Many of those 'small-minds' are within our own churches. WMU has never enlisted one-half of the women connected with our churches. We must reach that host of 'small-minded' southern Baptist women with the missionary message, seeking to 'Enlarge their minds to grasp God's thoughts, Enlarge their hearts to work His plan.' "

Olive Martin saw the needs of others from a wider perspective. She established good personal relationships with Negro Baptist women and then personally bridged the gaps between her white fellow members and the black sisters. "If Mrs. George R. Martin could," thought the women of the South, "surely we must." And as she traveled widely she sighted more than a tourist's view. She saw the need for better communication and joint endeavors by Baptist women around the world. She acted on her conviction by developing the Women's Department, BWA. In August, 1948, Virginia WMU sent Mrs. Martin to London to assist in the organization of the European Baptist Women's Union. Under her guidance a constitution was adopted and the wheels of the organization were set into motion.

Olive Martin from Tidewater Virginia had been true to her own desires to assure that WMU served its present age. She knew her generation of women and under her leadership they responded.

Mrs. George R. Martin, left, and Carrie S. Vaughan address Asian Baptist women in Hong Kong during their world tour, 1958.

MENFOLKS:
"The Man in the Shadows"

For almost 60 years George Roswell Martin lived in the shadow of his wife, the worldwide leader of Baptist women. Everybody knew Mrs. George R. Martin, known almost exclusively by her husband's name. Probably few women knew her as Olive.

Although only a privileged few knew *Mr.* George R. Martin, it must be understood that someone supportive assisted *Mrs.* Martin in all her endeavors. She traveled widely, at home and abroad, but when she arrived home, whatever the hour, Mr. Martin was patiently waiting for her at the train station or airport.

One summer he chaperoned the young people at the YWA Camp. In 1939, Baptist Lodge had been built but there were no funds left for mattresses. As the date for the campers' arrival approached, *Mrs.* Martin did the most sensible thing—she bought $1,500 worth of mattresses and charged them to *Mr.* Martin!

George R. Martin, superintendent of Lamberts Point Office of the Pocahontas Fuel Company, spent his working life on the waterfront. One WMU leader remembered that he was "well-read and an excellent conversationalist." She added that "he was kind and considerate." What more could have been needed for a man in the shadows? Supportive, encouraging, generous and, yes, sharing the same world vision so well articulated by his wife.

Olive Pauline Riddell: Missionary

*O*live Riddell was, in a word, a missionary. Whether on the foreign field of China or the home field of the Southwest Virginia mountains, she was a missionary. But even a missionary may be called by other names.

In China some called her a "foreign devil" while others hailed her as "honorable teacher." As reported in 1933, "both messages are used in bringing a crowd which follows her as she goes to the appointed preaching place. It may be a home into which the message has gone; it may be a little hall which has been rented; it may be a church building. Wherever the meeting is held, the message is faithfully given, 'Jesus, the Son of God, saves from sin.' "

"Through heat and cold, walking when she needs rest, riding on the piled-up wheelbarrows when she must, our Olive Riddell goes out in the villages in and around the Pochow District. When she tells of her experiences," reported the WMU page in the **Herald**, "we are reminded of the Acts of the Apostles during the first Christian century."

In 1950, she sent home a letter written with a borrowed pen on the back of a mimeographed program. She had been driven from her home in Kweiteh and had found refuge in the Canadian Episcopal Compound outside the city gates. She penned a few words just to keep the homefolks from undue worry: "The Japanese entered the city and I brought out very little except the clothes I was wearing. [When] we were permitted to [return], the house was empty of everything of any value except my books. Furniture, clothes, and food supplies all gone! I am not suffering for any of the necessities because the Lord has raised up friends. His word is still true, 'All these things shall be added unto you.' When He commands us to go, He also gives His promise, 'I am with you always.' "

In Virginia she served as an associational missionary for Lebanon and New Lebanon associations in the far southwestern corner of the state. "One of the first things I learned," she wrote of her mountain missions experience "was that there are many kinds of Baptists. It is always necessary to say Missionary Baptist when speaking of our own churches. I shall never forget the day I happened to stumble into the home of a Soft Shell Baptist. The mild suggestion that the Soft Shell must be something like the Hard Shell raised emphatic protest. Immediately she replied, 'Indeed we are not,' and was ready for an argument then and there. A confession of ignorance on the subject was all that saved us from an unpleasant visit." She reported on the Holiness people and warned, "If they would only have their own churches and minister to those of their own faith, they would do us very little harm. However they seem to think members of the small Missionary Baptist churches are their special mission field. They do much visitation and do not hesitate to tell the members of our churches they are not saved. A pastorless church is their happiest hunting ground and we have so many of them in the New Lebanon."

A Goochland County native, Olive Riddell experienced two distinct cultures, the Inner China Mission and the mountainfolk of her own state. She loved and served them both, proudly wearing her title of "missionary" until her death at age 90 in March, 1979.

Bessie Spraggins McGahey: "Missionary"

*I*t was about 1926 when a young woman named Bessie Spraggins stumbled into the Virginia WMU office, in search of a copy of **Royal Service** to use with her YWA group. She had already experienced a hard time finding the office, and the only person at work when she finally located 216 N. 2nd St. in downtown Richmond was Blanche Sydnor White, still new on the job. The meeting would truly be a turning point in her life.

Something in the two personalities instantly sparked; Bessie felt inclined to comment that if a vacancy ever occurred in the office, she would be interested in a position. Miss White quickly sensed the potential in this young woman and confirmed a present vacancy. Bessie accepted the offer, and the chance encounter changed the course of her life. She became Miss White's personal secretary, confidante and traveling companion.

Bessie married H.E. McGahey and he shared her with the WMU. He humored and honored her every request and was one of the faithful menfolks on whom the Virginia WMU office could rely for back-breaking labor.

Bessie even enlisted her mother into Miss White's schemes. For the Shuck Pageant in 1935, Miss White wanted everything as authentic as possible. She was especially horrified that the wigs for the Oriental women were blond. It was Bessie who, thus, recruited her mother to work through the night dyeing stockings black and turning them into wigs! Again Miss White was frantic because one of the main costumes was from the wrong period. Bessie was dispatched to fetch her mother, who quickly sewed another dress.

Bessie traveled across the country visiting missions sites and attending WMU annual meetings. Most of her time, however, was spent as a supportive staff member for her boss. Never was there a more loyal employee. Often Bessie would trick her hard-working boss into signing affidavits, pledges of slowing down or time off or some which simply read: "I promise to have no more bright ideas- . . . until after the annual meeting." Of course, everybody in the office knew her efforts were hopeless because Miss White was a wellspring of ideas.

After about 35 years of service, Bessie "retired" from Virginia WMU and wanted to "do missions" herself. She went to Africa to briefly help missionary nurse Eva Sanders and stayed months doing all kinds of tasks in the nurse's office. At home, she was devoted to summer missions at Camp Carey, the WMU-sponsored camp for black girls. She was devoted to the Chinese of Richmond and personally would fill her automobile with Chinese children and bring them to her church, Northminster, for Bible study.

In 1964, she began working at the Virginia Baptist Historical Soci-

The executive secretary, Blanche Sydnor White, on left, and her secretary, Mrs. McGahey, pose in front of the building of the WMU offices at 216 N. 2nd Street, Richmond, 1930.

ety as treasurer, office secretary, and research assistant. She typed the cards for Miss White's mammoth index to the first 50 years of the *Religious Herald*.

During her final illness prior to her death in 1988, a nurse on duty once inquired of one of her visitors as to her work history— "What kind of work did she do?" How would one explain the life spent in a multitude of works in the name of Virginia WMU? Secretary seemed so inadequate. There was a better word which came to mind: "Missionary. She was a missionary." It wasn't too far wrong. Bessie S. McGahey was a missionary in the finest sense of the word.

Louise Fletcher
The Lady with the Cowbell

*L*ouise Fletcher was the first director of the Good Will Center at a place called Stoney Lonesome near Norton, a bleak and forlorn mining community. One of the young lives she touched was William Jenkins who in adulthood devoted his entire working career to state missions as a staff member of the Virginia Baptist General Board. Among his significant contributions was developing student work in Virginia. Ask him to name his life's chief influence, and he will say Louise Fletcher. He calls her "the little lady from down East who talked funny."

A native of Middlesex County, Louise Fletcher may have "talked funny" to mountain lads in Southwest Virginia, but she also talked sense and exhibited love. She may have felt the mountainfolk "talked funny" too. Writing in 1933 about the local folks helping to build a Good Will Center, she quoted the people: "Miss Fletcher, I thought I'd come over this mornin' and see if there's anythin' I kin do to holp out. I hain't got no money, but I kin work." And work they did. Some of the women tended home gardens so the men could devote time for construction.

After three years of work she reported in 1933 that Sunday school attendance was over 180, all the WMU organizations were thriving except a YWA because she simply "lack[ed] physical strength and time to organize one," prayer meetings were led by the Baptist pastor at Norton, and Vacation Bible Schools, stretched out over five weeks, attracted well over a 100 children and young people. Although the Bible schools proved a genuine success story, Miss Fletcher did have one problem—habitually tardy pupils. With few alarm clocks in the Norton coal mining camps, the children were always late. One girl had a solution. She had a cowbell, a rusty old bell which her grandfather had given to her, and she offered it to the missionary. Standing on the front porch of the Good Will Center, Louise Fletcher would ring the bell, signaling the children to climb the hill and learn about Jesus.

Miss Fletcher also had a practical streak. Noticing that the local landscape was covered with black coal dust, she requested white paint from Blanche Sydnor White. She then painted the Good Will Center a stark white so, in the midst of all the bleakness, it would

*stand like a beacon on the hill. The picture of Louise Fletcher stand-
ing on the porch of the white house, ringing the cowbell, is an apt
symbol of Virginia WMU itself— standing on the world's front porch,
ringing and calling humankind to a better life.*

Virginia Baptist Women and their Quarters

By 1932, the situation was desperate. The Foreign Mission Board
had 398 missionaries under appointment to 13 countries. The
Board's budget was $600,000 but it owed $1,100,000 to the banks of
Richmond. Thirty-one missionaries were at home "clamoring to go
back." Thirty others were due furloughs but the Board had no money
to bring them home. Missionary volunteers were pleading to go. The
greatest anguish came as veteran missionaries remaining on the field
suffered under intensified burdens and heavy work loads.

In the spring of 1932, Barton Heights Baptist Church [now North-
minster] of Richmond sponsored a School of Missions with five days
of afternoon and evening services. The enrollment reached 736. Several denominational leaders and missionaries participated. Among
them was Blanche Sydnor White, speaking at an assembly period.

Wade H. Bryant, pastor of the church, long remembered Miss
White's message: "With her broad knowledge of and her burning zeal
for world missions she vividly described the evangelistic fires that
were blazing on our mission fields. She then pointed to the Foreign
Mission Board's crippling debt, to the missionaries who could not
return to their fields, to those whose furloughs were overdue, and to
the volunteers who were ready but could not be sent. She urged that
we pray and work to turn the tide for foreign missions."

The night after the school ended, one of the laymen asked Dr. Bryant to come by his home. The man shared that he had been unable
to sleep the night before. Then he said, "Surely, there is something
we can do to lift the burden from our Foreign Mission Board." The
two men talked and then went to their knees. Mrs. George R. Martin
captured the impact of that moment when she wrote: "They had
been given Christ's answer. And they dared not withhold from others
this plan—which was not theirs but His."

The plan was simple. It included securing 100,000 individuals to
give $.25 a week for one year—over and above all the other missions
gifts. The resulting amount would lift the entire debt from the Foreign Mission Board. Members responded when Dr. Bryant presented
the plan to his church. Next, when he presented the plan to the
Richmond Baptist Pastors Conference, a committee quickly began
work to promote it. When Dr. Bryant shared his plan with the executive secretary of Woman's Missionary Union of Virginia, the idea
gripped Miss White's mind and heart. The project was supported
largely by Virginia women. In 1933, $6,634 was donated and in 1934,
the amount towards debt reduction had grown to nearly $24,000.

Virginia women embraced the plan. From the Hilton Church WMU
came this note: "Eleven women promised to give and one more
promised to give what she could." From the Friendly Circle of the
Norton Good Will Center came news that several members were contributing. One declared that "We must; we must give 'till it hurts."
One newlywed couple, married but six weeks, decided that a quarter-

a-week was not sufficient sacrifice. The WMU Page in the *Herald* reported: "With brave smiles drew from the bride's finger the bright diamond which had been the pledge of their love and faith." The gift of the wedding ring indicated the depth of personal commitment for the missions cause.

The Doziers

"At the end of the Seminary course [in Louisville] when examinations were over, the young minister went down to Monroe, N.C., and was married to Mary Ellen Wiley. The wedding was unique. Before the ceremony, which was read by the bride's uncle, one of Miss Wiley's professors sang two hymns, 'We've a Story to Tell to the Nations,' and 'Have Thine Own Way, Lord.' The bridesmaids carried Bibles covered with white satin instead of the traditional flowers. The young couple hurried back to the Seminary where the husband received the degree of Master of Theology. 'In the fall of the same year, November 5, 1932, Edwin and Mary Ellen Dozier bade farewell to America and turned their faces toward 'The Island Kingdom.' " [In the summer of 1933, Edwin Dozier spoke at the RA Camp in Virginia Beach and "so inspired the hearts of the boys" that they urged Virginia WMU to add the necessary funds to send the Doziers to Japan. Edwin Dozier became the Virginia RAs missionary to Japan.]

Mildred Dodson McMurry
Constraining Love
1939

Mary Ellen and Edwin Dozier on their wedding day, 1932. Edwin Dozier was supported, in part, by the RAs of Virginia.

"Miss Elsie"

Elsie West Gilliam had a brief career as a foreign missionary, serving in China from only June, 1910, until the following June. But she had a lifetime of practical missions work at home. A native of Lynchburg and a fourth-generation member of its First Baptist Church, she was superintendent of the Strawberry Association WMU from 1926 to 1932. And for 14 years, from 1934 to 1948, she represented Virginia as a trustee of the WMU Training School.

Why was her foreign mission career so brief? She was teaching in the Eliza Yates Girls' School in Shanghai when a telegram arrived announcing her mother's sudden illness. The young missionary felt she must return home but thought the visit would be brief. Once home she became convinced that God meant for her to remain in Lynchburg. She found mission work at home. Yet someone said of Miss Elsie: "One city and one nation were not large enough to contain such spirit as hers; her field was the world." Everybody returned her love and one of the Strawberry groups and the Lynchburg Federation of BWC carried her name as an expression of gratitude and respect.

It was in her own home that the idea was born of organizing a Business Women's Federation in Lynchburg. Four Lynchburg churches formed the nucleus group from which the organization named "The Elsie Gilliam Business Women's Federation" grew. By

1968, there were 24 units in the federation with a total membership of 371.

From its beginning the School of Nursing at Virginia Baptist Hospital in Lynchburg received the special interest of Miss Elsie. In 1968, Virginia WMU established an endowment scholarship in her memory at the school. An initial gift of $2,500 from the State Missions Offering began the fund which grew with gifts from others who loved the woman who gave so much of herself.

Shockwaves!

*I*n 1949, the women of Virginia were stunned when Blanche Sydnor White announced her resignation after 25 years of "matchless service." While Virginia WMU is far larger than any one individual, the name, life, and imprint of Blanche Sydnor White was upon every good and great act of the Union for so long that many could not remember any other leader.

She had led the way in Cooperative Program support, debt retirement, education, student ministries, Good Will Centers, interracial understanding, home and foreign missions involvement, and after World War II, in international vision. She had made friends across the state and the nation and then across the seas. She supplied missions literature; when there was none available, she delved into the back issues of the **Religious Herald** and the old records and "made

Blanche Sydnor White's birthday party, 1952.

Sitting beside her president, Mrs. L. L. Knight, Blanche Sydnor White works on the little pillows which she gave each "soop" when they achieved their goals for the Virginia Baptist Historical Society wing of the Boatwright Memorial Library at the University of Richmond.

history come alive for us." She accomplished all this while keeping Virginia alert to the spiritual needs of the day. It is no wonder Mrs. E.D. Poe, historian of the Union, declared: "When we think of WMU of Virginia and of the future, like little children we can but ask where, oh, where shall her like be found again?"

The Executive Board confessed that their counterparts of 25 years before knew much about the woman they were selecting but did not know other things. One colleague said: "But what they did not know was the genius and the driving force of her dynamic personality. She was an indomitable advocate, never afraid to stand alone in her conviction, always however persuasive in her advocacy. Her courage, her keenness of intellect, her ability to speedily size up a situation, to make quick and sure decisions and to act boldly; and the rare gift of being able to turn seeming defeat into victory."

Mrs. George R. Martin, perhaps her closest ally, surmised that Miss White had "the double faculty of the wide sweep of the field glass and the deep look of the magnifying glass." She added that, "With wonderful accuracy and facility she is able to sense a situation in its perspective and relate it to the cause of missions."

Associational superintendents by the score provided tribute to her sterling life:
—"When a task seemed impossible and hopeless, you made me see that it could be done."
—"With all my failures your unfailing friendliness helped me to try again."
—"It never occurred to us to question any suggestion which you made."
—"You made us feel that the fate of the Virginia Union would be determined by us."
—"You have, as nearly as was humanly possible, done a perfect job."
—"You have given without stint and we have taken, often without realizing the cost to you."
—"You have skill in managing women. Few could have worked so closely with so many types of women, and have them all say now, 'What shall we do without her?' "
—"Sometimes the goals seemed unattainable, but we worked hard because we knew that you had confidence in us."

*At the annual meeting held at First Baptist Church, Roanoke, in March, 1950, the women heaped tribute upon tribute. They presented a book with notes of appreciation from 126 of the 151 association superintendents from her years of service. Then came the love gifts of bonds tied to the wings of a white plastic airplane with the suggestion that she travel to the African celebration of the centennial of the Nigerian Mission and also to Japan for the dedication of the Mallory Building of the Girl's Junior College. Those were the plans; but Miss White, who admitted her physician must decide "whether wings or a cane," kept chiding the Virginia women that, if they did not fully subscribe the gift of the Virginia Baptist Historical Society wing of the University of Richmond library, she would cash the bonds and donate them to the society's building. The wise Virginia leaders, however, knew she might give away her retirement gift and thus placed it in bonds which required a six-month "cooling off" period. True to form, the Virginia WMU came through with the funds for the Historical Society's wing and Miss White did not have to give her bonds. She would visit the society's library day after day to index the first 50 years of the **Religious Herald**, creating a working monument for Baptists for all years to come.*

Virginia WMU Emblem

WMU Emblem

Bank account book kept by Miss Lottie Moon in China.

Signing of contract for the camp.

Hunt Hall; dining, assembly, and meeting rooms.

At the dedication of Hunt Hall at Camp Little Cross Roads was Alma Hunt, former executive leader of WMU, SBC, for whom the assembly and dining building was named. She is shown at far right with her great-niece, Catherine Roe.

IF YOU WANDER OFF THE ROAD YOU WILL
HEAR HIS VOICE: "HERE IS THE ROAD
FOLLOW IT."   ISAIAH 30:21

JUNE 1985

Bullard Building; administration, housing, and infirmary.

Canteen

Cabin building

House of Happiness

Vesper Garden

Meeting unit

Dedication of the camp.

Peaceful surroundings of Camp Little Cross Roads.

Claybrook-Dunaway WMU group of Rappahannock Association staged a reenactment of the 1888 founding meeting of WMU, SBC, for their Centennial program.

Shelia Horton, at right, presides as the GAs of Providence Church, Appomattox, talk about their Centennial activities.

The ladies of Warsaw WMU held a Centennial Sunday with members in costumes, a display of mementos and an anniversary luncheon with a special cake.

Pearl Brooks and Agnes Land work on the Centennial quilt for Second Church, Petersburg.

Crozet Church's Joyce Davis BYW, Zeta Vess and Carolyn Saunders groups stage a Centennial program including a dramatic play.

GAs of Crozet Church participate in the Centennial celebration at their church.

Martha Delano prepares to serve Warsaw WMU's Centennial cake.

Parade of banners for the Centennial celebration of the member churches of Lynchburg Association WMU.

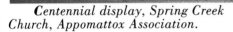

Centennial display, Spring Creek Church, Appomattox Association.

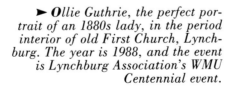

Mr. & Mrs. M. L. Heslop in period attire stand before the Centennial exhibit at Second Church, Petersburg.

▼ *The annual meeting of Mount Vernon Association WMU carried the Centennial theme. Candy Phillips, the new associational WMU director, stands beneath the Centennial banner.*

Mrs. Janet Andrews of Healing Springs Church, Natural Bridge Association, proudly stands beside her quilt.

► *Ollie Guthrie, the perfect portrait of an 1880s lady, in the period interior of old First Church, Lynchburg. The year is 1988, and the event is Lynchburg Association's WMU Centennial event.*

► *Centreville WMU presents an old-fashioned Chatauqua program for its Centennial observance. Among the booths were a photographic exhibit, items about youth missions trips to Jamaica and Maine, and even "a silent auction" table laden with homemade desserts. Proceeds went to missions.*

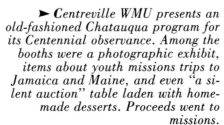

An archway of colorful balloons gives a festive air to the celebration.

Mission Friends of First
Church, Springfield, hold cupcakes
with candles as they, too, celebrate.

A lady from the past
suddenly appears to
promote debt reduction.

*"Yesterday and Today" was the theme for the Centennial program at
Spring Creek Church, Appomattox Association.*

The United States Postal Service offered a special cancellation for the WMU Centennial.

Richmond area women played hostesses.

Centennial finery at First Church, Monroe.

Glynn Buchanan participated in the celebration at Gwathmey Church, Dover, where activities included old-fashioned games such as apple bobbing, sack races and a tug-of-war. Mrs. Buchanan portrayed Abby Manly Gwathmey in the program.

"Celebration in the Park" featured a variety of events to entertain the crowds during the picnic dinner.

Friendly faces welcome visitors to the site of Broad Street Methodist Church where the organizational meeting was held in 1888.

Richmond Centre was transformed into a huge WMU"missions meeting."

Celebration Hall featured 85 exhibits including many historical artifacts. (Stanley Leary)

Here comes the parade!

The Richmond Coliseum was filled to capacity.

Women across the nation proudly displayed their authentic period dresses and handmade Centennial quilts. (Clay Allison)

Actresses recreate the founding meeting, in a sea of balloons while 11,000 watched.

People paraded from the foreign missions fields.

Old First Baptist Church, Richmond, site of the 1888 organizational WMU, SBC meeting, was restored and opened for tours just in time for the celebration.

Virginia comes in view!

Women ate from their official WMU lunch boxes wherever they could find space.

Ben Bruner, grandson of Abby Manly Gwathmey, views exhibit of his illustrious kinswoman.

The enormous montage of WMU leaders, past and present, covered one end of Celebration Hall.

135

"Let your light so shine!" The Richmond Coliseum in darkness except for the lights of the individual WMU members. *(FMB photo by Stanley Leary)*

Chapter 4

The Fulfilling Years,
1950–1974

*Y*ears cannot be neatly sheathed into distinct bundles. The influences and projects and personalities of any one era quite naturally fall into the annals of others. The great expansion of missions under Blanche Sydnor White's leadership from 1925 until 1949 spilled over into greater fulfillment in the next 25 years between 1950 and 1974. Led by two of Miss White's closest colleagues, Ellen Douglas Oliver and Carrie S. Vaughan, Virginia WMU's next epoch realized the work Miss White had begun. And Miss White herself continued her influence on WMU throughout the second 25 years, thereby providing both official and unofficial counsel to Virginia WMU for over a half-century.

Virginia WMU found new directions, supporting missions projects for migrants on the Eastern Shore, forgotten folks in the Shenandoah Valley, mountain people in far Southwest Virginia, and Indians in the Southwestern United States. "Motorcades" toured Virginia mission sites. Many new activities engaged the energies of an emerging force, women employed outside the home.

It was a time of effective leadership, as Virginia WMU women fulfilled their promise shown as GAs and YWAs. Among the notable leaders were Mrs. E.L. Dupuy, Mary B. Burke, Mrs. J.M. Bloxom, Mrs. Evan Lacy, Mrs. Jackson White, Mrs. E.S. "Emma" Stratton, Mrs. Curtiss English, Mrs. Bernard LeSueur, Mrs. Rolen Bailey, Mrs. Stone Landess, Mrs. Chiles Cridlin, Mrs. W.B. Sherman, Mrs. Lester L. Knight, Mrs. O.C. Hancock, and Mrs. A. Harrison Gregory.

In professional leadership the era marked the executive secretary tenures of Miss Oliver, from 1950 to 1957, and Miss Vaughan, from 1958 to 1975, and included the supporting work of Rees Watkins, Retha Tillman, Kitty Harwood, and Sue Hutton. The Union's missionaries in Good Will Centers and in associational work included Truman Grasty, Bobbie Black, Annie Mae Broyles, Edith Vaughn, Nell Culverhouse, Emma Lou McCraw, Laura McFadden, Elizabeth Thomas, Allie Candler, Olive Riddell, and Ann and Tommy Woo.

The epoch closed on the grandest occasion, the Centennial of Virginia WMU. Characteristic of the best in WMU work, the Centennial emphasized "Our Mission High Fulfilling" and kept before the women their valued theme—"The World for Christ! Hallelujah!"

> "Woman's Missionary Union of Virginia can do anything God calls us to do.
>
> "In 1874 He called this organization into existence to build a home for two missionaries in China. By the power of God it was done and even more.
>
> "Down through the years God has called this Union to undertake for Him many tasks seemingly as impossible as the first. This can be written across our history: He has never failed to give us the victory when we have undertaken with all our hearts to do His will.
>
> " 'A charge to keep we have,
> To serve the present age,
> Our calling to fulfill—
> O may it all our pow'rs engage
> To do our Master's will.' "
>
> Mrs. Lester L. Knight, 1956

BAPTIST LODGE

Let me live my life at Baptist Lodge
Where there's sand and dirt and girls to dodge, Where the
bunks are shaky and the insects crawl,
And there's homesick campers and wet beds and all,
Where there're eleven o'clock curfews and not enough space
Oh, how can I love this odd old place?

I could say I had a pretty bad deal—
What with peanut butter for many a meal,
A bug in my bed, being thrown in the shower,
or being awakened at most any hour,
Have I beach duty today, do I work in the store?
To play for Vespers; is there something more?

Oh yes, it's my turn to teach methods today
And give out the money . . . and get the ant spray!
And teach Sunday School and play in right field
And be in a skit—all with vigor and zeal.
And all during this constant, hectic rat race
I must keep a smile upon my face?!?

But what about these friends I made;
The flood of love that can never fade;
Life's experiences that I've earned;
Lessons in living and loving I've learned.

Then a letter one day for me:
"Dear Counselor, I'll be a missionary.
"While at camp I felt His call,
"And now I'm ready to give my all."

Now, Crusader, light up your face with that smile
Here's proof that it's all so very worthwhile.

Rose Ellen Stewart
Camp Counselor, 1966

MENFOLKS:
George A. Harris—"The WMU Camp Man"

In 1974, the employee of Virginia Woman's Missionary Union with the longest tenure of service was a man! George A. Harris, Jr., had served as superintendent of Virginia WMU's camp properties since 1947. Even earlier, in the 1930s, he served at the Royal Ambassadors' camp when it was under the women's sponsorship.

At his retirement, an article surveyed Harris' many contributions: "The development of the camp program has not been easy. The plans and dreams of a camp in the central part of the state [materialized] but only $5,000 was available for building. None of those dollars could be spared for an architect's fee. George Harris modified the blueprints used for The Cedars, scouted around for used materials, and began construction, doing much of the work himself. In 1951, Camp Viewmont operated for four weeks with only two cabins completed but the two were filled to capacity. Without George Harris this would not have happened!"

Harris' skills were again freely given on the relocation of Baptist Lodge from Virginia Beach to the Mathews County site along the Piankatank. When plans were made to move two old buildings to the new camp, Harris rallied men in his community and church to volunteer for the project.

On the WMU page of the *Religious Herald* at the time of his retirement, the women expressed their gratitude: "No one person is fully aware of the total contribution made by Mr. Harris through the years. However, many are aware of his deep concern for young people and his recognition of the importance of camp experiences in the task of missionary education."

GA and *YWA camp staff in the
summer of 1955 at Baptist Lodge, Virginia Beach.*

YWA camp at The Cedars, 1946.

Retha Tillman

*S*he was the picture-book perfect portrait of a lady—gentle, gracious, radiant—and yet those close to her called her by her last name, "Tillman," as if she were a commanding officer. And in many ways Retha Tillman was in command, especially whenever the GA queens "swarmed" Eagle Eyrie. For eight years, from 1958 to 1966, she served as Virginia WMU secretary for Girls' Auxiliary and planned the first state-wide Queens' court for Virginia girls.

As Mrs. Harold B. Tillman, the Arkansas native was a dutiful Newport News pastor's wife. As a widow she launched a new career direction when she received the GA leadership post.

"Tillman" possessed an effervescent sense of humor and the ability to make each girl believe herself to be the most important person the GA secretary knew. Through these qualities, she became endeared to Virginia girls and women.

Eva Sanders:
Virginian and Member of the British Empire

*I*n one of her earliest letters home from the mission field of Nigeria, Eva Mildred Sanders, a missionary nurse, closed her epistle thus: "Pray that we may seek to glorify God only." For Miss Eva glorifying God was the only worthwhile pursuit. Even when honors, long overdue and justly awarded, were bestowed upon her, she would reflect that the honors were to glorify God.

Born in Roanoke on December 30, 1902, Eva Sanders attended Westhampton College, the Jefferson Hospital School of Nursing, and the WMU Training School. In 1932, she was appointed to Lagos, Nigeria, as a medical evangelist. Help was so scant on the missions field that Eva Sanders was expected to be in three places at once. She recalled once: "Dr. Green expected me to go to the Baptist Hospital at Ogbomosho; Idi Aba Girls' School, Abeokuta, was expecting me; and for some reason, I was expected to stay in Lagos, studying the language and teaching in the Baptist Academy there. Well, I went to Lagos." For six years she remained in Lagos working alongside Lucille Reagan.

In 1943, Eva Sanders returned on furlough to Virginia. As a visiting missionary, expected to address church groups on field missions work, she went beyond expectations. She spoke throughout the state, helped in the WMU camps, and "advanced the cause of missions in many ways." In a war-torn world, she journeyed through dangerous and troubled waters on the long voyage back to Africa, returning safely accompanied by other missionaries.

In 1946, Miss Eva became a nurse-midwife specialist and founded the Baptist Welfare Center at Ire, Nigeria. In the course of a 22-year career in supervising births, she either delivered or oversaw the delivery of approximately 14,809 infants. It might be said that Eva Sanders became the great white mother of Ire! By 1948, the Ire Dispensary was serving 72 villages and administered well over 60,000 treatments in one year.

Eva Sanders and her Virginia WMU-supplied automobile, "Virginny," even rode in a king's royal procession when a young man serving in the Baptist Hospital was honored by his tribe as their new king. Miss Eva had worked with him at the Baptist Hospital, inspecting the work he performed at the leper colony. He invited his Baptist friends to join in the celebration.

Miss Eva recalled the great inaugural day: "I went in the new car Virginia WMU gave me, but dust followed by rain had made my car look like a muddy lorry." She transported several Baptist friends and as she laughingly recalled: "Suddenly, we met the procession. The new King rode in a spick and span car, but he halted the procession, got out of the car in his gorgeous king's robes and, with his wife, came to our car. He wanted to ride in our car to the Church of England church in which he was to be consecrated as ruler. So, dirty, but triumphant 'Virginny' and I led the procession, preceded by the drummers and trumpeters." Afterwards, the Baptist missionaries were among the honored guests at a luncheon given by the British district officer.

In 1954, Eva Sanders was the honored one. A native messenger had come to her door and in African fashion had clapped his hands together rather than knocking. It was her summons to the local British official's headquarters for a presentation naming her a member of the Most Excellent Order of the British Empire. She received a certificate signed by the Monarch and a medal.

Two years later Queen Elizabeth II visited Nigeria and her subjects, real and honorary, were to pay proper respects. Miss Eva wore her medal, the second and last time, expressly for the Queen. On leaving for the event, she realized that she had forgotten to wear the requisite hat. Her only one was a rat-eaten straw hat with a hole. True to her no-nonsense approach to life, she plucked a flower to cover the hole and went to meet the Queen.

On her retirement in 1968, Miss Eva returned to Virginia as camp nurse at Baptist Lodge. Mary Lou Burnette, who served as director of Baptist Lodge, declared: "Miss Eva's care and concern soothes the pains of camp. Her cabin [wistfully called Nigeria] is an open house all day. All kinds of problems are carried there. None seem quite as impossible after Miss Eva has heard them. One staff member is quoted as saying, 'I felt sorta down so I stopped by Miss Eva's to feel better.' "

Thousands of people had done the same in Africa. They stopped by Miss Eva's to feel better. And she helped them with medications and Scripture—and by the warmth of her personality radiating a singular purpose—to glorify God.

Eva M. Sanders holds her framed citation and her medal from Queen Elizabeth II upon the occasion of presenting these to the Virginia Baptist Historical Society, 1984.

An Ambulance for Ire

"Smooth as silk," declared Eva Sanders, the veteran missionary nurse at the Baptist Welfare Center of Ire, Nigeria, describing the new ambulance, a Peugeot, purchased by Virginia WMU. "You can't imagine the confidence a new car gives as we take patients to the hospital," she declared. Miss Eva could appreciate the new ambulance since she knew "Sunbeam," the old Ford station wagon, was doomed. "I was conscious of every turn of the wheels. I had a flat tire with only a hemorrhage case in the car. The time before that the whole exhaust pipe dropped out. I had reason for trepidation!"

Eva Sanders needed good transportation. The Welfare Center had no resident doctors and seriously ill patients had to be transported 60 miles to the Ogbomosho hospital.

Miss Eva's ambulance was supplied by Virginia WMU.

Pearl Nunnally Burke

*A*s a girl Pearl had gazed upon the face of a missionary heroine, Lottie Moon, whose picture graced the child's bedroom wall. The selfless service of the Virginia missionary had surely served as early inspiration for the girl's life.

A native of Cumberland County, Pearl Nunnally was reared and educated in Chesterfield County. She taught school in Richmond until her marriage to Kenneth E. Burke, a young pastor in Southampton County, after which she assumed every responsibility of a pastor's partner. The church members and the community became her concerns; later, with her children, she became a devoted mother. She found another channel of service in Woman's Missionary Union and reached out to others, leading the way in interracial and migrant work.

The Burkes lived in Norfolk where Kenneth was pastor of Burrows Memorial Church; in 1950, the couple moved to Richmond when Kenneth Burke became treasurer of the Baptist General Association of Virginia and, of course, of Virginia WMU.

Wherever they lived, Pearl Burke involved herself in local WMU work. In Southampton County she was the young people's leader for the Blackwater WMU. She compiled a handbook for counselors of WMU youth organizations.

In Norfolk she helped persons displaced by World War II. Pearl Burke brought the needs of migrant workers to Portsmouth Association WMU, and they conducted Daily Vacation Bible Schools in the migrant camps for several years. Broad Creek Village Mission, established during her administration as a group leader, became a Baptist church.

In 1945, she began a decade of service as state literature chairman for Virginia WMU. Subscriptions increased by about 20,000 to a total of 54,825. In Richmond she devoted time to Camp Carey, the Virginia WMU camp for Negro girls, and from 1956 to 1960, she served as Virginia WMU's Interracial Committee representative. As someone observed: "Fearlessly, untiringly, enthusiastically she pressed on, exercising keen insight and foresight. She won the admiration and friendship of the Baptist women of both races throughout Virginia."

She also suggested the name of Viewmont for the WMU camp. WMU Board members had suggested other names—"Seven Springs" and "Spring Hill"—but Mrs. Burke declared: "What's wrong with you? With the birthplace of Miss Lottie Moon just three miles from the camp entrance, you can't possibly call it anything but Viewmont!" She contended the name would be a keen daily reminder to the campers of Lottie Moon's missionary zeal. Possibly she was recalling the influence of Lottie Moon upon her own life as a child.

When Pearl Burke died in June, 1960, someone discovered the following thought among her papers: "Death is not extinguishing light; it is putting out the lamp, because the dawn has come."

Ellen Douglas Oliver:
"A String of Matched Pearls"

*I*n 1930, Mrs. W.C. James presented to the Virginia WMU Executive Board the name of a young Irvington woman for the position of young people's secretary. On observing the "good looking" Ellen Douglas Oliver, affectionately called "Doug" by her friends, Mrs. James had been suitably impressed—this young woman knew how to dress and present herself well. Mrs. James felt that the first hurdle in winning the attention and respect of young people was in creating a favorable first impression.

Mrs. James shortly realized that her good judgment had been confirmed. Years later she reflected that Miss Oliver's life and works were like "a string of pearls carefully graduated and matched, each reflecting the light, the changing colors, the glow of the Pearl of Great Price."

The young graduate of Westhampton College, where she wore her blue-tie as the best goalie on the hockey team, and the WMU Train-

ing School, became an instant favorite of the young people to whom she gave devotion and creative service. In her first greeting to the young people, she borrowed the verses from the hymn, "I would be true, for there are those who trust me . . . " and added, "You are indeed trusting me when you give me the wonderful privilege of serving as young people's secretary, and I shall strive each day to be true to that trust and to you. Do you know what being your friend means to me? It means that I am always 'at your service,' ready to give to you whatever little there is worthwhile in me."

Miss Oliver developed the camping program for Virginia's young people. She enjoyed every moment and every activity, as she planned outstanding programs and invited only the best leaders and great missionaries.

From 1947 to 1948, Miss Oliver experienced what may have been the happiest, most fulfilling year of her eventful life when she served as a teacher of English at the Eliza Yates Girls' School in China. While in China, she "broke ground" for the University of Shanghai Village Project, a dream held fast by Elizabeth Ellyson Wiley for Virginia WMU to erect a Baptist Center near the gates to the university. It was to include a chapel and clinic and serve as a Good Will center.

Ellen Douglas Oliver, who taught at the Eliza Yates School in China (1947–48), enjoyed an unusual rapport with the children. The high point of her trip was the journey to the villages where Margie Shumate worked.

She also visited Margaret Jung, the Chinese-born woman who had grown up in Norfolk and attended the WMU Training School. In 1947, she, too, had gone to China to teach. Miss Oliver reported on her visit: "She [Margaret] seems happy in her work and is already making a place for herself in the school. I went to her home for a Chinese meal and met her parents for the first time. It hasn't been easy for any of them to readjust to China." Miss Oliver's letters home included suggestions to Virginia WMU for items which would *assist Margaret's work.*

In 1950, with the retirement of Blanche Sydnor White, Virginia WMU looked no further than "the next desk" where Ellen Douglas Oliver had been promoted only the year before to associate secretary. The Union selected their own daughter to serve as the new executive secretary.

In 1955, Virginia WMU sent their executive secretary to London to attend the Baptist World Alliance meeting and to tour the mission fields. On her 25th anniversary and her royal "send off," Virginia WMU presented Doug Oliver with a miniature silver chest filled with silver dollars from the Executive Board members. With characteristic good humor, Miss Oliver laughed and declared "I am trying to decide whether to bring home an English castle or the crown jewels of Austria or Spain. Really, I am overwhelmed and I can't possibly tell you the things I'd like to say about my 25 years working with Virginia WMU but you know I do love you and appreciate you with all my heart."

By 1957, Miss Oliver was totally exhausted. As President, Mrs. O.C. Hancock explained to the Virginia women, "overwork" and no vacations for years had led to a lapse of strength. The Executive Board granted a three-month leave of absence.

Unfortunately the months passed with no improvement and in May, former executive secretary Blanche Sydnor White was elected acting executive secretary. In September, Miss Oliver resigned. The resolution of the Executive Board expressed "deep regret and sorrow" and praised "her many talents, ever-ready smile and buoyant nature" which bore witness for the Master. Editor Reuben E. Alley of the *Religious Herald* declared: "Conscientious in response to every trust, Miss Oliver dedicated 27 years of her life and many unusual talents in Christian ministry on behalf of young people and women in the Baptist churches of her native state. This gentle Christian woman has the abiding love of a multitude of grateful friends."

In time Miss Oliver's strength returned. She found employment at the Baptist Book Store in Richmond; then in 1967 an opportunity arose for her to find meaningful use for her vast knowledge of Virginia Baptist life, past and present. From 1967 to 1979, she served as librarian for the Virginia Baptist Historical Society. She was a friendly and gracious contact for all who sought information about Virginia Baptists. Miss Oliver remained in demand as a missions study leader and speaker for missions programs. In February, 1983, she died peacefully, kneeling as if in prayer beside her bed in her Lakewood Manor residence. Sixty years earlier her Westhampton annual had described her as "Good, lovable, attractive, true; she does just the things she ought to do." The same inscription could have likewise been her eulogy.

***E**llen Douglas Oliver, also served Virginia WMU as executive secretary (1950–57).*

"Miss Mary"
of Dan River

"*Mrs. W.R. Barksdale, superintendent of the WMU of Dan River Association from 1897 to 1899, was one of the pioneers in the organization of the Union. Her daughter, Helen, led the Dan River WMU as its superintendent from 1910 to 1916. When she resigned the mantle of leadership fell on the capable and consecrated shoulders of her sister, Miss Mary Barksdale. From 1917 to 1951 'Miss Mary,' as she was lovingly called, continued to serve as associational superintendent. This she did in addition to heavy responsibilities in her own church and as a teacher in the high school in South Boston and, later, as supervisor of Halifax County elementary schools.*

"*In her first report to the Union, she said: 'During the past year, the Dan River Woman's Missionary Union has determined to establish a memorial for the Church Building and Loan Fund of the Home Mission Board, has contributed $1,690.03 to missions—a marked increase over last year's contributions—and has added eight societies.' In 1920, 'Miss Mary' asked the Association to rejoice with her for there were only four churches in which the women were not organized. It was not long before every church reported a Woman's Missionary Society.*

"*Closest to her heart was the missionary education of young people. Missionary societies for each grade were established and fostered. In this service, Dan River took and held a place in the front ranks of State and Southwide Woman's Missionary Unions. The women of Dan River would have been ashamed to report to 'Miss Mary' less than their best for her life was to them an abiding challenge.*

"*'Miss Mary's love for young people and her firm belief that missions should permeate every facet of their lives, led her into the summer camping program of Woman's Missionary Union of Virginia. She served at the Baptist Lodge and The Cedars as Camp Director for many of the GA and YWA camps from 1939 to 1946, touching hundreds of young lives with the quiet radiance of her life and service.*"

Blanche Sydnor White

When "Miss Mary" died in 1958, the women of the Dan River Association wanted to establish a memorial to their beloved superintendent. They also remembered another daughter of Dan River, the missionary Elizabeth Hale then serving in Malaysia, and designated the memorial gift for use as Miss Hale directed. She decided that the Baptist seaside campgrounds, called Golden Sands, needed a proper gate. "Remembering how much Miss Mary believed in and gave herself for such camps," Miss Hale explained, "I thought a memorial here would be most fitting. The entrance was most unattractive; the old wooden gate was broken; and pigs came in and ruined the flowers." The new silver and blue gate was practical and decorative. Far across the world in a place where few from Halifax would ever visit, the strong gates of Golden Sands would swing open to campers and *secure the grounds from unfriendly intruders. Miss Hale declared: "It will be a joy to tell campers about the one in whose memory the entrance to Golden Sands was made beautiful. As they come through the gate I trust it will be with open hearts and that they will go back home through it to obey what has come into their hearts from Him during the days here."*

The Lady from Portsmouth

*I*n 1946, when elected president of Virginia WMU, Mrs. Lester L. Knight proclaimed: "I would like to throw down a challenge to every woman who is a member of a missions group from the seashore to the mountains . . . Pray! Enlist! Give! These are simple, fundamental, essential to our cause."

Carol Roper Knight never strayed from the fundamentals. She gave her life over to prayer in joyous times as well as in tragic ones. She enlisted, reaching first to women of her Portsmouth area and then to women across Virginia. And she gave of herself.

Outside of her family, Woman's Missionary Union claimed her time. She served as the leader of YWAs in her own church, Court Street in Portsmouth, as superintendent of the Portsmouth Association WMU, from 1938 to 1946, and as president of Virginia WMU, from 1946 to 1956. She and Blanche Sydnor White were co-workers in every endeavor.

A native of South Carolina, she attended Greenville Female College which later was incorporated into Furman University. In 1918, she married Lester Lloyd Knight and the couple settled in Portsmouth, where her husband had a distinguished career with Seaboard Coast Line.

In her seventh year as president, Virginia WMU collectively "looked over their shoulders" at all which had been accomplished during Mrs. Knight's tenure—two "Virginia girls," Edith Vaughn and Kay Sanderson Culpeper, had left for missionary service; Diamond Jubilee foreign students had been brought to America to pursue studies; Ellen Douglas Oliver had been sent to China for missions service; Rees Watkins and Jo Norwood had joined the staff; and the Diamond Jubilee had been a time of celebration and commitment.

In addition to the dedicated hands that gave of WMU service on the home front, there had been the outreach represented by European relief after World War II; fund-raising for a building for the Virginia Baptist Historical Society; and "the hundreds of missionary triumphs" through seasons of prayer and offerings, in Virginia, in the homeland, across the seas. As her presidency closed, the number of persons involved in Virginia WMU had grown from 79,000 to 114,000.

Carol Roper Knight had a queenly presence, the embodiment of aristocratic old South Carolina. When the WMU, SBC, met in Norfolk in 1976, Christine Gregory, a fellow Virginian and yet a fellow native South Carolinian, was to preside. Mrs. Knight, affirming their common bonds, presented to Christine Gregory a piece of family crystal. It was just like Mrs. Knight, always giving, always affirming.

Mrs. Lester L. Knight, president (1946–56), center front, at an annual meeting in the 1940s. WMU leaders also pictured are Mrs. A. G. Carter, left, and Ellen Douglas Oliver, right. Mrs. E. L. Dupuy and Blanche Sydnor White are in the background.

"There is danger, that in the midst of multiplied activities, we shall forget the fundamental verities on which Woman's Missionary Union was founded.

"Meetings are important but not as important as the purpose for which the meeting is held or the spirit of intercession which should permeate every meeting.

"Adding to our membership rolls is important but not as important as leading all our women to lift up their eyes and look on the fields at home and abroad."

Mrs. Lester L. Knight

"Churchwide Offerings' Round One"

In 1956 a highly controversial issue exploded on the Virginia scene. It concerned whether the seasons of prayer offerings should be strictly those funds collected by and from WMU or whether the offerings could be church-wide including "the brethren" and others not members of WMU. Virginia WMU clashed with Southern Union and with others within the state on the issue.

Blanche Sydnor White saw the proposed change as a conflict of basic WMU policy. "Without pausing to consult with the state Woman's Missionary Unions, the Executive Board of the Southern Union adopted a resolution to 'invite the entire church membership to participate' in her seasons of prayer and the offerings," wrote Miss White. "The Virginia Woman's Missionary Union believes that the cause of missions is best served by preserving these seasons of prayer and offerings for home, state and foreign missions as definite Woman's Missionary Union projects."

She noted that if promoted in Sunday school classes, training unions, and Brotherhoods and yet reported as WMU-collected funds, the results would become "not an accurate—even an honest—report." She added: "As a long-range program, we believe that much less money will be given to missions."

Three major objections were cited as follows:

"1.   The churches (certainly the great majority of those participating) have not followed the policy of preparing for these offerings by seasons of study and prayer. History reveals that a number of general concerts for prayer for missions have been launched, but have not continued. We fear the same fate would befall the three seasons of prayer . . .

"2.   Many churches will make them budget items rather than over-and-above gifts.

"3.   There will be the temptation, on the part of the church leadership, to divert the gifts to other causes. . . . In time of depression, missionary funds have been *borrowed* by some Virginia Baptist church officers to meet local expenses."

Virginia WMU leadership across the state supported the old plan. Their stance was "Let us 'hold the line' " in Virginia. The women love having their very own special seasons of prayer and offerings" (Mrs. D.P. Anderson, Potomac); "They should continue as a free will, woman's gift" (Mrs. Lonnie Busic, New River); "We should keep our 'over-and-above,' sacrificial offerings" (Mrs. H.C. Epperson, Lebanon); "When they get to be just another plea for money—which they will be if we do not emphasize the prayer services—they will have lost their reason for being" (Mrs. Willard Chandler, Accomac).

In December, 1956, Miss White took her appeal to the larger arena of the **Religious Herald**. In a letter to the editor, she outlined the history, nature, and purpose of the WMU-sponsored offerings. "A house to house canvass was not the policy," she declared. The Virginia leader also suggested that if the WMU and the Foreign Mission Board desired change in regard to the Lottie Moon Offering, they should take the matter before the constituency "in a straightforward and regular manner."

In a private letter to Mrs. L.L. Knight, she reflected on the heated issue. "I do not know when I have felt more unhappy. That you should have felt defeated because I advised that you refrain from an open and heated fight hurts. To have fought and lost—as you would have—really would have been defeat. Your part before the General Association was dignified, one that subsequent events will prove wise. No bid for thoughtful consideration would have helped. There was mob spirit to contend with and mob spirit does not permit thought.

"What has been accomplished? This matter has been brought out of the background or underground and put squarely before both the General Association and Woman's Missionary Union. The pastors are alerted and, believe me, the leading pastors will begin to think what they are facing. Woman's Missionary Union has been put on the spot. I hope every associational WMU meeting will be called upon to rate their sentiments."

Virginia WMU "held the line" in round one of the great debate. Twenty years later a different approach would be taken to the same controversial issue.

Virginia WMU launched Baptist student work with campus directors in the late 1930s. Grace Landrum Watkins was supported by the Golden Jubilee Offering for her student ministry at Westhampton College.

Student Workers

Miss Caroline Holladay, Virginia WMU "College Correspondent," who wrote and visited college girls to enlist them for missions. 1911–16.

*O*livia Stephenson

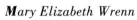

Student Workers

*M*ary Elizabeth Wrenn

*S*arah E. Poole

*E*ris Anderson

Missionaries' Library Fund, 1955

"My heart has been singing ever since I received your Christmas card, your note and check. I am so happy and thankful to you and the WMU of Virginia for remembering me at Christmas. The gift came as quite a surprise. You have no idea how very much needed this check is. When I opened the letter, the first thing I thought was, 'Thank you Lord for friends.' "

Geneva Edwards
Carver Good Will Center

"Go Forward"

*F*or 40 years Alma Hunt's warm smile, captivating speech, keen administrative sense, and ability to work well with the denomination's brethren and sisters have been assets for WMU. Long after her official "retirement," she was useful to the Union's cause, responding to speaking engagements in both major cities and remote towns. During the Centennial year of 1988, she was in constant demand. She poked fun at herself, declaring that, in her late 70s, she was the "oldest thing around" in the WMU. Almost anyone would have been hard pressed to keep such a hectic schedule. When she was caught cat-napping in an airport terminal, she confessed that such occasional rest periods were part of her secret.

Alma Hunt also served the denomination well just simply by being herself, the best goodwill ambassador any organization, any country could have. She was comfortable with those from all walks of life. Her correspondence, steady and engaging, was another secret of her friendships and her ability to spread good feelings among Baptists. Once her mother, a tremendous source of strength in her life, chided Alma for sending so many Christmas cards. Alma protested that she really knew all the recipients and had been a guest in many of their homes around the world. Simply put, she was genuinely interested in every single one of those folks.

The Executive Board of WMU, SBC, must have been looking for a "people-person" when they selected Alma Hunt in 1948 as their Union's executive secretary. The Roanoke native was then serving as Dean of Women at William Jewell College, a position her former pastor, Walter Pope Binns, had selected for her after leaving the Roanoke pastorate for the college presidency. He once let it be known that only for Southern Union would he release his dean.

Alma Hunt had grown up in Virginia WMU. Baptized at age 10 by John F. Vines, she came under the influence of the Virginia WMU leader, Mabel Vines, her GA leader. Miss Hunt served as leader in the YWAs of her home church, First Church, Roanoke, and in the Vines YWA Council of Roanoke. As a young career woman she became involved in the BWC and enjoyed the excitement associated with assemblies at Ridgecrest.

It was obvious to everyone that, except for devotion and commitment to missions, Alma Hunt stood in sharp contrast to her predecessor, Kathleen Mallory. At 38, she was young and free-spirited and shocked the dour older Baptist women with her painted nails, makeup, and stylish attire. She represented a new generation of Baptist women; and although visibly different from her predecessor, she received her public support. "Personally and as the Union's former executive secretary," wrote Miss Mallory in Royal Service, "I commend her unreservedly." Miss Mallory even drew comparisons between the new executive and the first, the legendary Annie Armstrong. Both were 38 at the time of office, both reared "in the eastern part of SBC territory," and both "nurtured, converted, baptized, and habitually helpful in the church of [their] Christian parents."

In her first printed message to Southern Union, Alma Hunt reflected upon the old motto of WMU, "Go Forward." Readying herself and her constituency to move ahead, she stated, "The growth of the work through the years is a thrilling study, but not a satisfying one. This is no time to be complacent." Indeed the lively young woman from Virginia was ready and eager to promote missions. And Alma Hunt never lost her zeal to "go forward" in Christ's service.

"Through the years my heart has been made glad many times by the gift of Virginia women through the Missionaries' Library Fund. Now that I have had to leave my beloved work in Nigeria, it is just as sweet to be remembered, and I hope to have more time to read now than when I was an active missionary. May God bless you all."

Ruth Kersey
Nigeria

"Thank you for your Christmas gift which you call 'Missionaries Library Fund.' I really do use the money for magazines and books and often think of you as I enjoy reading them."

Margie Shumate
Thailand

▼ *Among Southern Baptist women, Alma Hunt was known by all. Pictured,* left to right, *are Alma Hunt, Mrs. R. L. Mathis, and Mrs. Robert Fling.*

◄ *Alma Hunt became a goodwill ambassador for WMU after her retirement as executive secretary. In this photo, she stands at the podium of Bon Air Church, Richmond, with the local church WMU president, Mrs. James Todd.*

Richmond women hosted the annual meeting in 1960. Seated, from left, at the planning meeting are Mrs. Theodore F. Adams, Carrie Vaughan, and Mrs. W. B. Hackley, who was associational superintendent.

Norfolk hostesses meet to plan the 1967 annual meeting. Mrs. Frank M. Barr, associational superintendent, is flanked by Mrs. George R. Martin, left, and Carrie S. Vaughan, right.

Norfolk women hosted the annual meeting in 1962. The planning committee takes time out for a group photograph.

Rees Watkins:
Missions Education

*W*hen Blanche Sydnor White toured mission stations in Nigeria in 1947, she met a young Alabama woman, Rees Watkins, who was principal of the large day school at Ogbomosho. Miss White was impressed enough to remember the young missionary.

Rees Watkins contracted chronic malaria in Africa and was sent home to the states. The Executive Board of Virginia WMU had been considering for some time the need of "lightening the load" upon its small staff by adding another person. Miss White, remembering the woman she met in Nigeria, employed her as assistant young people's secretary. Within months Ellen Douglas Oliver had become associate secretary to Miss White and Miss Watkins received a promotion to the post of young people's secretary.

Rees Watkins arrived on the Virginia scene just in time for the fall group meetings. By her own account she made "31 speeches in 28 days" in a whirlwind of speaking engagements.

Two women had new responsibilities in the fall of 1948 and both wanted to look their best at the next meeting of Virginia WMU in March, 1949. Rees laughs that she and Alma Hunt, the newly-elected executive secretary of WMU, SBC, and a native of Roanoke, passed each other to purchase suitable clothes. Miss Hunt left Birmingham to shop in her native Roanoke and Miss Watkins left Virginia to shop in Birmingham in her home state. "I remember that first Virginia state meeting," recalls Rees Watkins. "Somebody pinned a camellia on me. I sat there worrying whether she had made a hole in my new suit or whether the flower would stain it."

At her first meeting Miss Watkins referred to her own astonishment at the turn her life had taken: "From the Ogbomosho Baptist Day School in Nigeria to fall group meetings in Virginia is a long, long step. From fall group meetings as a visiting missionary to assistant in the Young People's Department, getting acquainted with the intricate process of mailing out Season of Prayer materials is another long step. And from there to the desk at 1 West Franklin as your young people's secretary is the longest step of all. I am amazed. I am awed. But I am here—and I am filled with a sense of deep humility as I realize that it is my privilege and duty to prepare a report of the young people's work for the Diamond Jubilee Year."

"The sound of trumpets of the Diamond Jubilee is caught up into the melody of time past," declared the new secretary, "but the song of achievement is captured forever on records and becomes a triumphant march for the future." On the negative side, she exclaimed: "From every side we hear the cry, 'We have the children but we do not have the leaders.' Oh, the tragedy of it! 'First they give their own selves to the Lord,' said the Apostle Paul. Too few among us have been willing to give ourselves. Too few of us know the glorious privilege of leading children to a broader understanding of Christian missions."

In the years ahead Rees Watkins advocated involving adults in missions education of youth. She led camps, seminars, and conferences and spoke at thousands of missionary meetings. She used her pen to compose stirring sermonettes from missions lore. She reveled in the history of her adopted people, the Baptists of Virginia, and read, studied, and communicated that history through the WMU page in the **Religious Herald** and in **They Made It Happen**, the story of Baptist women in Tidewater, as well as in a history of the House of Happiness, the oldest Good Will Center in the SBC, and in 1987, through a young people's history, **A Backward Glance**, published for the Centennial of WMU, SBC.

For nearly 10 years as young people's secretary, she carried sole responsibility for all four WMU youth organizations. Under her leadership the organizations grew. She could be as effective with rambunctious RAs as she could with the girls—who were not always sweetness and light. Rees was forever involved with teaching youth, as her posts reflect: Young People's secretary, from 1949 to 1958; YWA secretary, from 1958 to 1960; YWA and Sunbeam Band, from 1960 to 1969; Acteens and Baptist Young Women's director, from 1970 to 1975. In September, 1975, her responsibilities changed with her assignment to the new position of editorial research director. The role was the same—missions education—but the new position tapped her writing skills and her vast knowledge of the organiza-

tion's past and purpose. The Centennial activities of 1974 also prompted the need for promotional literature.

Even after her retirement from Virginia WMU in 1983, she continued her pursuit of missions education by part-time service at the Virginia Baptist Historical Society as education assistant. She produced missions education literature including a widely-distributed booklet on Virginia Baptist women and their contributions, as well as a playlet for the Shuck Sesquicentennial. She researched and designed the 35 panels in the Virginia Baptist History Mural painted by Sidney E. King. In 1988, she participated in the Society's annual meeting held in conjunction with the grand Centennial of WMU, SBC.

In her first annual report after arriving on the Virginia scene, Rees Watkins asked an essential question: "Have you a vision of a nobler, happier world? Tell the children. They will build it for you." For 40 years Rees Watkins helped Virginia Baptists share that vision of "a nobler, happier world." And she taught the children who would construct it.

Rees Watkins, soon after her arrival on the Virginia WMU staff, as she prepares promotional material for young people's work, 1948.

Coronations

GA coronation at First Baptist Church, Bluefield, 1962. (Photo courtesy of Tyler Easley)

GA coronation in a mining camp of Southwest Virginia.

▼
The Queens have been crowned! Rees Watkins, young people's secretary, center, 1955.

▶
GA coronation with Retha Tillman, at left.

The Story of Vaughn Summit Mission

"Vaughn Summit community joins the Shenandoah National Park. It is located eight miles from Luray in Page County. Shenandoah WMU was concerned when it learned of this mission field in its midst. When approached, the people hid and peeped out from behind the trees. On some occasions they called the dogs on the inquiring friends. Finally a man met one of the WMU ladies; and when she told him of their desire to start a Sunday school at Vaughn Summit, he replied, 'It ain't no use lady. It ain't gonna work. We don't want none of your religion.'

"Some groups have been stopped by such behavior, but not the WMU! This only caused them to pray more and work harder. After many discouraging hours, their faithfulness was rewarded when in 1945 a chapel was dedicated. It was rebuilt from an abandoned store building and made into an attractive house of worship.

"The people attended! They came out of the fields with their boots and mud, and left most of the mud in the chapel. The men came with their hats on, and left them on during the service. They yelled at each other, regardless of whether there was a hymn, prayer or sermon.

"The question was asked in the Adult Bible Class if the members could imagine what it would be like to live in an area that did not know Christ. A lady replied, 'We do not have to imagine. We know! We know what it was before the Mission was put here. We know the hatred, the stealing, the lying, the immorality that reigned here. We know the difference between having Christ and being without Him, and that difference is all the difference in the world!'

"Following one of those discouraging periods, I stopped to see the community missions' chairman. She lives near Vaughn Summit and probably knows that section better than any Baptist. I asked her the question, 'Is it worthwhile?'

"She replied, 'Certainly, it's worthwhile!' She continued, 'I worked up there seven years. I know what it is. I get discouraged. But if you think conditions are bad now, you ought to have seen Vaughn Summit before the WMU put the Mission there. Worthwhile? Yes! Every cent of money spent, every hour of work given, every prayer uttered to God on behalf of Vaughn Summit has been more than worthwhile!' "

Judson Baldwin
State Missions Offering
Promotional Material
1958

Vacation Bible School group, Vaughan Summit Mission, 1970.

"Each One, Teach One"

Her prayer was simple and direct. "Lord, you know how badly I want to read. Please let me learn how!" For an adult woman who never learned to read it was a heart-wrenching prayer—one which seemed to require a miracle.

Virginia WMU had just begun a literacy ministry and it was an answer to the woman's prayer. She attended the Newport News Good Will Center where Mrs. Russell G. Joyner was her teacher. At one point as many as 18 teachers were active in teaching reading.

The ultimate goal of the reading ministry was to teach pupils so they could eventually read the Scriptures. Several professions of faith were made, including one from the woman who uttered the prayer above and one from her daughter.

Another who worked in the literacy ministry was Mrs. Norvell W. Hunt of Colonial Heights, literacy chairman for Petersburg WMU. About 20,000 adults in her area were non-readers and functional illiterates. Representatives from 23 of the Baptist churches in Petersburg Association attended training workshops for teachers, and they achieved phenomenal success. One pupil, a Japanese woman, a Buddhist, began attending her teacher's Baptist church where she could learn about Jesus. One woman taught her husband to read and with his new skill he found a better job. Mrs. Hunt and the many others involved in teaching adults achieved their purpose. As she stated: "The underlying motive and ultimate goal is to make Jesus Christ known. This is always the primary function of community missions." By 1967, some 18 district association WMUs in Virginia were participating in the literacy ministry.

Annie Mae

From 1948 until her retirement in 1964, Annie Mae Broyles was a state missionary through Virginia WMU, working in the mountains of Western Virginia, first in Strawberry and later in Highlands and Roanoke Valley Associations. Of course, Annie Mae remained a missionary at heart and in action until her death. She had been trained as a missionary, attending the WMU Training School and gaining practical missions skills at Petersburg Good Will Center and at the Virginia Baptist Children's Home.

She was a rare person, generous, selfless, and possessed of a love for "the little people of the world." Mrs. Joe McGhee, superintendent of the Strawberry WMU, remembered Annie Mae as an "humble, sincere, beloved servant of Christ." She also remembered that when the Strawberry churches were pastorless the people could look to their lady missionary for guidance. In Strawberry, Annie Mae organized and taught Vacation Bible Schools—sometimes at three schools a day.

For the Highlands Association she became "the link" between the various places tucked away in the hillsides and hollows. "Through rain, sleet, snow or summer heat, she made her way, adding support and encouragement," said Mrs. C.V. Eames, superintendent of the Highlands. In that association she revived sleepy churches, conducted Vacation Bible Schools, and taught a Bible School for the Negro children of Elliston community. It was not unusual for her to travel over 2,000 miles a month performing missions duties. In ranking her hobbies, she placed hiking and reading on the short list, but the hobby of the first order was "teaching Mission Study Classes."

Mrs. Chiles J. Cridlin, superintendent of Roanoke Valley WMU, called Annie Mae a "nagger" and explained: "She nagged us in Roanoke until we went out to Craig County and started missions work in New Castle which she nursed along when many of us would have given up. Thank God for her nagging!"

A Christmas to Remember

"The week before Christmas [in 1963] fire struck in the Virginia Lee Mining Camp, destroying one home located just a few feet from the George Braxton Taylor Good Will Center. Only because the Junior RA Chapter was there was the center building saved. Louis Cody, the counselor, and the boys carried pails and pans of water from the small creek nearby until the fire truck arrived. They saved the building.

"The house that was destroyed was occupied by the family who had been taking care of the center building. They lost all their own possessions plus the 140 gifts that were wrapped and ready for the Christmas party at the center.

"Under the leadership of Mrs. Earl Hedrick, WMU superintendent, and Alan Moor, pastor of First Church, Pennington Gap, folks went to work to replace the Christmas gifts. A check went out from Woman's Missionary Union of Virginia. On the very day that the group began work to replace the gifts, seven boxes arrived from across the state. One from a Sunbeam Band had the exact number of dolls needed for one age group of girls! Mrs. Hedrick says all the boxes were wonderful, but that surely God had a hand especially in the packing of that one box.

"Between Monday and Sunday 140 packages were assembled and prepared. Every person at the center received a gift. Mrs. Hedrick has written, "We made 140 people at the Good Will Center happy. I just wish every WMU member in our state could have shared this time with us and gotten some of the joy.' "

Religious Herald,
January 23, 1964

Allie Lee Arendall was the first director of the George Braxton Good Will Center, St. Charles.

Spanish children at Santa Fe talk about God's nature. Love reached from the Old Dominion to the Southwestern United States as Virginia WMU supported missions work among the Spanish and Indians.

In 1946, Edith Vaughn of Pulaski served as a state missionary, shown here with a group of her missions children in the Norton area of Wise County. After her work in Virginia, she served on the staff of the WMU Training School in Louisville and later as a foreign missionary in Brazil.

1st Row (L to R) Nell Culver-house, Alice Crutchfield, Gwen Oliff; standing (L to R) Emma Lou McCraw, Laura McFadden.

►►
Elizabeth Thomas served for nearly a quarter-of-a-century as a state missionary in the old Blue Ridge Association.

►*Walter A. Hash, Virginia WMU's first state missionary.*

172

Manassas Baptist Center missionaries Phyllis Weems, Patricia Bailey, and Nell Culverhouse.

Nonie Gravett.

State missionaries employed by Virginia WMU gather at an annual meeting.

Nell Culverhouse (front row, right) surrounded by friends at her retirement reception.

Nell Culverhouse and Allie Candler.

"The Joy of Being a Missionary"

"It is a privilege and a joy to be called a missionary, and the blessings are many. One privilege is that of having my name on the calendar of prayer and knowing that hundreds of people are praying for me and our work on that particular day. Another is the joy of receiving cards and 'love letters' from GAs and other friends. Being a missionary from Virginia has added pleasures, especially in December, as I receive a love check as my part from the Missionaries' Library Fund.

"The real blessings go much deeper. One of these joys is seeing people come to Bible classes and eagerly study God's Word. It is the catch that comes to my throat when I hear a Mexican woman read in English—haltingly, stutteringly, at first—then with more confidence as she continues to learn and proudly stands to read the story of the first Christmas before the other adult women in her class. There is the heart-filling joy of helping a woman become an American citizen, desiring all the more to have her become a citizen of God's eternal Kingdom. There is the inexpressible joy of being able to talk with a young Negro mother and assure her that her baby will be all right because we, too, had the same experience with one of our little ones. Then comes the joy of showing her in God's Word how He provides grace and strength to those who need Him, and of seeing the expression of relieved assurance come over her face as she surrenders to Christ, knowing someone does care for her and her little one. These are the joys that cannot be bought with any kind of money."

Ann B. Woo
Religious Herald, 1968

Carrie S. Vaughan

When Carrie Vaughan was recognized in March, 1975, on her retirement, President Christine Gregory declared the occasion "the Queen's Day." Miss Vaughan, always humble and retiring, beamed as regally as any royalty. In her message at the annual meeting—"Rejoice in the Past, Present and Future"—she traced her spiritual pilgrimage from Sunbeam experiences through youth organizations involvement and finally to personal contact with Blanche Sydnor White, who recognized the potential within her.

In that address she commented: "Mission action is not just looking after our own families and the church family. It is sharing our faith and God's love to those who know not the Father." In her life, Carrie Sinton Vaughan had gently and gracefully led Virginia women in the direction of which she spoke including helping the Indians in New Mexico.

As she departed the office of executive secretary, which she had filled for 17 fruitful years, she expressed several abiding concerns: "That our women and young people may learn truly to abide in Him and to pray without ceasing. That our members may recognize participation in missions is not optional but is an obligation assigned to all believers by Christ Himself. That priority may be given in all our churches to strengthening and enlarging missionary education of young people and that many may be sent out to tell all men everywhere of God's love and His forgiveness. That we may never forget that this work is not ours: it is His."

Carrie Vaughan also "rejoiced in the future," with optimism for the second century of work. She closed her address with I Corin-

thians 15:57–58. "Therefore, my beloved brothers, stand firm and immovable and work for the Lord always, work without limit since you know that in the Lord your labors cannot be lost."

Julian H. Pentecost, editor of the **Religious Herald**, was a colleague in missions education and a close observer of Miss Vaughan's contributions. On her life's work, he commented: "Commitment to missions and missions education has been the hallmark of her years as executive secretary. She has given of herself unreservedly to enlist members in study of, prayer for and gifts to missions. Her interpretation of Christ's Great Commission has rightfully been holistic— from each local 'Jerusalem' to 'the ends of the earth.'

"Through the years she has recognized the necessity of new strategies and methodologies in the teaching and practice of missions. A person of deep convictions, supported by reason and experience, she is capable of discussion and dialogue with persons who disagree with her. She also possesses the maturity to accept and warmly relate to individuals of genuine dedication with whom there is an honest difference of opinion.

"She is sensitive to the needs of other persons, always courteous and gracious. Her capacity to perceive and to be appreciative of the support and efforts of her co-laborers is rare indeed!"

The retirement years were kind to Miss Vaughan. She had admired and appreciated Blanche Sydnor White and wanted the new generation of Virginia women to know of her accomplishments. She and her long-time friend and fellow WMU worker, Mary Lou Burnette, recorded the essence of Miss White's unusual life and captivating personality in their book **For Such A Time As This.**

At the end of her life, Miss Vaughan taught Virginia women yet another lesson, observed by only a few close friends. It was a lesson on how to die. The dignity which characterized her entire life remained dominant as the days narrowed.

"Christ has no way of speaking to the church except through the heart and mind of the individual believer. Surely our thinking has been wrong in dividing mission responsibility between those who go and those who send. Regardless of whether the individual goes or stays, he is under obligation to go and preach the Gospel to all nations."

Carrie S. Vaughan, 1965

Virginia leaders at Ridgecrest are, left to right, *Inez Fletcher, Charlene Staples, Christine Gregory, and Carrie Vaughan.*

Virginia BWC group at Ridgecrest, 1944.

BWC Motorcade visits Eagle Eyrie.

What's In a Name?

The new decade of the 1970s brought change in the WMU, SBC, organization and Virginia WMU followed suit. At the March, 1970, annual meeting of Virginia WMU it was approved that the name of the adult organization would be henceforth "Baptist Women—Missionary Society"; those from high school graduation, or age 18 through 24, would be known as "Baptist Young Women." The children and youth organizations also had new names: Mission Friends, Girls in Action and Acteens.

If local societies had followed the age-grading as recommended by Virginia WMU since 1948, regrouping of children and girls was unnecessary. "Leave organizations just as they are," explained Virginia WMU officials. "New names will be used, but the organizations may stay the same in number and set-up. Primary Sunbeam Band boys remain with the girls and become Children in Action."

Virginia BWC members at Ridgecrest, 1944.

Norma Rock and BWC friends

Centennial!

Fourteen years before WMU, SBC, celebrated its Centennial, Virginia WMU had already experienced its 100th anniversary. For three days in late March, 1974, the sanctuary and chapel of First Church, Richmond, overflowed with "missionary ladies" and with the excitement of being part of history in the making. An estimated 2,500 to 3,000 persons attended the annual meeting which brought a grand and sacred conclusion to 100 days of prayer. The meeting emphasized "worship, praise, recognition and commitment."

Mundus Christo Jubilate—"The World for Christ! Hallelujah" was the Centennial Year's theme, and the March meeting's theme was "Our Mission High Fulfilling," taken from the hymn "O Zion Haste." Editor Julian Pentecost of the *Religious Herald* characterized the event as "wisely conceived and inspirationally implemented" and provided a few carefully chosen words in review of the organization's worth: "The record of Virginia WMU during its first century has been characterized by commitment, cooperation, patience and perseverance. In unnumbered ways, both large and small, they have strengthened the cause of Christ, particularly through their study of missions, their prayer for missions and their gifts to missions."

Imaginative women could pretend they were transported to the founding year of WMU. The "actors" of First Church, Richmond, presented several dramatic episodes from Virginia WMU history. Even the ushers wore period costumes.

On one evening a "Birthday Party" was held and included a procession of Girls in Action and Acteens carrying the banners of each district association. Special recognition was given former executive secretaries, Blanche Sydnor White, who provided *in absentia* a message to the women via a tape recording, and Ellen Douglas Oliver. Three former presidents, Mrs. Stratton, Mrs. Knight, and Mrs. Hancock, were honored with "roses and kisses."

Officers during the Centennial were Mrs. A. Harrison Gregory, president; and Mrs. Chiles J. Cridlin and Mrs. Clifford W. Randall, vice presidents. The annual meeting included presentations by Virginia's own Alma Hunt, then in her 25th and final year as executive secretary of WMU, SBC, as well as by Marie Mathis, president of WMU, SBC. Carrie S. Vaughan, at a high point in her service as executive secretary of Virginia WMU, guided Virginia women to remember the best of their history and to claim the future for expanded mission service. She knew that at the heart of Virginia WMU was one burning theme: "Mundus Christo Jubilate!"➤

Virginia WMU Centennial included a formal tea held at First Baptist Church, Richmond, in March, 1974. Here Betty Sherman, Centennial chairman, visits with Emma Stratton, president, and Retha Tillman.

Admiring a century-old dress at the Centennial are, left to right, *Mrs. R. L. Mathis, Christine B. Gregory and Louise Fletcher.*

Centennial visitors are native Virginian Alma Hunt, left, *and Mrs. R. L. Mathis, both of WMU, SBC, shown here with two GAs, 1974.*

Centennial excitement is registered on the faces of WMU women, left to right, *Marie Van Lear, Rees Watkins and Mrs. L. L. Knight, 1974.*

*Virginia WMU past and future
are represented at the Virginia WMU
Centennial with a young Queen and
former missionary, Olive E. Bagby.*

Juliette Mather happily autographs copies of her Virginia WMU history, Light Three Candles, *1973.*

Virginia WMU Centennial Aided the Zuni

"When the Zuni mission building was decided upon to be the Virginia Centennial Memorial, it was not by chance. For over 40 years Virginia WMU has been involved in the Spanish and Indian work in New Mexico. There is none of this work in which Virginia women have not had some part—a well here, pews there, a building here and song books there.

"In December, 1974, my husband and I visited 'Zuni Baptist Mission.' Our entry into the building was somewhat disappointing for, instead of seeing the eastern chapel-type mission, we saw what resembled a good-sized high school gymnasium. The kitchen was beautiful and several times we were reminded to thank the Virginia women for the kitchen cabinets!

"It was not until well into the dedication service that I fully comprehended the Hand of God in that building. The Governor of the tribe thanked Virginia women, and told of the prayers he and his wife had prayed for 18 years—prayers that some Christian group would place a building on the reservation which would minister to the total personality of the Indian youth. I then recalled Jesus' admonition that He had come to make men whole. In recalling the dozens of Indian youth I had seen that afternoon and evening with nothing to do but walk the streets and get drunk, I saw the desperate need for a place for fun and fellowship and where someone could talk of God's love and feel it among His Children.

"As a beautiful little Indian girl was baptized that afternoon in a small baptistry above the basketball goal, I saw this as a beginning of the countless members who would find in that building a completed life.

"The story is not done. The building thus far has been a labor of love. Virginia gave the money, but many hands did the work."

Christine B. Gregory
Religious Herald
March, 1975

Mrs. O. C. Hancock

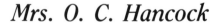da Burroughs Hatcher Hancock was Baptist through and through. Born in 1900 on Jeter Hill in Bedford, she was closely related to J.B. Jeter and W.E. Hatcher, two prominent early Virginia Baptist ministers. She attended the local schools and received advanced education at Radford College and the University of Virginia. In 1933, she married Ollie C. Hancock of Bedford and was thenceforth known by her husband's name as Mrs. O.C. Hancock.

In 1955, when Virginia women gathered for their annual meeting in Roanoke, Mrs. Hancock, a member of First Baptist Church, was their chief hostess. In March, 1956, she was invited to follow Mrs. Knight as president of Virginia WMU. "When the nominating committee presented Mrs. Hancock's name," stated the WMU page in the Herald, *"they did it with a feeling that God had definitely led them to her."*

From 1956 to 1964, she accomplished a great deal in service to Virginia women, including the establishment of three Good Will centers. She was a woman of great dignity and her public presence—in a room or on the platform—was in itself a statement. In her history of Virginia WMU Juliette Mather stated: "She had faced difficult decisions, but looking back, she rejoiced in the marked progress in state missions and the larger part the associational superintendents were taking in the meetings of the Executive Board."

Three presidents in a row, left to right, *Emma Stratton (1964–71), Christine Gregory (1971–75), and Mrs. O. C. Hancock (1956–64).*

Emma Stratton

"*Emma Mantiply Stratton was one of my most unforgettable characters. We became acquainted when I assumed the pastorate of First Church, Waynesboro, in 1957. Since that time our families have enjoyed a warm and meaningful interpersonal relationship.*

"*I knew her as devoted wife and caring mother [and] as faithful and responsible participant in her local church. And I knew her as an informed and committed supporter of our denomination in this state and around the world.*

"*Emma was deeply appreciative of the family into which she was birthed and nurtured. She cherished her memories of the consistent Christian witness of her father and mother. She was profoundly grateful for her family—husband, Eddie, and children, Betty Sue, Edward and Jane. She loved them, encouraged them, did for them, and stood by them.*

"*Emma's most important concern was to be pleasing to her Lord. That was her number one priority. She was careful to maintain devotional disciplines and to be loyal to church commitments.*

"*'Miss Emma,' as she was affectionately called by some of us, had a special knack for establishing and maintaining close personal friends. She took time for them through personal visits, telephone calls, letters and cards. Keeping in touch was important to her.*

"*Emma Stratton could walk with those in the most prominent places of denominational and civic influence or with those of modest means and ability and be equally comfortable.*

"*Her record of involvement in Christian missions is indeed impressive. It began and it should have begun, in her local church—her beloved First Baptist Church of Waynesboro. It moved beyond there into the Augusta Association and subsequently, into the Baptist General Association of Virginia and the Southern Baptist Convention.*

"*Emma was unreservedly committed to the Great Commission of her Lord. She was convinced that commission had her name upon it, calling for her time, her ability, her prayers and her money. No place of denominational involvement afforded her more genuine satisfaction than her service as a trustee of the SBC Foreign Mission Board.*

"*She could not have done all she did in Baptist life without the understanding and support of her husband and children and she knew it. Her experience of family undergirding is a reminder that only those who have been recipients of grace* within *family can be channels of grace* beyond *family.*"

Julian H. Pentecost
Religious Herald
August 14, 1986

She was a tall, commanding figure who would embrace her fellow Baptists with bear hugs and obvious concern. She opened her heart and her home, that landmark on Afton Mountain, to everyone who came calling. She opened her hands for generous giving of self and means.

Emma Mantiply Stratton was a woman of service. She provided sterling service as president of Virginia WMU, from 1964 until 1971. In November, 1970, still ahead of her times, she was nominated by a man, Howard Lee of Danville, for president of the Baptist General Association of Virginia, the first woman ever nominated for the Virginia office. Four others—all men—were nominated. Although the votes were fairly evenly distributed on the first ballot, by the second ballot, she had lost.

In 1972, she was again nominated. Theodore Adams of Richmond urged the messengers present at the Virginia Beach meeting to break precedent and begin the General Association's Sesquicentennial with a woman as first vice-president. This time, there were three men in the balloting, but the times were ripe for Emma Stratton's election. She was possibly the first woman to hold the office of vice-president of an association or state group within the SBC.

Denominational affairs had been "a man's world"; if a woman were going to work effectively in that world, she needed the valued experience provided by WMU. "Miss Emma" moved very assuredly through a man's world, blazing the trail for those to follow.

Virginia's office staff and president meet with WMU, SBC leaders. Pictured, left to right, are Alma Hunt, executive secretary of WMU, SBC; Sue Hutton, GA secretary; Emma Stratton, Virginia WMU president; Carrie S. Vaughan, Virginia's executive secretary; Rees Watkins, young people's secretary; and Marie Mathis, president, WMU, SBC, 1971.

*M*any times, the Executive Board filled up the choir loft during the annual meetings as they "backed up" their officers during the business sessions.

Christine B. Gregory:
At the Height of Service to WMU

*T*he unpretentious Cape Cod style *house on Franklin Turnpike outside Danville is an unlikely head-quarters for an internationally known and highly involved leader of one of the nation's largest religious bodies. There is a vegetable garden to tend in the growing season, yardwork to be done, dishes to be washed. It could be anyone's home. Yet from these modest scenes plans are made which affect denominational affairs.*

Only a scrapbook casually placed on a bookcase gives visible evidence of a busy life. There are many items tucked in the pages by a woman too busy to paste in the clippings: a candid snapshot taken with Theodore Adams, a former world leader among Baptists; a press photo taken on an SBC platform with Bailey Smith, a recent president of SBC; a color photo taken "bird's eye" of that diverse group of Baptist folks who comprised the SBC "Peace Committee"; and the cover of Royal Service *in 1975, showing the newly-elected president of WMU, SBC, from Virginia, Christine B. Gregory.*

A housewife in the 1950s whose full potential emerged in the 1970s and 1980s, she always preferred her married name, Mrs. A. Harrison Gregory. Anyone who has ever met her loving and supportive husband, "Greg," instantly knows why. He is the one who pridefully shares the news that she has been placed in her hometown high school's hall of fame along with distinguished judges and politicians.

The couple met at a training union party on New Year's Eve during Christine's student days at Winthrop College. But it was 10 years before they decided to marry. Greg explained: "I had to get an education, fight a war, and get a job so I could keep her in the way in which she was accustomed to living or her Daddy might object." Even after 41 years of marriage there is still a spark of magic between the two, evident in secret winks and warm smiles. "Greg has been the biggest plus I have," she confesses. "I am who I am because of who he is."

Their home is "lived in." Although their three sons are long gone, it remains a homeplace—warm, inviting, cozy, comfortable—like its owners. But make no mistake, the house is solid, formidable, again like its owners.

On the dining room wall is a hand-stitched hanging made, interestingly enough, by a son, Harry. It shows places important in his mother's life including Averett College, the local Baptist school where she has served as an advisor; First Baptist Church, Danville, which has been the family's local community of faith since coming to the city; and the house on Franklin Turnpike.

From this house Christine made weekly trips to Richmond in the months between Carrie Vaughan's retirement and Kathryn Bullard's arrival when, as president of Virginia WMU she sought to keep buoyant the confidence in the organization. From this house she made countless trips to Greensboro for air flights to Birmingham during her long and demanding presidency of the national women's missionary organization from 1975 to 1981. From this house the couple made the annual trek to wherever the SBC was holding its yearly meeting. It was at the 1981 meeting that Christine Gregory was tapped as first vice-president of the Convention. At first she resisted even the suggestion of such service, until she spoke with her long-tine mentor, L.D. Johnson, in the crowded convention center. He put it plainly: "But you must!" She reflects that "without that push" she would not have given assent to place her name in nomination.

From 1982 to 1983, as president of the Baptist General Association of Virginia, the first woman to hold the office since the group's founding in 1823, she filled speaking engagements across the state from rural churches to big city ones. Often accompanied by Greg, she would repeatedly depart early on a Sunday morning to drive across Virginia for some church service.

Christine Gregory received the Christian Citizenship Award from the trustees of the Religious Herald. *At the luncheon hosted in her honor are Mrs. Gregory and Editor Julian H. Pentecost, 1985.*

From her suburban house in southside Virginia she traveled widely and frequently on Baptist business. In 1985, with the denomination almost rent from controversy, a "Peace Committee" was appointed and Christine was one of only two women assigned to the strategic committee. She went to the Baptist summit meetings, leaving tranquil rural Virginia to join the committee in considering the forces dividing the Convention.

Reflecting upon the whole sweeping range of the SBC controversy, she surmises: "You cannot speak to every issue. You have to choose your issues and then you have to speak in such a way that you never undercut someone else if you want to be heard. I am afraid that we often do not extend the courtesy to others that we expect for ourselves." She established a personal mission to secure a friendship with a vocal leading figure in the controversy. And she, one on one, was successful.

Christine Burton Gregory was a woman of rare abilities long before coming to Virginia. Growing up in Greenville, South Carolina, she experienced a strong church-going influence in her mother, Bessie H. Burton. "She set every example that you would want a mother to set," remembers the daughter, "and she saw to it that we went to the [missionary] meetings." She also credits her pastor's

wife, who was her GA leader, as a strong influence. Mrs. E.P. Driggers encouraged her husband to invite missionaries to share his pulpit and then to help the young people at East Park Baptist Church meet the visiting missionaries. Christine's parents made sacrifices in the post-Depression times to enable their daughter to attend summer mission camps and participate in all the activities. Christine, elected to a state BSU office, fulfilled the duties of that early position as seriously as the demands of later top national offices.

When the Gregorys moved to Danville, they came under the loving watchcare of Marion and L.D. Johnson. The popular pastor of First Baptist Church and his wife "took us under their wings," as Christine has termed it, and encouraged the couple to keep an open mind, examining all sides to a question and accepting individuals at odds with their own particular viewpoint. For awhile Christine "filled in" as religious education director at the Danville church, where she developed skills in motivating and teaching people. Another local pastor, Luke Smith, made a significant impact on Christine's life. "He had the capacity to stretch your mind," she reflects and adds that "he could do it without your ever being really aware of it." From a distance she observed Virginia WMU leaders, among them Mrs. George R. Martin, whom she greatly respected as "the parliamentarian of all the parliamentarians." Soon Christine joined the ranks of those serving in major offices.

During her presidency of Virginia WMU, Christine Gregory had two chief objectives. "I felt the tenure needed to be set for officers.

We were bringing young women up to a point and then there was nothing for them to do." Solving that problem, she tackled another. "We had talked over and over about the church-wide offerings and I knew that there would be a time when we would not have to push [the matter] so hard." In time, massive resistance turned to genuine acceptance and, finally, to change. She also shared the dream of establishing a camp which could be used throughout the year.

At the height of a large and useful denominational service, Christine Burton Gregory reaffirms her affiliation: "Even at our worst, I am glad I am a Baptist," she shares, "because I still have the freedom to fuss and say and do what I think is right. No one has ever made me feel that [a certain way] is the way I have to believe. As a Baptist I still have the choice of freedom."

Christine Gregory has approached her relationship within the denomination as a Christian servant. Once during her presidency of the General Association she provided her personal philosophy as follows: "To know Christ is to serve. A servant takes risks. A servant is open to ridicule but a servant is also open to joys of service. A servant takes the risk of rejection but the important thing in service is ferreting out the person of no charisma and building him up until he blossoms. It is only under the power of the Holy Spirit that we can serve."

Continuously since 1971, Christine Gregory has fulfilled the role of Christian servant through state and national denominational service. The lady on Franklin Turnpike has been mighty busy!

Southern Baptist missionary Georgia Mae Ogburn interprets Christine Gregory's message for the members of First Baptist Church, Santiago, Chile. Mrs. Gregory traveled the world over for WMU. (Photo by James Lee Young)

Chapter 5

The Years of Expectation,
1975–1988

*A*fter her first month in office, Kathryn Bullard, in an open letter to Virginia WMU, told her fellow members that her days had been "filled with many exciting and challenging experiences." She drew on the distant past for guidance, sharing a statement from the first paid leader, Mrs. Julian P. Thomas, whom she quoted: "Shall we learn from our successes where our strength lies and from our failures wherein our weakness? If we shall do this, we have heard the voice of God calling us to Go Forward."

Kathryn Bullard built upon the solid foundation of WMU's past, while helping Virginia women to construct new programs for the future. While she encouraged the women to "move boldly toward new goals," she recognized that Christianity faced great contests. "Never has the church in our lifetime been tested more than today," she once observed. But Miss Bullard saw the tests as challenges "to strengthen the home base for missions."

In 1975, during her first year as executive secretary of WMU, SBC, Carolyn Weatherford made the first of numerous visits to Virginia and sounded high themes: "Today is the greatest time in history to be alive." Reminding Virginia women that their foremothers of the 1880s were the "feminists of their day," the national leader declared: "We have found our place! We have education. We have money. We are liberated! We don't have to fight back anymore. In Christ we have found freedom."

Yet another key leader challenged Virginia women. In 1979, Bobbie Sorrill, director of the education division of WMU, SBC, returned home to Virginia and issued five challenges in a resounding message: "Keep the purpose of mission education clear and unchanged; establish priorities; make wise, quality plans; pray for the presence of the Lord in our lives and for laborers for the harvest; and pray for the power of God."

The leadership thus communicated to Virginia women the expectation of great tasks to be executed. From organizational changes and policy shifts, including the momentous change regarding church-wide offerings, to new directions for ministry, it was generally agreed that Woman's Missionary Union, Auxiliary to the Baptist General Association of Virginia, remained a viable force for good.

One of the most visible signs of expectancy was in the fulfillment of "the Great Camp Vision," which resulted in the closing of existing camps and consolidation into one centrally-located new facility.

> "It is time for us to look back and evaluate and continue to build upon the solid mission foundations of the past. It is also a time to look forward, listen to the voice of God, and move boldly toward new goals."
>
> Kathryn Bullard,
> 1975

It was an era of sterling leadership from presidents, Christine B. Gregory, Mary Jane Thurman, Jane Clarke, Jean N. Woodward, and Margaret Wayland. Mrs. Gregory gave Virginia WMU renewed pride as she led in wider circles, including top leadership posts in the BGAV, SBC, and BWA. Other leaders in the period included Rebecca Cridlin, Kitty Martin, Ruby Vest, Cornelia Rayhorn, Alleen Wheeless, Ethel Dickerson, Phyllis Randall, Helen Simms, Emily Daniel, Dolores Bailey, Marie Bailey, Frances C. DeFoe, Thelma Kiser, Elizabeth Axselle, Martha Hudgins, Mildred Jenkins, Mary Cherry, Louise Harris, Norma Rock, Edna Bradley, Helen Riley, Susan Grant, Madelyn Jones, and Weeksie Carmines. In the state office several gave devoted service, including Rees Watkins, who served under four executives. Several new staff members also added creative touches to the on-going direction of WMU programs and activities.

In gathering up the years the volume closes with 1988, the year of the grand Centennial of WMU, SBC. Observed locally by WMU groups and in associations and in the state meetings, the Centennial came to an impressive finale in Richmond on May 13 and 14, 1988, when some 11,000 women, and a few men, came from across the world to participate in the event. It was a fitting close to an era of great expectations as the women observed "A Century to Celebrate—A Future to Fulfill."

Virginia WMU: Its Purpose

At the 1982 annual meeting the Constitution was reworded to reflect the following expression of Virginia WMU's purpose which "shall be to promote Christian Missions by training the associational and church WMU leadership to teach missions, to engage in missions action and personal witnessing, to support missions and to interpret and undergird the work of the church and the denomination to women, girls and preschool children."

"Step by Step—By Step!"
A History of the Clinchco Mission

"When WMU became interested in a spiritual ministry in Dickenson County, the church at Clintwood was the only functioning Baptist church. For three summers, 1938–40, Baptist young women, under the leadership of Louise Fletcher conducted Vacation Bible Schools in the mining community of Clinchco. WMU wanted to establish a permanent work but all properties were owned by the mining company which refused to sell. By 1959, policies had changed and the company was selling houses in the community. WMU bought three houses on adjoining lots—remodeled one for the missionary home and the other two for mission center activities.

"Emma Lou McCraw was WMU's first full-time missionary to serve in the area. In 1960 Laura McFadden joined Miss McCraw to make a great team. Under the leadership of these missionaries, the work grew—men, women, youth and children participated.

"In 1962, with resources from the State Missions Offering, WMU purchased another lot next to the existing property and constructed a church building in which members and families of the center could worship.

"Anticipating the retirement of Emma Lou McCraw and with the resignation of Laura McFadden, who accepted employment at the Baptist Children's Home, WMU conducted a study to see what goals

Clinchco Chapel was built next to the Good Will Center cottages.

should be for the 1980s. Believing that the members of the Clinchco Baptist Mission had reached a point in history when it was time to look toward being constituted into a church, it was the findings and recommendations of the WMU Executive Board that guidance and help from a sponsoring church, the association, and the Division of Ministries of the General Board was needed.

"At the request of WMU, Clintwood Baptist Church agreed to sponsor the mission. Monetary assistance was given from Wise Association, and the General Board gave its support as well as WMU. The group of believers at Clinchco took another step forward and called a full-time pastor."

Religious Herald
January 3, 1980

Two visitors from Colombia, South America WMU visit Virginia WMU state offices. Fannie de Perez, president, and Amparo de Medina, executive secretary, to the right under the portrait, toured America in 1981.

Remembering WMU's Richmond Roots

On May 14, 1981, a group of Baptists and their special Methodist guests, including two bishops, gathered on Broad Street in downtown Richmond to commemorate the events of another May 14th so long ago. It was the 93rd anniversary to the day of the founding of Woman's Missionary Union, Auxiliary to the Southern Baptist Convention, in a borrowed hall at the Broad Street Methodist Church. The brethren of the SBC in those days of woman-less annual meetings were in session about two blocks away in the First Baptist Church.

A permanent marker was unveiled at the site where the church was located across the street from the present-day City Hall. The occasion attracted numerous Baptist leaders, including representatives from 12 of the 15 states present for the first meeting. The event offered a small preview of larger things to come when the WMU, SBC Centennial would be held in Richmond in 1988.

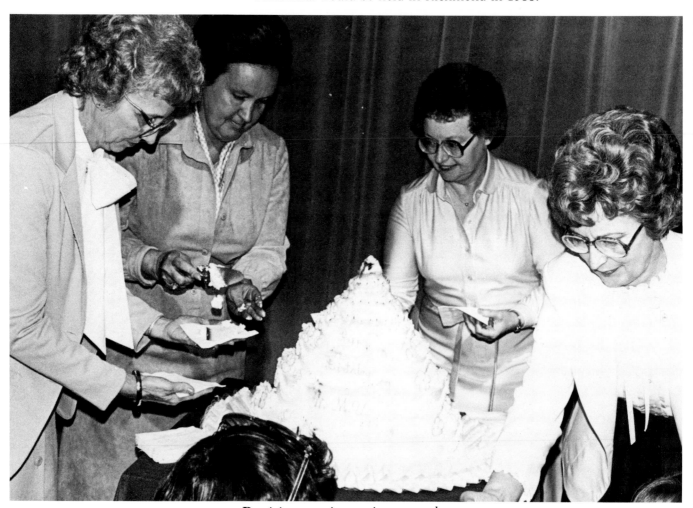

Participants enjoy anniversary cake.

*B*ronze plaque presented to Broad Street Methodist Church in the Jubilee year of 1938. In recent years it was presented to WMU, SBC.

A large group gathered on Broad Street in downtown Richmond for the placing of a marker at the site of organization of WMU, SBC.

Methodist Trustee, Fred C. Forberg and Kathryn Bullard at Marker Dedication.

Keith Parks, president of the Foreign Mission Board, SBC, was present for the occasion.

Christine Gregory and Carolyn Weatherford light the candles for the 93rd anniversary celebration.

Alma Hunt presented one of her captivating speeches on WMU history at the anniversary banquet.

Marjorie Bailey And Her Tough Love

*M*arjorie Lee Bailey, a state missionary, was a trailblazer. When she was ordained to the Gospel ministry in 1972, she was the first woman ordained by a Virginia Baptist church and the third in the SBC. An all-male council examined the candidate and unanimously recommended her ordination by Bainbridge Street Church, Richmond. After missions work in the Baptist Center of Richmond Association, she found her life's calling among the inmates of Virginia's correctional facilities. Again she would be listed among the "firsts." She served as chaplain at the Virginia Correctional Center for Women in Goochland for over 20 years; in 1977, on becoming senior chaplain at the Virginia State Penitentiary in Richmond, she was believed to be the first female chaplain in the United States to serve in an adult maximum security prison. She earned the respect of the male prisoners and some on "death row" even requested her to witness their executions.

Virginia WMU had a part in Marjorie's missions career by the inclusion within the State Missions Offering of funds for the Chaplain Service of the Churches of Virginia. Marjorie could go where few others could; therefore through her ministry, Virginia WMU members went behind the bars in maximum security prisons to carry a helping and comforting ministry. Marjorie Bailey exhibited what someone has called "tough love." From her missions center work in 1951 throughout all the years "behind bars" when she served over 1,200 prisoners until her death in 1988, she loved and cared and served with intensity. The following are remembrances from two adult male prisoners:

"I met Chaplain Bailey in 1979 at the Virginia State Penitentiary. I had only recently accepted Christ; and while I didn't know much of my new-found faith, I was sure I had all the answers. I often spent more time talking than listening during our early relationship. I often undercut and opposed her. I had heard, 'Women aren't supposed to preach,' yet Chaplain Bailey was my staunchest supporter in my opposition although I made her job much more difficult. She taught me valuable lessons—tolerance and acceptance of others and forgiveness.

"One day Chaplain Bailey overheard a conversation between another inmate and me and my language was not the kind you hear in Sunday school. I explained to her that I had actually been telling the guy about why he should come to the chapel. I had spoken as I did because that was the language he used and understood. She simply smiled and said, 'It isn't the way I would do it, but I won't say it is wrong.' I had never heard any Christian be so accepting and I began to look at her in a new light.

"Eventually, through her constant efforts to be both a friend and a minister and to include me in chapel activities, I became aware that she loved me in spite of everything. Because I had been so public in my opposition, I felt that I should be public in my apology. One night in chapel I publicly confessed the error of my actions and asked her to forgive me. With typical grace, charm, and love, her face split into a big ear-to-ear grin, and she hugged me and said, 'It's okay. I knew all along you would make it, Brother.' She had been forgiving me all along and I just hadn't realized it. She made a difference in my life."

Tony

"As senior chaplain, Marjorie conducted Sunday worship services and it was while attending one of those services that I first met her. I had no inkling of how significant she would become in my life.

"She later exercised trust by arranging my assignment as chapel aide. I was one of her 'rascals' for years and she knew my heart and my secrets as no one else.

"When I met Marjorie I was a new-born Christian with no real strength in Christ or direction in my life. My time shared with her brought out strength and loyalties within me that I did not realize existed.

"One situation carried the probability of violence and Marjorie knew it. The problem dissipated and later I asked her, 'Why didn't you do something . . . why didn't you have me transferred?' Her reply was, 'I was not worried. I felt that I was enough to hold you!'

"Whenever I was about to do something wrong, she used to say firmly, 'I wish you wouldn't! I wish you wouldn't!' She knew I would never go against her wishes."

"Clyde"

Expecting Great Things

The era from 1975 to 1988 thrived upon high notes of great expectancy. Missions work in familiar fields was enhanced and new areas opened, while the revamping of the camping program resulted in one new central camp through concentrated and sacrificial efforts of Virginia women. The women held steady anticipation of increased enrollment through Vision '88, a membership enlargement campaign, and of celebrating their shared organization's heritage with the Centennial to culminate in 1988 with a world-wide focus upon its origins in Virginia. ➤

Mrs. Candy Phillips

Executive Board.

Mrs. Mildred Jenkins

Geneva Thomas

Mrs. Dorothy Allen.

Early in the era two significant changes were made with far-reaching effects. First, the Virginia WMU Board was re-structured to give all Board members more involvement in making decisions. Secondly, Virginia WMU adopted the WMU, SBC, plan of work which included church-wide offerings.

With activities throughout the year, every season held something new. In March of each year the annual meeting continued as the great focal point of activities, as motivating themes and dynamic speakers encouraged large attendance. The women conducted their business sessions with dispatch and harmony while delegates expressed their concerns and opinions. The program highlighted inspirational features which made the "women's meetings" often stand in contrast to the state and national Baptist meetings which became increasingly absorbed with the "political" changes and problems within the SBC.

Dramatic sketches enliven an annual meeting, as Sarah Tatum of First Baptist Church, Roanoke, portrays an early WMU leader.

A sampling of themes through the years reflects the emphasis: "You Shall Receive . . . and Witness," 1979; "The Gift of God Within Me," 1980; "Commit . . . Trust . . . Live," 1981; "Given to Become," 1983; "Laborers Together with God," 1985; "Gifted to Serve," 1987; and in the year of the national organization's Centennial, "Constant Through the Ages," 1988.

Outstanding program personalities over the years included Carolyn Weatherford, Bobbie Sorrill, and Catherine Allen of the WMU, SBC, staff and Mary Saunders, Christine Gregory, Dorothy Sample, Carrie S. Vaughan, Helen Jean Parks, Mildred McWhorter, Alma Hunt, Gerhard Claas, Winnie Pearce, Edith Vaughn, Marjorie McCullough, Peter James Flamming, Roberta Dorr, Barbara Joiner, Wendell Belew, Beverly Sutton, Edna Frances Dawkins, Beth MacClaren, Sara Ann Hobbs, Nancy Curtis, Carolyn and Claude Rhea, and Edna Lee deGutierrez.

Standing before the watchword banner, "Laborers Together With God," president Jean Woodward's daughter, Claire, offers a prayer on behalf of the officers, staff and members of Virginia WMU.

Checking her watch to ensure arriving at an annual meeting session on time is Cornelia Rayhorn shown here with Beulah Hooper.

Several WMU members gather for an annual meeting held in Richmond.

In the spring, Acteens looked forward to their "Weekenders" at Eagle Eyrie. Just like the "old days" when YWAs would gather at camp to learn and laugh, these were times for fun and fellowship. Thankfully, some things never changed!

The 1978 Acteens Weekender featured a "Missions Mania" experience. The girls presented missions work throughout the world by using costumes, playing games, staging puppet shows, displaying flags, and playing music.

Executive director of the Virginia Baptist General Board, Richard M. Stephenson, was a frequent visitor at WMU meetings.

"Clowning Around" at an Acteens Weekender!

Missions volunteer team to Colombia.

In the summer a week of activities was planned for the WMU at Eagle Eyrie, the state Baptist assembly grounds. These were opportunities for Bible study, mission study, leadership training, and "plenty of Christian fellowship." The relaxed setting atop the little mountain overlooking Lynchburg offered a retreat where Baptist women assembled from across Virginia, learned from each other and established lasting friendships through work and study. It was a time to meet missionaries; through the years, special guests included Linda M. Bridges, Taiwan; Barbara Deal, Colombia; Bonita Leary, a missionary serving in New York under the HMB; Sarah Scanlon, Guatemala; Linda Boswell, Peru; Marian Phillips, Nigeria; Jean R. McEntire, Paraguay; Anna Keeling, a state missionary assigned to the Norfolk area; Lucy Wagner, Korea; Virginia Highfill, Japan; Ada Young, a home missionary serving in New England; G.C. and Pat Harbuck, the language missionaries serving in the Richmond area; Martha McAlister, Tanzania; Betty Vaught, Hong Kong; Sarah Williams, India; "Virginia WMU's own" Jean Teague, Japan; Lois Woodson, Chile; Harriett Lennon, Thailand; Linda Rice, Uganda; Evelyn Berry, a home missionary serving in a Baptist center in Richmond; Betsy Herman, Ecuador; Lillian Isaacs, a home missionary serving in Florida; Marie Van Lear, Nigeria; Joyce Wyatt, Colombia; Hazel Watson, Japan; Martha Franks, Taiwan; Nancy Hern, Lebanon; Carol Leigh Humphries, Nigeria; Arlene McGlamery, Colombia, Gaza, and India; Mary Ann Davis, Paraguay; Annette Hall, Gaza; Dottie Williamson, church planter with HMB; Mary Ellen Divers, Argentina; Cornelia Leavell, Hong Kong; and Ann Dwyer, Yemen. Other outstanding speakers included Alma Hunt, Baker James Cauthen, Malcolm Tolbert, Helen Falls, Ken Chafin, Isam Ballenger, David Burhans, John Jonsson, Julian H. Pentecost, Theodore F. Adams, and Beverly Hammack. ➤

The WMU camera catches the action at Eagle Eyrie events.

"Vision 88" was the WMU, SBC, bold new enlistment plan to secure new members.

Virginia WMU staff and leaders visit the quilting workshop of the Powell River Association.

Christmas-in-August, conceived of by Virginia WMU, remained a project of Virginia women in the 1970s and 1980s. Girls and women sent packages to the mission fields, a project which was really a celebration. "Children, bearing gifts, learn the joy of sharing with others," promoted *Virginia Lines*, the official newsletter of Virginia WMU. "Help them celebrate the love of Jesus by giving to others."

At the era's opening, Virginia WMU continued operating Good Will centers at Clinchco, Trammel, and Manassas. In 1978, the Baptist Center at Manassas was enlarged with construction of office and storage space and a deck. In time the relationship shifted and responsibility for the center was given to the Potomac Association.

Interracial understanding and cooperation remained a priority of Virginia WMU. In 1977, a conference was held at Eagle Eyrie sponsored by the Interracial Administrative Committee of Baptist Women in Virginia, the group contributing so much through the years to greater interracial understanding. It was aimed at attracting "Baptist Women and high school girls who are interested in learning to know women and girls of other Baptist conventions and in participating together in missionary endeavors." Among the program's personalities were Theodore Adams, the beloved pastor emeritus of First Church, Richmond; Cessar Scott, then with the Virginia Baptist General Board; Norma Burruss, a missionary to Liberia through the Baptist General Convention; and Dora Mae Moss, a home missionary in the SBC.

By 1976, Camp Carey, the WMU-operated camp for black girls, was closed "due to lack of interest." Virginia WMU had not, however, forgotten the needs of black youth. The Fletcher Mae Howell Scholarship Fund provided funds for black students to attend college.

In 1977, Virginia WMU was recognized by the WMU, SBC, as second only to South Carolina in the percentage of churches with WMU organizations. The plaque passed from Virginian to Virginian as Christine Gregory, president of the national organization, presented the award to Mary Jane Thurman, Virginia's president.

White Cross remained an area of practical missions for Virginia women. In 1980, *Virginia Lines* carried letters of appreciation from several Baptist hospitals. "It would be very difficult to carry on much of our work without the assistance in providing bandages," reported the Baptist Medical Centre in Ghana; Eku Hospital, Nigeria, reported over 76,000 patients in a year's time and appreciated Virginia's gift of rolled bandages; Gaza Hospital used Virginia's "sheet bandages."

An exciting international friendship developed between 1981 and 1982. In March, 1981, two leaders from the Colombia WMU, Mrs. Fanny de Perez, president, and Mrs. Amparo de Medina, executive secretary, visited Virginia WMU. That following January, Virginia WMU accepted an invitation from its Colombian sisters to visit their country. Representing Virginia WMU were Jane Clarke, president, accompanied by her husband, George, Kathryn Bullard, and Peggy Smith. Miss Bullard chose the theme "Send Me" and the text of Isaiah 6:8 for her address before the Colombia WMU, "La Union Feminil Bautista de Colombia." Missionary Mrs. Zach Deal translated Miss Bullard's message. The Virginia women presented leadership training sessions for the Colombian women; and they visited the foreign missionaries with Virginia ties.

Lasting ties were forged between Virginia WMU and the Colombian women. The Virginia Acteens wanted to participate and in 1982 sent half of their Weekender offering for Colombian youth.

Another international contact was made in March, 1985, when Kathryn Bullard journeyed to Hong Kong to participate in the dedication of the Blanche Sydnor White Library at the Baptist Seminary. The gift had been approved by the Virginia Union in 1973 as part of the Centennial Offering. Miss Bullard reported: "The missionaries, many of the Chinese leaders, and the Seminary's president asked me to express their profound appreciation for your love and financial gift."

The plaque in Hong Kong records Virginia's contributions.

Yet another opportunity came in 1987 as Virginia WMU participated in the Virginia-Tanzania Partnership, providing over $33,000 for "food, linens, pots, pans, and other equipment." The gifts of Virginia WMU helped undergird the many volunteers who served from Virginia.

President Jean Woodward presents a check to Bill Russ for Tanzania missionary support.

Margaret Wayland and Alleen Wheeless receive gifts from local women on a visit to Tanzania.

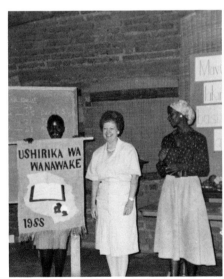

Banner made by Executive Board of Virginia WMU presented to a Tanzania women's group recognized for achievement.

Among the period's highlights were special conferences sponsored by Virginia WMU in 1979 and again in 1983 for ministers, their spouses, and children. The overall purpose of the family-centered conferences, which were aimed at younger pastors, was to stir anew a

commitment to missions. These also encouraged fellowship between WMU staff, officers and the ministers, and helped create contacts from which lasting relationships could be strengthened.

Possibly no other denominational service received as much attention and improvement in this period than did the camps. The era began with the three existing camps, Baptist Lodge, Viewmont, and The Cedars, and closed with the successful operation of one contrally-located new camp in the beautiful mountains of Amherst County. The story of Camp Little Cross Roads is a saga of vision, sacrifice and commitment.

In 1986, Virginia WMU staff relocated to the new Virginia Baptist Building on Emerywood Parkway. The new facility offered expanded office space for the Union. ➤

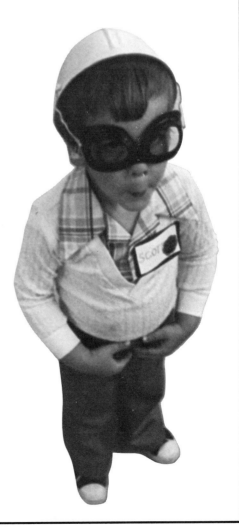

Acteens on the go.

Muriel Butler displays Centennial quilt made by the women of First Baptist Church, Bristol.

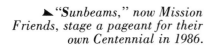
▲ *"Sunbeams," now Mission Friends, stage a pageant for their own Centennial in 1986.*

The future of WMU is found in its young women and children.

Beginning in 1987, Virginia women joined their sisters in the larger Southern Union to study their common history and to affirm their heritage. It was the initiation of the WMU, SBC Centennial, the biggest event in the history of an organization full of grand events. Local WMUs were recording and writing their histories. Women were reading Catherine Allen's superb history of the national organization. Everyone was making costumes, staging dramas, holding missions

fairs, making quilts, and drawing posters. And they were making plans to descend upon Richmond, Virginia, for the grand Centennial weekend of May 14, 1988. Virginia would play hostess once more to SBC women and this time over 11,000 would come calling. Kitty Martin served as Virginia's State Centennial chairman. Virginia women also gave nearly $70,000 to the WMU, SBC Centennial Thank Offering. June Bass was chairman of the Local Arrangements Committee for the national Centennial celebration in Richmond, which entailed the enlistment of many sub-chairmen as well as hundreds of committee members.

Gathering up the years of 1975 through 1988, it is evident that Virginia women were expecting great things for their future. Kathryn Bullard touched upon that future in her dedicatory remarks for Camp Little Cross Roads. She quoted another when she said: " 'Vision, purpose, and missions are closely related. Vision is the perception of a need, a sense of call to do something about the need, and the confidence the need will be alleviated. Purpose is an individual's or an organization's reason for being. Mission flows out of vision and purpose.' " The members of Virginia WMU had caught the vision, were secure in the purpose, and moved ahead from victory to victory.

June Bass coordinated the local arrangements in Richmond of the national Centennial Celebration.

The Great Camp Vision

Since 1917, Virginia WMU had operated summer camps as training grounds in missions education, group fellowship and personal commitment. Three great camps developed across the state: Baptist Lodge by the sea, Viewmont in the central Piedmont, and The Cedars in the mountains.

Visiting the construction site are, left to right, *Kay Maroney, Frances Appel, Elizabeth Axselle* and *Emma Hutchins.*

Plans are revealed for Camp Little Cross Roads.

After a thorough study from 1974 to 1977, the 1978 annual meeting featured a recommendation regarding a major change in WMU camps. The proposal was to sell the existing camp properties and purchase a larger site in a central location. Instead of three camps, Virginia WMU would operate one camp in a year-round facility. Cornelia Rayhorn, as chairman of the Long Range Camp Committee, delivered the report, which emphasized the rising operations costs for three camps needing "extensive repairs and renovations" to meet regulations. The committee recommended in 1979 operating only Viewmont while the other other camps were being sold. It also suggested the appointment of a fund-raising committee. With the approval of the proposals, the "Great Camp Vision" began to unfold.

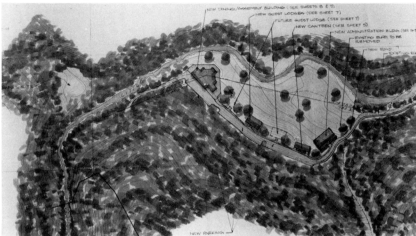

June Bass, left, and Kathryn Bullard break ground for the camp.

In 1981, 423 acres bordering the George Washington National Forest were purchased in Amherst County. At the May, 1981, Executive Board meeting a fund-raising plan was adopted. The WMU membership was asked for commitments over three years. The camp funds were to be over and above the regular contributions. The Virginia women who removed denominational debts, financed buildings at home and abroad for many causes, and early learned the value of small change, of pennies, nickels, and quarters were called upon to give in dramatic proportions. A promotional statement declared: "Investing in a project like the camp is another way of sharing the resources which God has entrusted to us. [It] is eternal in the end results. Many respond to God's call to Christian service and some to career missions . . . others [experience] examination and renewal. Any commitment that draws a person closer to the Lord has eternal values."

The majority of Virginia women embraced the new plan with their usual enthusiasm. Several women reported special promotional methods used in their groups: Anna Sanders of Warsaw Church commented that they made "tree bookmarks" to give to each member "as a reminder of her pledge"; Mrs. H.W. Halstead of Grove Park, Portsmouth, had a tree design cut from plywood and painted green as the group met its goal; Mrs. Edwin Watson of Virginia Heights, Norfolk, reported that "We are making offering boxes for the small children." A small paper bank was even designed to resemble a log cabin for children's gifts. The GAs of First Church, West Point, sponsored a *"movie show,"* and requested and received money for the camp. Women across the state began to share the vision.

Through the local WMU organizations, Virginia WMU established two levels of goals, *"silver"* and *"gold."* By 1982, it was reported that the Southside Association had the highest percentage participating with 12 of the 23 WMUs accepting target goals.

In the spring of 1983, Kathryn Bullard appealed for increased support. "We must make it happen," she urged. "That simply means *everyone* sharing. Missionaries testify to the importance of the camp-

ing experiences in their lives as they have responded to God's call to career missions. Leaders recall with enthusiasm the contribution a camping experience has meant in their lives. Parents have stated that attending the WMU camps has brought about definite changes in the lives of their children." She added: "History will reveal that WMU's finest hours have been in the camping program. God has blessed this work with nearly 90,000 campers over a 65–year period."

By mid-1983, the Executive Board had sufficient funds to warrant beginning the camp's construction. The funds at the time amounted to $1.5 million towards a goal of over $2.6 million in the first section of Phase One of construction. J.E. Jamerson and Sons of Appomattox were chosen as the contractors. Finally contracts were signed, and in 1984, June Bass, chairman of the Building Committee, and Kathryn Bullard donned hardhats for the groundbreaking. Still more money was needed and continued appeals were made. Many responded. Four cabin meeting units were given by families in memory of loved ones; one lady at retirement gave her accumulated sick leave pay "because God had blessed her with good health."

For six months in 1984, Virginia women responded to a request for submissions suggesting names for the new camp. Out of over 100 submissions, one stood out. The Executive Board approved the name of Camp Little Cross Roads, a reminder of Lottie Moon's house in China, purchased in Virginia WMU's formative years by Virginia women. The name also "would symbolize the crossroads a girl may come to at camp and the life-changing commitments that can be made there." The camp, too, had been placed in the literal center of the state, at the crossroads of Virginia.

The camp fund was boosted when Richmond WMU donated proceeds from its sale of the House of Happiness Good Will Center property. The money funded a guest lodge, named after the former House of Happiness. ➤

Camp Staff

After years of preparation, the day of dedication had arrived on a Saturday in June, 1985. In her remarks Miss Bullard used the women's ability to arrive at the financial goal as evidence of their unwavering spirit: "When this missions project was launched, our nation's economy reached one of the highest inflation rates in her history. But the steadfast faith of our members was undaunted. Our goal was to raise the four million dollars needed and not borrow money. Thus far, we have paid all bills and have not borrowed any money. We have raised the money for the construction of these buildings . . . and are confident we will go on to victory!"

Kathryn Bullard chose the Little Piney River, flowing through the site, as a natural metaphor for the women's ability to meet and overcome challenges. The river encounters obstacles in its formative years, which she compared with those faced by individuals. She quoted Isaiah: "If you wander off the road to the right or the left, you will hear His voice behind you saying, 'Here is the road. Follow it.' "

Across the wooded landscape were several buildings: Bullard, housing administrative offices; Hunt Hall, the dining and assembly building; and House of Happiness, the guest lodge. Soon the camp would echo with the happy sounds of campers just as the three old camps had through the years.

Construction costs reached over $3.8 million. The Virginia leadership declared in 1986 that by "putting hearts, hands, and prayers into this mission project" it had been realized.

Kathryn Bullard

*K*athryn Bullard is a product of the rural life of the Carolinas. She was born and reared where North and South Carolina meet in Gibson, Scotland County, North Carolina, across the state line from McColl, South Carolina. She was the daughter of a farm overseer and his wife, and Mary Elizabeth "Lizzie" and Joel Bullard taught their six children more from their actions than their words. The lessons remain exemplified in the values held by their youngest child, Kathryn Elizabeth Bullard.

Her mother kept a starched white tablecloth on the dining room table, always ready for unexpected company. Lizzie Bullard also kept her six children in church. "Sunday we all went to church. There was never any discussion of whether or not we would go to Sunday school or church. If we said we were sick then the medicine bottle was pulled off the shelf and we knew that." Church, the social life for the local farming community, early became the center of Kathryn Bullard's life.

When people came to buy corn from her father he would heap the corn into the sheller. Kathryn remembers telling him, "Daddy, you put in more than a half-bushel." And he would reply that he wanted people to go away feeling that they got more, not less, than their money's worth. Throughout her working career in denominational service, Joel Bullard's daughter has given far more of herself than anyone could have rightly expected.

218

And she gained other values. "I came along in the Depression and we had very little of this world's goods. My father worked very hard to provide for his family. I remember him working all day on the farm and then working at night in a peach orchard to bring in a little extra money. We all had to work. We worked in the fields. I know what it is to pick cotton. I know what it is to drop peas in a corn field with a mule coming right behind you, breathing down your neck with my father saying, 'Walk faster, Kathryn, the mule's right behind you' and he didn't have to tell me that because I could feel his breath on my neck. And my little legs were going just as fast as they could go trying to drop the peas in the corn rows as he was coming along down the middle covering up the peas." Accordingly, she has done what she had to do without regrets. Even when problems were breathing down her neck, she never dwelled upon them. "I just believe," says Kathryn, "that when you have done the best you can do, you don't dwell on the problems. You just go ahead and tackle them." Kathryn Bullard has been tackling problems one-by-one whenever they occurred ever since she left home for Mars Hill College so eager for an education, and later, at business school in Charlotte.

The childhood world in Gibson had been very narrow—no more than a 10-mile radius. However, at the Gibson Baptist Church there were three ladies—Mrs. O.W. McManus, "Miss Maggie," the pastor's wife; Frankie Stubbs; and Clevie Stubbs—who cared about the chil-

219

dren and Kathryn credits them as key influences in her childhood years; through the Sunbeams and GAs Kathryn learned that there were other people living far beyond her 10-mile world and that people in China and Africa had never heard about Jesus. She also learned that she could do something about that fact. As a farm girl, Kathryn knows all about seeds and sowers; and she believes those three Christian ladies were planting seeds in her young mind.

In GAs, the Gibson children were told that they could earn a pin if they memorized all that was required within the Forward Steps. Kathryn remembers: "For a little country girl who had no jewelry, to get a pin was just fantastic! I am not sure my motive was in proper order in working on my Forward Steps but I do know that, as the years have passed, what I memorized back then, I have continued to use. As important as that pin was to the child, what I memorized has been a sustaining force in my life. I still have that GA pin. It's my prized jewelry and quite a reminder to me."

After business school Kathryn applied for a secretarial position at First Baptist Church, Kannapolis, North Carolina. Soon she was doing the work of an educational director and, before long, the work of an associate pastor although she was called promotional director. She visited the sick and homes where there had been deaths and helped in many ways. The church had a very active WMU and everyone, including the men, looked forward to the Weeks of Prayer. At Kannapolis the WMU was having church-wide promotion long before it became popular.

After 10 years a letter arrived "out of the clear blue" from a lady on the personnel committee of the North Carolina WMU, advising her of a position on their staff. Kathryn protested that she lacked sufficient formal education but the woman again made contact and persisted. She met with the committee and thought there would be no further contact. A couple of weeks later the telephone rang at 6:30 a.m., the same time a train always rattled the walls of her garage apartment every day. She kept yelling to the committee member, "You will have to wait till the train goes by."

The committee wanted the young energetic woman from Kannapolis for the state job of Baptist Women's director but she was unsure about the position. "I would cry and agonize and be miserable with myself and finally I said, 'Lord, you seem to be telling me something' and then I had a peace about it. I said to myself that the Lord was leading and it will not always be easy but I will go and stay until the Lord leads me somewhere else." She stayed 16 years.

Kathryn Bullard found significant differences between local and state church work. In the local church a worker sees immediate results; but from the state office the fruits of one's labors are seen more slowly. Yet Kathryn Bullard was developing a reputation as a hard worker, a woman who completed tasks, and by whatever measuring rod, got results.

One day Kathryn's telephone rang and the voice on the other end said: "Hello, I'm Liz Payne of Richmond and we are looking for a state executive secretary." The approach Liz Payne took was simple yet profound. "I am calling not to ask you to do anything except to pray about talking with us about this position." Kathryn Bullard prayed and let her heart be open to the direction in which the Lord *might lead her. She had one, two, three good excuses why she shouldn't take the position, but each one was removed.*

The years were filled with exciting challenges. Kathryn Bullard reflects: "It has been a happy experience. The people have been warm, responsive, gracious. It has not been easy but it has been great joy and fulfillment in the Lord's service. It has challenged every gift I had and those I never knew I had. It's an opportunity to use everything you've got and it's just fun to be a part of WMU. If I had it to do all over again, I would not choose any other place to use my energies."

Kathryn Bullard had brought an air of expectancy to Virginia WMU. Everyone sensed that the timing was right to take new directions, while taking along the best of the past. Among many other accomplishments she led Virginia WMU in meeting needs around the world, building a $4 million camp in the foothills of central Virginia, and restructuring the Executive Board for wider participation.

The years of service have been fulfilling for the farm girl from Gibson, North Carolina. In 1987, the University of Richmond bestowed the honorary degree of Doctor of Humane Letters. While she walked across the platform and the academic hood was placed over her shoulders, echoing in her brain must have been the words of her father in the field: "Walk faster, Kathryn, walk faster." Kathryn Bullard has walked fast, worked hard, and achieved results.

"I am humbled by the trust you have placed in me by electing me executive secretary. I believe God has brought me to this place, and I want to say to you today what I expressed earlier to the personnel committee. I realize I bring nothing to this great office of responsibility except as the Holy Spirit works through me. And this is my whole desire!

"I have had great respect for your leaders in the past; and as I come to work with you, I want to continue to build upon your strong missions foundation. I'm totally committed to missions and the mission organization. I will give my total support to Woman's Missionary Union's being one of the program organizations of the church.

"I believe that a church which has a strong mission organization is a stronger church because of it. I also want to be a part of that kind of church.

"As I accept your trust in this leadership position, I am keenly aware of the tremendous responsibility which goes with it, and I pledge to you, with God's help, my best.

"Let us covenant to pray for one another that we may know His Will—His Power—for the facing of the hour—for this day— for all the days to come in His glorious service—that we may glorify our Lord.

"The words of the Psalmist express my feelings: 'Accept my grateful thanks, O God, and teach me your desires.' Ps. 119:108."

Kathryn Bullard's *first*
speech as executive secretary, 1975

"CO-LABORERS"

During the last 15 years Virginia WMU has been blessed with several capable persons in diversified staff positions. There were only three professional staff positions and employees in 1974: executive secretary, Carrie S. Vaughan; Baptist Young Women and Acteens secretary, Rees Watkins; and Children, Girls in Action, and Mission Friends secretary, Sue Hutton. When the new period began in 1975, Miss Watkins moved into the newly created position of editorial/research secretary; in time, as other positions were created, Kathryn Bullard, executive director, attracted creative women to develop specialized areas of work.

In 1976, Maxine Bumgarner directed Baptist Women and Baptist Young Women and Ann Kilner led the Acteens. Linda Kay Morgan, a graduate of Southern Seminary, directed Mission Friends and Girls in Action from 1978 to 1979. After Maxine Bumgarner resigned in 1979 to head women's missionary work for the West Virginia Convention, Jean Teague, who had served as a missionary associate teaching English to nurses at the medical school in Gaza, joined the staff to direct Baptist Women and BYW. Peggy Jo Smith began serving in 1980 as director for Girls in Action and Mission Friends. A graduate of Southern Seminary, she had served as a missionary journeyman in Korea. She expressed her commitment by declaring, "I enjoy being with children and respect their strengths as well as their fragility so I think it is essential that their adult leadership be well-equipped."

Ann Kilner resigned from her Acteens post after five years to serve

on the WMU, SBC staff. Ardith Williams, a graduate of New Orleans Seminary, headed Acteens work from June, 1982 to 1987.

Others who served in supporting positions included Emma Hutchins, administrative assistant, who brought her years of practical experience from secretarial positions at First Church, Richmond, and the Virginia Baptist General Board to the WMU state office; Dorothy Alley, financial secretary; Elsie Mae Weaver, receptionist and secretary; Jan Westbrook, materials secretary; Cathy Banton, receptionist and services secretary; and Teresa Crow, office secretary. Continuing the long tradition of cooperative work with black churches, Grace Williams served as a special worker in this area. With a new camp came a manager, Carl Davis, employed along with his wife, Bonnie, as food service manager.

In December, 1982, Virginia WMU gained a new missionary to support from their own ranks. Peggy Jo Smith, the Girls in Action and Mission Friends director, was appointed as a missionary to Brazil. That event reminded some of the time years before when "Our Elizabeth" Ellyson Wiley went directly from the Virginia WMU staff to the foreign missions field of China. Now "Our Peggy" was going to serve and Virginia women took a special interest in her. In 1983, Jean Teague returned to foreign mission service as a missionary to Japan.

Donna Britt began serving in the GA/MF area in 1983. An experienced youth worker, she graduated from Southeastern Seminary. Margaret Myers also joined the staff in 1983 as BW/BYW director. The daughter of missionaries to Vietnam, she specialized in ethnic missions.

Betty Merritt, Donna Britt, Carol Kidd (seated), Kathryn Bullard, Pamela Smith, Cathy Banton, Emma Hutchins, Teresa Crow, Earlene Jessee (seated). (Photo courtesy of Mark Mitchell.)

Carl Davis, Camp Little Cross Roads Manager; Bonnie Davis, Camp Little Cross Roads Food Service Manager.

Jean Teague in her Japanese attire.

In the summer of 1983, Rees Watkins, the last of the long-time staff members from Miss White's era, retired as editorial/research secretary. From 1948 to 1983 she had served Virginia WMU in several capacities. Kathryn Bullard remarked: "Rees always had a vision for the future. Once a decision was made, she put her hands to work to accomplish the goal. Many have grown in their spiritual life because of the excellence in programming which Rees has provided through the years." Miss Bullard added that Rees' quick wit often was a relief for everyone in the daily office routine.

In December, 1984, Kay Maroney become BW/BYW director. She served as a career missionary in Ghana, Ethiopia, and Kenya. In 1986, Karen Kendrick (*Toalston*) became consultant for BW/BYW.

In June, 1987, Ann Cross (*Compton*) became Acteens consultant. She had served as a missionary journeyman in Surinam. In 1988, Steve Law joined the staff as an accountant and Betty Merritt became BW/BYW consultant. A graduate of New Orleans Seminary, she served as a missionary in Nigeria. As the period closed Earlene Jessee joined the staff as WMU consultant, Pam Smith as Acteens consultant and Carol Kidd as accountant.

Virginia WMU's small but dynamic staff coordinates missions support and education for the thousands of women who comprise the organization. They are capable and effective professionals, "denominational servants" in the best sense of the old-fashioned term, and truly "co-laborers" with each other, with their larger constituency, and with God.

Winds of Change

At the annual meeting in March, 1976, at First Church, Roanoke, Virginia WMU affirmed significant directions. The winds of change had been blowing for several years, and finally action was taken on the critical issue of the State Missions Offering. It was the woman's offering and had been since the Day of Prayer for State Missions and the Thank Offering were inaugurated in 1902. Three years later, in 1905, the offering was designated for a specific need as the women rallied to support Walter A. Hash in his missionary endeavors in Buchanan County. Through the years a myriad of worthy causes benefitted from the women's offering.

By the mid-1950s, the question had surfaced as to retaining the State Missions Offering exclusively within WMU's domain. "Churchwide promotion" became the key words of those within the organization (and without) who sought change.

Juliette Mather reviewed the case in *Light Three Candles*: "The Executive Board prayed and discussed again and again. In 1955, the Board recommended that the Virginia WMU continue as previously in promoting the Lottie Moon, Annie Armstrong, and State Missions Offering as expressions of love from its members (or others who of their own volition wished to give), with WMU promotion to be channeled only through its own organizations.

"Reasons for reaffirmation of this policy were valid. The SBC had approved these offerings as offerings of WMU; promotion of church offerings on the state level was the function of the General Association. The conviction continued that the Cooperative Program was the regular channel of missions gifts from Southern Baptist churches, and the plan needed constant emphasis. Seasons of prayer offerings came as the result of prayer and study at special seasons of the year and were promoted as over-and-above love gifts. The offerings were increasing year by year, and wisdom decreed caution in changing a course which had proved so gratifying to the cause of missions. WMU of Virginia reaffirmed its policy first in 1955, and again in 1957 and 1964."

In 1976, the issue again was brought to the floor. Frances C. De-Foe of Roanoke, who had long been active in the life and ministries of Virginia WMU, delivered a report and recommendation. She began her remarks by declaring, "Some years ago Virginia women requested the men in the churches not to help them with the State Missions Offering. They have been considerate in honoring our request! I spoke to a Brotherhood meeting about state missions and the men asked why they couldn't help. We would now like to undo what we did in the past and have the men participate with us." She proceeded with a bold change: "That the Virginia State Missions Offering be co-sponsored by the WMU of Virginia and the Virginia Baptist General Board. That the allocations be approved by the Executive Board of WMU in consultation with the VBGB. That the Executive Secretary of WMU and the Executive Secretary of the VBGB be responsible for the promotion. The Executive Secretary of WMU, in consultation with the Executive Secretary of the VBGB will be responsible for program materials." The WMU delegates approved the recommendations unanimously and subsequently the change was approved by the VBGB. The first jointly-sponsored State Missions Offering was in the fall of 1977 for the 1978 budget year. The winds of change had indeed blown.

Also at the 1976 meeting Mrs. Elizabeth Payne of Richmond presented a recommendation "that the Virginia WMU adopt the plan of work of the WMU, SBC." Kathryn Bullard, still new to her work as the executive leader of the Virginia Union, cautioned, "This is in no way a change of our interest or purpose in the past. It will permit greater flexibility in structure, and provide a valuable tool to assist WMU of Virginia to do its task. *The Virginia Supplement* would then deal only with matters specifically related to Virginia WMU."

In the fall of 1976, at the General Association meeting the WMU president, Mary Jane Thurman, referred to the changes and stated: "Let me assure you that the changes are not in principles but only in methods. More emphasis will now be placed on missionary education for the entire church family. We are committed to doing a better job."

Gentle winds had permitted change.

Mary Jane Thurman

*A*s a young girl, Mary Jane Cubbage would get into the family's big Dodge touring car and accompany her mother to the missionary meetings of Goshen Association (Kentucky) WMU. *"It always seemed [as if] it [were] raining for the*

missionary meetings," Mary Jane now laughingly recounts, "and driving through the unpaved back roads of Grayson County it seemed the car was always covered [with] mud on WMU day!" Of paramount importance is that her mother, superintendent of the local association WMU, introduced her daughter to WMU at an early age and Mary Bassett Cubbage's daughter became president of a state WMU in adulthood.

Mary Jane followed in her mother's footsteps. Like her mother she attended Bethel Women's College and afterwards her father, a country banker, insisted that the young woman receive practical skills at a business school. This opportunity took her to the city of Louisville where her life would take new directions. She met a young man who was working on his doctorate. Peyton Thurman's proposal was straightforward—if Mary Jane got a job they could get married. And she got a job.

Peyton Thurman, like his bride, was a product of Sunbeams and was receptive to the idea of missionary service. As a young man he was approached by Inabelle Coleman of the Foreign Mission Board *with the tempting idea of accompanying a missions group to the Balkans. As a Georgetown College student he lacked expendable funds for such a venture so "Miss Inabelle" contacted the generous "Miss Elsie" Gilliam of Lynchburg and she helped finance his trip.*

The Thurmans lived in several Kentucky communities where he was pastor—a student pastorate at Frankfort and pastorates at the First Baptist Churches of Russellsville and Hopkinsville. The pastor's wife chose to serve in missions study in those churches; and during Peyton Thurman's long tenure at Southern Baptist Theological Seminary as dean of students, Mary Jane had a "double dosage" of WMU, attending the missionary meetings at the Seminary and at Crescent Hill Church.

When the couple moved to Charlottesville, where Peyton was pastor of Belmont Church, the newcomer from Kentucky found that Virginia women appreciated and welcomed her. She presented a series of missionary messages at Eagle Eyrie and was invited to serve as a member-at-large of the Executive Board. In 1975, she served as the state mission study chairman.

Early in 1976, she was standing in her kitchen when the telephone rang. The caller wanted to nominate Mary Jane Thurman for president of Virginia WMU. "It's easy to turn down something when I am alone," she reflects, "but my husband was standing nearby and kept shaking his head while I was trying to say 'no.' I agreed to give it prayerful consideration. After I put down the receiver, Peyton said: 'You know you could, so therefore you should.' It's hard living with a preacher who delivers a two-line rhyming sermon!"

Mary Jane Thurman served as president of Virginia WMU from 1976 to 1978, and gave support to the new executive secretary, Kathryn Bullard, a lady whom she admires. The two women—both "come heres"—respected Virginia tradition and moved cautiously to determine whatever changes might be sanctioned by Virginia women. They traveled with the Virginia staff across the state to leadership conferences, listening to Virginia women discuss past successes and future WMU needs.

Mary Jane Thurman has held fast to memories. As a girl she assisted at the missionary meetings by passing the refreshments and

by passing a heart-shaped cut glass dish which became the offering plate for her mother's WMU. She remembers that the ministers who served her home church at Litchfield, Kentucky, were always inviting missionaries and nationals to speak on "faraway China and darkest Africa." Once when she was about six years old a guest speaker compared a missionary to a penny. The girl's mind wandered and for the first time she considered the idea of giving to support missionaries; when she focused again upon the speaker's message she caught his point: a missionary, like "one cent" is, of course, "one sent."

The illustration stayed with Mary Jane Cubbage Thurman; although she was never sent as a missionary herself, she devoted her time and energy to helping those sent.

Jane Matthews Clarke:
Like Family

*W*hen Jane Clarke stood on the platform at the Virginia Beach meeting in March, 1979, following her election as president, it was as if she were standing on her own front porch, welcoming everyone with her warmth, natural enthusiasm, and unaffected love. Jane Clarke believes in family and resides in an old homeplace where family is always calling. During her presidency she just made Virginia WMU and all the Baptist folk her extended family.

Jane Matthews Clarke was born in Brunswick County into a nurturing and caring large family. The Matthews women were strong influences upon the young girl. Her Aunt Viola, "a reserved and rigid" lady, had served as a missionary to Brazil. Jane attributes her earliest missions interest to those long fascinating stories about life in a faraway land told under the oak tree in the yard. Aunt Pattie Sue taught the Beginners Sunday school class and was president of the local WMU. One day, when she was about six years old, Jane came home and told her mother, "I know what I want to be when I grow up! I want to be president of a Woman's Missionary Society."

But the greatest influence was her mother, Elizabeth, who from the age of 28 suffered with Parkinson's disease. She was an "encourager" for her daughter.

Jane Clarke was reared a Methodist. At age seven she made a profession of faith. When she was 15 she went to a summer youth conference at a Methodist school, Randolph Macon, and heard two missionaries from China speak on their work. The teenaged girl made a commitment to full-time Christian service. As a student at Ferrum College she came under other strong influences but rheumatic fever struck while she was a sophomore. She returned home and for six months, confined to bed, she was nursed by her mother. With tears she recalls that Elizabeth Matthews called those six months of constant care "the happiest time" of her life.

Jane transferred to High Point College, from which she was graduated in 1949 with a B.S. degree in Bible and religious education. She taught in Halifax and everybody expected the Bible teacher to lead missions courses. Every week she was speaking somewhere in all the denominations. Halifax was old-line Baptist territory and Jane Matthews was surrounded by Baptist influences including the gentle tugs of Camilla Lacy and Mary Barksdale and associations with several Baptist ministers and their wives, including Frank Riley, Walton Connelly, Ray Brown, Bill Smith, and the Rossers, "Buddy" and Ann. After five years in Halifax, George Clarke entered her life. She told her groom that, if the Baptist minister in Kenbridge wanted to call on them before she joined the Baptist congregation, he had better come soon because she intended to join the first Sunday she was there. And she did.

As a bride she moved into the Clarke family home on Fifth Avenue in the small friendly town of Kenbridge, bringing only her antique rope bed. Jane was 28 and George was 39 when they married and

began a family. The old homeplace was kept lively by two daughters and a son, all of whom frequently return home.

The new Baptist quickly became acquainted with "the WMU ladies" of the old Concord Association, Mrs. George Wilkerson, Mrs. Kidd, Mrs. Jeffries. Jane Clarke began serving as Acteens director, GA leader, president of Baptist Women, circle chairman, and then she was asked to serve as the state's Mission Study chairman. At first she declined but she did serve later. It was for that work that she travelled across the state, "wearing out an automobile," leading programs. She moved in 1979 to the presidency. The girl's dream had been fulfilled in unimaginable ways. She has declared that if she had been born 20 years later, she would have become a woman Methodist minister!

One of her tenure's highlights was the development of a sister relationship between Colombia WMU and Virginia. When Virginia's leader visited Colombia, Jane lead a children's workshop. She recalls one woman's remarks: "I knew you cared because you gave money and sent supplies but I didn't know you cared enough to come."

The "Great Camp Vision" was a most ambitious project yet the president never doubted the ability of Virginia women to make it a reality. She once told the women that "millions of dollars will not build the camp" because it would be built with "five-ten-twenty-dollar gifts." She has reflected: "It was those small gifts from many women, giving every week, keeping the money back and sending it in monthly, that built the camp. I had been in the homes across the state, from Arlington to Southwest Virginia, from Jonesville to the Eastern Shore and I just knew the women were going to do it."

There was one concern. Some members of the Virginia Baptist General Board might oppose the camp's fund drive. After all, the Virginia Baptist Homes were in a financial crisis. Whatever opposition might have surfaced was quieted when Meredith Roberson, executive director of the Virginia Baptist Homes and a Kenbridge native, spoke at the Board meeting, saying: "Jane Clarke says there's enough money among Virginia Baptists for both the Homes and the camp. She helped take care of my mother and I know we can trust her."

Jane Clarke's capacity to help others is well known. She attracts the entire span of ages, from children in town who ring her doorbell for a friendly chat with the lady they admire to the church's oldest member, a lady who is 101, who received a bright red party dress from Jane for her birthday. But, after all, to Jane Clarke they—the women in Colombia, the "circle ladies" in Kenbridge, the children, the young couples in her Sunday school class—are all just like family. And Jane Clarke believes in family.

Virginia WMU commissioned and presented portraits of three former WMU, SBC, presidents for the national building in Birmingham. The Virginians in the portraits are, left to right, *Abby Manly Gwathmey (1894–95); Mrs. John A. Barker (1903–06); and Mrs. W. C. James (1916–25). At the presentation in 1980 were,* left to right, *Christine Gregory, then the current president of WMU, SBC; Kathryn Bullard, executive director of Virginia WMU; Jane Clarke, president of Virginia WMU; and Carolyn Weatherford, executive director of WMU, SBC.*

Jean Woodward

"*Everyday is a Beautiful Day*" reads a framed cross-stitch piece in Jean Woodward's bright blue-painted kitchen in her Richmond home. Actually, the saying was a favorite which her husband, Robert F. Woodward, coined from his pulpit at Winchester where he served for 12 years; the hanging was stitched as a gift by a church member. It is clear to a visitor that Jean and Bob Woodward share many things—a love for all things beautiful, a flair for creative touches, the willingness to nurture seedlings, whether plants or people, into maturity and, yes, a philosophy that life indeed is to be lived joyfully to the fullest.

Jean Woodward has met the last 15 years in Virginia with a zestful enthusiasm and, one by one, unsought but gratefully accepted blessings for service have come her way. She has been involved in every phase of denominational life and as she says, "Whatever I am involved in is important to me or I wouldn't be involved in it." Previously, in Maryland, she was active in the local WMUs in churches where her husband was pastor, first at Princess Anne from 1949 to 1952, and then in Frederick from 1952 to 1974. She usually accepted the positions of mission study chairman and then "fell into" associational WMU jobs on the Eastern Shore and in Frederick.

In Maryland, two women were significant influences. Mamie Clause, president of the Maryland Union, gave Jean her first opportunities to preside; as she explains, "Mrs. Clause walked me through the paces." Even today Jean Woodward expresses "a debt of gratitude" to the older woman for her affirmation and guidance. The other key influence was Maryland's indomitable executive secretary, the Virginia-trained Josephine C. Norwood. Jean Woodward correctly surmises that "Jo Norwood brought Virginia to Maryland" and so from her Jean learned about Virginia WMU long before living in the Old Dominion. She also caught Jo Norwood's passion for missions history.

When the Woodwards moved to Winchester in 1974, they vowed to steer clear of denominational work. After all, Jean had been busy with Maryland WMU and Bob had served two terms as president of the Maryland Convention, as well as serving on the committee which wrote the Baptist Faith and Message. They also had reared four children. Enough was enough. Although new responsibilities in Winchester were demanding, within a year they both again were involved in denominational affairs; Bob was serving on the Virginia Baptist General Board and Jean was named a member-at-large of the Executive Board of Virginia WMU. From 1979 to 1983, she served as second vice-president of Virginia WMU.

When several within the WMU organization began suggesting Jean Woodward as a possible president, she registered a quick "no," realizing the travel demands upon the president. She felt needed at home. Someone made her promise that, before she made a final decision, she would discuss the matter with her husband. She agreed and then just as quickly put it out of her mind. Now she muses: "Without ever knowing I had been asked, Bob began saying things *that just countered and evaporated all my excuses. He commented that a minister's wife as president might be helpful in securing support from ministers for the new camp. Little by little the rug was being pulled out from under me. Another provision I had considered was that the request to serve had to come from many people and not just a few. The telephone rang and it was the chairman of the nominating committee saying that so many had been asking if I would consider having my name placed in nomination. And then, of course, I did what any woman would do at the time, I cried." From the perspective of time and opportunities for service, she adds: "It was an affirmation from the Lord and I believe the Lord prepares us in many ways and not just in intellectual gifts. If indeed a minister's wife was needed because of the camp project, then I felt that I could do it."*

As president from 1983 to 1988, Jean Woodward guided the "great camp vision" into reality. The Virginia leadership role placed her in a strategic position in the planning for the new headquarters building in Birmingham for WMU, SBC, and to assist through chairmanship of the national organization's Finance Committee. The project required close work with the staffs of Virginia and Southern Unions and Jean Woodward affirms the capable and creative employees of

both organizations. She especially is appreciative of Kathryn Bullard whom she cites as an administrator who routinely seeks advice from her elected officers and who has gently effected positive changes in the Virginia organization.

In 1988, following her tenure as president of Virginia WMU and service on the Virginia Baptist General Board, Jean Woodward again was tapped for service. At its annual meeting in Virginia Beach, the Baptist General Association of Virginia elected Jean Woodward unanimously as president. She has been only the second woman in its history to hold the office.

She came to the presidency at perhaps the most trying time in Baptist life. At the 1988 meeting Virginia Baptists responded to the decade-long struggle within the SBC by adopting a "memorial" or lengthy statement of views to be presented to the national body. Among other things the document labeled the controversy a "crisis." The new president would have to shepherd the memorial and appoint a special committee to address the critical issues which had surfaced. It was not the easiest time to serve as president.

"God has gifted each one of us and expects us to use our gifts," the new president observed, "and I feel that He has placed us in particular places. When I ask the Lord if this is something He wants me to do, I do not have to worry about my inadequacies."

Jean Nelson Woodward received gifts from both parents. From her father, Lee Thoren Nelson, she received her outgoing personality. She credits him with "leading me to the Lord." From her mother, Ebba Anderson Nelson, she learned compassion and a rare ability to embrace the needs and interests of people from diverse situations. There were other strong influences including a Sunday school teacher, Ruth Ziemer, the daughter of her minister. She admired Ruth, later a missionary to the Philippines, and was impressed by her skill on the violin. Jean's mother wisely counseled that her daughter "could do whatever she wanted to do" because she was as "equally capable" as Ruth; such affirmation of individual self-worth helped Jean find her own gifts. In developing those, she attended Wheaton College where she met her future husband.

Today, as a homemaker with grown children, she has time for denominational service; when the demands of the presidency recede,

Every president needs a loyal aide. President Jean Woodward confers with Robert F. Woodward, her own chief aide.

she expects to volunteer at one of the local Baptist Centers. Clearly, she will always find useful work to be done.

To a casual observer it may seem that the poised, confident, strikingly-attractive lady with the bubbly personality and gentle humor is never flustered or bothered. When problems do come, she finds strength in her husband and in her Lord. "My feeling of self-worth helps as well as just knowing to whom you belong, for God's love never fails. His mercies never fail. They are new every morning. It's true. I am an early riser and the time early in the morning is my time to speak to the Lord. And in this way I find that every day is a beautiful day."

Margaret Wayland

*M*argaret Buck was born two weeks after her father's death and her entire life has been evidence of answered prayer. After Elizabeth Breeden Buck lost her husband she went into her room, where she remained for a long period. Naturally her family was concerned. She was nearly ready to deliver a child, this young widow with several children. She already had the care of four children from her husband's first marriage and their daughter, Marie, and now an unborn child. When relatives knocked on her door and inquired about her, she gently explained that she needed time alone with her Lord. Among her prayer requests were for strength to rear her family and a life long enough to see her unborn child grown. Her prayers were answered.

Margaret Buck Wayland is quick to select her mother as a lasting influence along with her half-brother, William Thomas Buck, who became a father figure. Her mother was an excellent seamstress and she used this talent to support her family. As an adolescent Margaret wished that she had a store-bought dress, but now she would "give anything" for one of her mother's handmade items.

Mrs. Buck would work all day sewing, come home and prepare the family's evening meal and then would sew again for others at night. She was a perfectionist, a trait still evident in her daughter with her attention to detail. She also gave her daughter other values. She would say: "Where there's a will, there's a way," and "anything worth doing is worth doing well." She praised her yet impressed upon her that one never quite obtains perfection. Whenever Margaret would try her hand at sewing, her mother would take time to help her over the rough spots. Most of all, she was affirming. "I attribute where I am today and the things in which I am involved to the roots that my mother gave to me and to the wings that she gave to me."

Margaret Buck has striven for perfection: she excelled in both commercial and academic courses and became valedictorian of her high school class, scholarship recipient at Averett College, and "a proud Spider" graduate of Westhampton College. She was a guidance counselor for the Pittsylvania County schools.

She used to fantasize that she might marry a minister one day.

Margaret Wayland participated in the Diamond Jubilee Pageant, 1949.

The man she did marry was not a minister although Lee Wayland's mother once hopefully inquired if he had received direction from God to the ministry. "No, mother," replied the son, "God has called me to be a Christian scientist." Today the chemist teaches Sunday school at West Main Church, Danville, which has been the center of the couple's life. "If ever any of my children were neglected," Margaret muses, "they were only 'church orphans.'"

As a young girl she was active in missions organizations. While in college she worked in all the Baptist camps and as head counselor one summer. It was in camp that a fellow counselor, a Japanese girl attending Baylor University, affected her deeply when she questioned why the older girls did not talk individually to the younger ones about Christ. The surprised young Americans answered that they probably just took their faith for granted. The Japanese girl responded: "Oh, you must never take Him for granted." The comment made a lasting impression.

Dean Mary Fugate of Averett presented the idea of Margaret transferring to her alma mater, Westhampton College. "I am grateful," Margaret says today. "Westhampton was small enough that you could feel a part and yet large enough that you could have the diversity of offerings. I felt very close to my professors . . . Dr. Holtzclaw, Dr. Wiley, and Dr. Solon B. Cousins. I took a class in Paul under Dr. Cousins and I can see him now, standing in a chair and portraying Paul calling to the Macedonians."

Another role model was a prominent Danville woman, Mamie Wyatt Hall, a leader in West Main Church. She was always "doing for everybody else, visiting the sick and bereaved." Margaret reasons that Mrs. Hall had the freedom through financial privilege to give of herself yet believes she could have found a way even if lacking advantages. "I grew up in her shadow," she says, "and I had the dream that . . . I wanted to be like Mamie Hall. I never really attained it but I have tried to serve in any capacity in which I was asked."

Today the Waylands' spacious brick home is directly across the street from the old house once occupied by Margaret's mentor. From her porch, she can view the white frame Victorian house from which Mamie Hall operated her own personal missions work.

Howard Lee, her former pastor at West Main, was a strong influence. Like a father, he was there when she was making decisions about college, during the death of her mother, her courtship and wedding, and the baptism of her sons.

Margaret Wayland likes to be a homemaker, still enjoys counseling with others, possesses a gift for fancy lettering, and treasures private quiet times for reading and reflection. "My life has been so full and so blessed. Life has been so good to me and I feel that I need to respond by giving of myself to others."

Long before her election as president of Woman's Missionary Union of Virginia in March, 1988, Margaret Wayland had been freely giving of herself to others in her community. In her own church, West Main in Danville, she served in numerous capacities including Sunday school director, chairman of the Weekday Early Education Center, and director of Training Union and Vacation Bible School. She was the first woman in her church to serve as a deacon and later became chairman of the Board of Deacons. She was director of both the West Main WMU and the Pittsylvania Association WMU. She was the first woman to be a trustee of Hargrave Military Academy, a Baptist-related preparatory school; and she represented Pittsylvania Association on the Virginia Baptist General Board.

In Virginia WMU Margaret Wayland found many opportunities for service. Through the years she was a member of every phase of WMU: Sunbeams, GAs, YWAs, Baptist Young Women and Baptist Women. As a college student she participated in the Diamond Jubilee pageant of 1949.

Virginia WMU repeatedly selected Margaret Wayland for leadership roles: Executive Board member, Mission Action chairman, parliamentarian for nine years and first vice-president, 1987 to 1988. By 1988, it was a short step to the presidency of the Union which she had loved and served for so long.

Virginia WMU's president serves on the Virginia Baptist General Board. Shown here (l-r) are Nathaniel Kellum, treasurer; Reginald M. McDonough, executive director; Kathryn Bullard and Margaret Wayland.

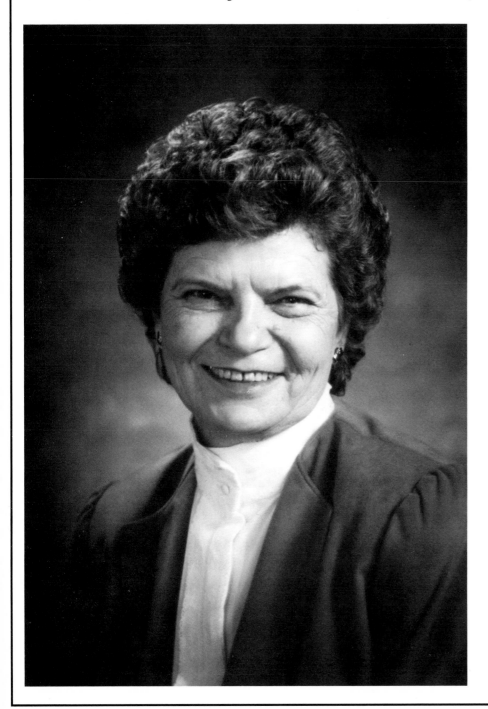

SECOND CENTURY

Standing on the edge of WMU, SBC's second century, far removed from the early years of Ann Hasseltine Judson, Mary Webb and Ann Graves, the Baptist women of the 1990s must wonder at the future. Is the purpose of the organization the same? Is there still a need for WMU? How can younger women be encouraged to join? Several Virginia leaders were asked their views of the present and future.

Is the need for WMU over? "Not if you believe the Lord's call," declares Jane Clarke. "Because He said to go and teach and win and all those things still need to be done. It's our job!"

Jane Clarke tells her Sunday school class in rural Kenbridge that their children will never learn unselfishness unless they themselves do something for others outside the home. She feels WMU is "one of the greatest places to share your life" because it offers service in one's own community, as well as foreign lands.

Jane Clarke

Should WMU change? Margaret Wayland sees a need for the organization to be flexible in reaching the woman of today—a person who is often a career woman as well as homemaker. She believes meetings should be creative, innovative and suggests that they even be held in unconventional places such as the workplace, during coffee breaks. She advocates that women adapt the official materials to suit their circumstances. She also emphasizes the importance of group meetings. "After all, you are with each other; you pray together; you share mission stories together. We convey by being together that we are truly 'Laborers together with God' and there's strength in numbers."

Margaret Wayland wants to span age groups, by including the older women, "our prayer warriors," and yet involving the younger

Margaret Wayland

ones. She has heard the suggestion that every WMU member should adopt a younger woman and instill in that one woman the member's passion for missions so that the younger woman will catch the vision and herself reach others. "The purpose of WMU and [its] needs will not change," she declares.

For Margaret Wayland, there is an air of expectancy particularly as the WMU launches the second century. Yet she tells women, "The future of WMU is not in Birmingham or Richmond. The future of WMU is in the hands of the many women working in local churches."

For Jean Woodward opportunities for mission service through WMU are "exciting" and she believes that missions action must remain in a "front and center place" especially to attract younger women who are service oriented. "Women today want to see results," says the former president of Virginia WMU, "and we need to understand our audience and go where they are." ►

Jean Woodward

"I believe with all my heart," says Christine Gregory, "that, if you had a missions organization where young women could be involved along with their husbands, the couples would become active in volunteer missions."

Kathryn Bullard views the needed thrust as motivational. "I think that the people who are in WMU have to be motivated to see the bigness of it and the far-reaching effects of it and see that it's worth their time. Women today are busy and they want their time to count for what's good. They want to be on the cutting edge and WMU can place them there. But it's work!"

Mary Jane Thurman acknowledges that "there is an aura to missions" that surrounds Baptists even today. She also believes there remains a challenge for local churches to address missions and "create a kind of environment in the local church for young people to become involved."

In the summer of 1989 a new executive director for WMU, SBC, was chosen, and she came from among Virginia Baptists. Dellanna West O'Brien of Richmond, a former missionary and educator who started her own educational testing business, is very much like her

Christine Gregory

Baptist peers of this last decade of the twentieth century— a married homemaker balancing career and family life. Over and over again, without exception, Virginia WMU leaders have expressed highest hopes and expectations that the new leader would serve as an appealing role model for Baptist women and lead the national organization into innovative approaches to reach members and prospective members.

The future of WMU, the thrust of missions education and support, belongs to the great-granddaughters of those pioneers, to a new generation of the "King's daughters," and they are equal to the task. They still are "laborers together with God."

Kathryn Bullard

241

Executive Board (Photo by Jean Lynn)

*H*omes of Virginia WMU through the years are (top, left) 1 West Franklin St., 1944–62; (top, right) Monument Ave., 1962–86; and (bottom) since 1986 the new modern home at 2828 Emerywood Parkway.

Woman's Missionary Union
Gives itself to weighty tasks, not
With the blare of trumpets, and the
Beat of drums, but with a mighty
Faith. Lowly may seem the sphere of
Any woman, gifts meager, with
Uneventful passing of the
Days; but if she walks the way that
Leads to God, potent is her life.
Along the path across the years
Of history that woman's feet
Have trod in the service of her
Lord, few names may blazon forth, but
The glory of that highway is
In the great multitude of lives,
Uneventful and unacclaimed,
But lived with steady purpose for
The holy things of life. Lead on,
O Woman. But whither? Lead us
To the heights where purest breezes
Blow; where vouchsafed to us will be
A clearer vision of our God,
And man's duty to his fellow.
May the work of the
Woman's Missionary Union
Go on until the end of the
Days; until the angel shall stand
Upon the earth, and upon the
Sea, and proclaim that time shall be
No more.

             Thorburn Clark